Dick Sheppard

Dick Sheppard

a biography

by

Carolyn Scott

HODDER AND STOUGHTON
LONDON SYDNEY AUCKLAND TORONTO

For Austen Williams
who is there now

Contents

Acknowledgements

I would like to thank the numerous people who have given their help with such generosity and enthusiasm, especially Mrs. Gordon Richardson and Mrs. Rosemary Pearse, Dick Sheppard's daughters, who, while in no way initiating this book, nevertheless gave so much kindness, time and assistance.

I would also like to thank the Vicar and Churchwardens of St. Martin-in-the-Fields for permission to reproduce Sir Gerald Kelly's portrait of Dick Sheppard.

Of all the volumes I have consulted in the preparation of this book, I would like to acknowledge particular indebtedness to the following: *Dick Sheppard by his Friends* and *The Impatience of a Parson* by H. R. L. Sheppard (Hodder and Stoughton); *H. R. L. Sheppard*, by R. Ellis Roberts, and *The Human Parson* by H. R. L. Sheppard (John Murray); *Testament of Experience* by Vera Brittain (Gollancz); *What Do We Believe?* by Laurence Housman and H. R. L. Sheppard (Jonathan Cape); the *Sunday Express* for extracts from articles written originally for them and printed under the titles *Some of My Religion* and *My Cry For Christianity*, both by H. R. L. Sheppard (Cassell); Faber and Faber for permission to quote from *The Hollow Men* by T. S. Eliot; and for access to material in the *St. Martin's Review*.

I am also grateful for background material in the following; *Dick Sheppard and St. Martin's* by R. J. Northcott (Longmans); *Dick and Jef* by John Edward Francis (Joseph Sault); *St. Martin-in-the-Fields Past and Present* (St. Martin's Review); *St. Martin-in-the-Fields Old and New* by Katharine A. Esdaile (SPCK);

H. R. L. Sheppard (Cobden-Sanderson); *Two Days Before* by H. R. L. Sheppard (S.C.M.); *Fiery Grains* Ed. H. R. L. Sheppard and H. P. Marshall (Longmans, Green and Co.); *We Say 'No'* by H. R. L. Sheppard (John Murray); *Bridge into the Future*, the letters of Max Plowman (Andrew Dakers, Ltd.); *Woodbine Willie* by William Purcell, *Cosmo Gordon Lang* by J. G. Lockhart, *The Unutterable Beauty* by G. A. Studdert Kennedy, and *Memories and Meanings* by W. R. Matthews (Hodder and Stoughton); *Portrait of Soper* by William Purcell (Mowbray); *Max* by David Cecil (Constable); *Aldous Huxley* by Sybille Bedford (Chatto); *William Temple* by F. A. Iremonger (O.U.P.); *Undiscovered Ends* by W. H. Elliott (P. Davies); *Editor* by Kingsley Martin (Hutchinson); *Faith Under Fire* by John L. Collins (Leslie Frewin); *Letters to a Sister* by Rose Macaulay, Ed. Constance Babington Smith (Collins); and *I Renounce War* by Sybil Morrison (Sheppard Press).

Introduction

From *The Human Parson* by Dick Sheppard

IF THE DISCIPLE can maintain a constant conversation with his Lord, the greatest of all gifts will inevitably be his. It will be as natural for him to love as to breathe. Love in its highest manifestation is the richest, most persuasive, loveliest, nicest thing God has to offer—it is the only weapon we need.

It is full of understanding—it knows how easy it is to sin, how difficult to live nobly. It sees with the eyes of those it loves. It never makes quick harsh judgements. It gets to the heart of a situation as nothing else. It thinks in terms of men and women and children, and never in terms of statistics. It prefers to give itself to the individual. It shuns expression on public platforms. It has no ulterior object except to serve. It would gladly lead if it could—it would never drive. It asks nothing for itself, but it is human enough to long for love in return.

It knows when to speak and when to be silent, when to be patient and when to be impatient. It is at home with all sorts and conditions of men and women and children, and it makes them laugh, for it has a real vein of humour. It gives and gets a joy in loving. It believes in all men and women. There is no such word as 'hopeless' within its vocabulary. It feels; it is sensitive to the moods of all to whom it is given. It is never clumsy, and yet it often steps in where angels fear to tread.

Perhaps its greatest characteristic is its power to understand. It anticipates man's needs; it can see a situation sometimes before it occurs; it has an almost super-human instinct for what ought to be done and how to do it. It knows what is in the heart of man. It is not always declaring itself. Like all creative forces, its best work is done in quietness. It prefers action to speech, it would

prefer to visit someone in want to making any oration on fellowship. It likes best to do small things that no one else has seen need
doing. It sees sorrow where sorrow is thought to be hidden, and
virtue and grandeur where it is least expected. It is for ever on the
watch for those who need it.

It runs to give itself as the father ran to the prodigal son, not
because he pitied, but because he could not do without his son.
It washes the disciples' feet as He did because it wants to—not
because there is a lesson in humility to be taught. It is like a
window through which can be heard all the cries of the market-
place without. It knows no barrier of rank or class, of creed or
colour. It overflows the boundary of its own denomination—no
official channels can hold it entirely. It flows, perhaps, most
tenderly to those who never enter church and care little for the
love of God. It sees the crown of their need on their foreheads,
and longs to be of service.

It could not patronise if it tried—it understands too much. It is
generous, yet strong in controversy. It seeks to win without
wounding—it never descends to personal abuse or bitter speech.
It is sometimes angry, for there is nothing sickly or sentimental
about it. It is never shocked. When it is angry it is because
another is hurt—in soul, or mind, or body. It knows nothing of
jealousy—it rejoices in another's success. It is never petty or
mean. It has all things in their right proportion. It is ever seeking
to disentangle itself from irrelevancies.

It learns more in listening than in speech. It is never sarcastic,
for it knows that by such means no soul was ever won. It is the
property of no clique – it wears no ecclesiastical badge. It cares
nothing for its own status – there is nothing professional about it.
It is not always trying to buy up the opportunity, to point the
lesson and draw the moral. Above all, its faith in God is massive.
It is confident always that in the end darkness must flee before
light. This love which comes of God through Jesus Christ is the
one weapon we need. If we who are to serve in the Society of
Christ could possess it from constant conversation with our Lord,
we shall not have lived in vain.

Men who see it will know from whence it comes, and they will
give praise to God who can do such great things. They will
know also why we are what we are and what are the essentials of
Christianity.

I

The First Fence

ST. JOHN ERVINE called him a good man. Max Beerbohm called him an enchanter. Shaw called him an actor: 'WHAT an actor!' His parishioners said, 'He knew Jesus, preached Jesus, and made him real. He loved us – and we loved him.'

Dick Sheppard was a man of extremes, so complex that his Dean called him four or five characters in one. He was a man at once practical and mystical, gay and sad, popular and reticent, an autocrat and a democrat, struggling within himself, and yet sublimely confident.

He called himself a failure: but it was in his nature to dramatise.

The son of a court ecclesiastic, he was determined not to go into the Church. Working at an East End settlement, he was happy, bewildered, and beaten up, but he made friends for life, and when illness forced him to leave, they said, 'We dare not speak of how he loves God.'

Tempted into the Church by Cosmo Gordon Lang, he left the East End of London and went to the West End, where he re-vitalised a dead Mayfair chapel. 'If Christ came again,' he said, 'he would weep over Park Lane and Poplar.'

Vicar of St. Martin-in-the-Fields for twelve years, he pioneered broadcasting and popular religious journalism, and made the church one of the most famous centres of social work in London, with people queueing to come inside and sit on the chancel steps to hear him preach.

His most famous book, *The Impatience of a Parson*, antagonised his enemies and his closest friends. So did his work for Church unity and his persistent fight for pacifism. 'I would like to smash Canterbury and then try to rebuild it again,' he said.

Towards the end of his life, outwardly and militantly cheerful, he was so disillusioned and lonely that he considered leaving the Church. 'Faith?' he said. 'I don't believe I know anything about faith. Jesus is my God. I don't think I have any faith except that. But I have a love for men: somewhere in me I have love. I hang on to that.'

He died alone in his canon's house at St. Paul's Cathedral, at odds with the Church leaders, broken-hearted because his wife had left him, apparently unable to preach love ever again, because he felt he had failed to love well enough himself.

'When Dick Sheppard died,' said Rose Macaulay, 'the world's temperature seemed to drop.' As his body lay in state, over one hundred thousand people came to pay their respects.

Illness had forced his resignation from St. Martin's. In 1931, illness had again forced him to resign his position as Dean of Canterbury. He called himself a coward and a failure, and he planned to write an autobiography.

It was an un-typical venture: perhaps even he didn't know why he was doing it. Whether it was done for money or self-justification, it remained unfinished, as if the handful of vivid childhood memories, comic and horrific, had served their purpose.

At a time of wandering in the wilderness, it provided a scape-goat less painful than the truth.

On the back of a scribbled list of contents, he wrote some words of Bismark: 'When you want to take any fence in life, throw your heart over it first, and then you and your horse will follow.'

All his life Dick Sheppard threw his heart over the highest fences without a moment's hesitation, only to be pulled up short the other side when his horse stumbled.

This first glimpse of him, then, is from the book he began at a time of failure — and then failed to finish.

*   *   *

'Nothing would induce me to go over my childhood days again,' he wrote. 'I thought I was happy because my mother said I was.

I was very frightened of my father, whom I grew to love more than any other man in the world. I was lucky, compared with others, and I was brought up to tell God how much I loved him, which I didn't.'

His father, a minor canon of Windsor, was courteous, dignified, and conventional, 'loyal to his sovereign, discreet beyond the discretion of most wise men'. He had written official court biographies, mercilessly censored by the Queen, but felt that 'either we should have our sovereign off the throne, or else we should shield him and his family from abuse, even if they were a little comic'.

His mother, probably to his father's discomfort, detested protocol and snobbery, and was 'delightfully independent of Castle patronage.

'Queen Victoria never forgave my mother because on one occasion when my mother was told to go to dinner at the Castle, she said she couldn't, as a new curate was arriving, and could not be left alone to have his dinner on his first night in a new job.

' "Most strange", Queen Victoria said.'

Dr. Sheppard's name, like that of his own father and elder son, was Edgar, and his insistence on good manners was such that he once brought in the boat when he and Dick were on a fishing expedition, so that Dick could write an overdue letter of thanks.

We were not an intellectual, but a conventional family. It never entered my head to be blasphemous enough to consider if God—a God of the Jehovah kind—was lovable or even likeable. Mr. Gladstone represented the devil, and every ill that happened in the world was due to him.

The minor canons had fine singing voices, but so far as I was concerned, my father's tenor surpassed them all.

The house where Dick was born, he called a miserable affair. The doorway of No. 2, The Cloisters was half hidden beneath a dark arch. Beyond the crooked lintel, the hall was dim and dark and silent. From the window of the low-ceilinged room where he was born, Anne Boleyn is said to have first seen Henry the Eighth.

I am told I was a beautiful baby, while my brother, with
whom I fought, looked like a rabbit. Later he became very good-
looking, which has never been an accusation brought against
me.

'What a plain man, Mr. Sheppard is', I heard one old lady
say to another on the porch of St. Martin's. 'Undoubtedly', said
her companion. 'But what a pleasing expression.'

With that I must be content.

Baptised formally as Hugh Richard Lawrie, at a service which
he was later to denounce as futile and irritating, he was known
among Windsor servants as Mr. Lawrie.

In 1880 when I was born [he says], Windsor was indeed
the Royal Borough, with all the romance of a nightly password
and a challenging sentry and the prospect of running into the
great men of the world at every corner. Nothing was done
without the approval and patronage of Queen Victoria or one
of her several daughters.

My parents were not enamoured of the Queen, and I think
the distaste was mutual. She was a tyrant first and last, however
kindly she may have been to servants and lesser people, and it is
false history to write of her otherwise.

Canons of Windsor were blameless old pluralists of courtly
manner and comfortable circumstances. They blossomed out
when the weather was fine, and withdrew when it wasn't, and
were decorous, gracious, and Anglican to the backbone. Unless
they were ill they were only in Windsor for three months each
year, and were not then greatly active. Later, my experience as
a Dean taught me that active Canons can be out of place in the
Cathedral precincts unless their main activities are, so to speak,
out of the place.

There was also a Chapter Clerk who was a considerable
figure, and who, towards the end of his life, on fine afternoons,
took gentle exercise on the flagstones that flank St. George's.
He was very deaf, and once, on a damp and blustering day,
when my mother asked him how he was, he answered, 'Very
wet and windy.'

Gerald Wellesley was Dean of Windsor, and 'he looked the part: Deans of Windsor always do.'

The Queen was very fond of him and sought his advice on many occasions. I once had in my possession several of her letters to him for which the sensational press would have paid highly.

It is no good pretending that the great lady knew anything about theology.

Mrs. Wellesley was so admired that crowds gathered outside the Deanery to watch her start for her afternoon drive. Her humour was irresistible—she smoked cigarettes on the roof of the Deanery with the future King Edward when smoking was taboo at the Castle—and she adored my mother and her sincerity. She did not give her affection easily and she had a tongue well capable of expressing her disapproval, which caused her to be feared by great and small while she held a formidable position, and to be forgotten when the Dean died.

She was lavish in generosity to us children, giving away with both hands things that were of value. Among the gifts we received was a scabbard used—as it was said, though I doubt it—at the battle of Waterloo by the Duke of Wellington, Dean Wellesley's uncle, a lock of the Duke's hair, and a walking stick of black ebony with a whistle which he used when exercising his dogs.

Also in the house there was a watch and a china tea-set which had belonged to Napoleon the First, and an engraving of the Emperor with the young King of Rome asleep on his lap. Later, when Dick's younger daughter was born, he loved to point out a resemblance.

Marmont, Napoleon's famous marshal, disowned his wife with the terse comment that 'My marriage was entirely unhappy.' Exiled on Elba, Napoleon denounced Marmont, and welcomed Madame Marmont as one of his few visitors. The girl who was born from their brief liaison was said to have come to England and married Edgar Sheppard in 1819.

It is interesting that this tradition, which fascinated him in his youth, was left out of Dick Sheppard's autobiographical notes. Much later, Harold Anson, Master of the Temple, and one of his oldest friends, was to describe his character as a dichotomy between the descendant of Napoleon and the profoundly humble servant of Christ.

Few people [he said], realised how much there was in him of his great ancestor. Not only had he that strange, uncanny power of being able to sway great masses of men to do and believe anything that he wished, but he had also that capacity in a very high degree, of meticulous attention to detail, and a grasp of all the essential points of a complicated programme of business which is one of the marks of a great organiser.

He was a great saint, but he could quite as easily have been a magnificent sinner. He had it in him to be a ruthless and eminently successful employer of labour, or an infinitely subtle and unscrupulous politician, or a leader of devastating armies, overrunning the world. It was only by continual prayer and humility that this great elemental and passionate force was so completely turned to the service of God.

Some people find it easy to be good and innocent and innocuous. I cannot imagine that Dick could ever have been all that he was without a very conscious and deliberate surrender of all this torrential energy to the service of humanity.

From Windsor, the Sheppards moved to St. James's Palace in London, where Dr. Sheppard took up a new appointment as Sub-Dean of the Chapels Royal. Lady Meresia Nevill, 'an intrepid but dangerous whip' terrified Londoners when the horse pulling her phaeton bolted up the steps of the Albert Memorial, and Dick marvelled at the sight of Gladstone and Lord Salisbury attending the altar rail side by side without kicking each other in the pants.

In those days [he says], I lived in a fear that the end of the world was about to come. Its date was often announced on pamphlets that were pushed into the letter-boxes, bidding us flee from the wrath to come, but in the dreams I had of the Day of Judgement, my limbs wouldn't work and I had to sit still amidst the prelude of banging and thumping and trumpets and shriekings as twilight began to fall on the face of the world.

Night after night I awoke sweating with fear and hoping that the noises I heard might herald a thief in a mask rather than the cataclysm which I had been told would also come like a thief in the night.

If I dared to mention my dream, 'Don't be so silly' was the only consolation vouchsafed.

When he was sent away to prep. school at Albion House in Margate, Dick's mother told him how lucky he was —a fact she never ceased to impress anxiously on his mind —and his grandfather, as awesome and unlovable as Jehovah, tested him on Latin, sitting on a bench in Leicester Square.

I feared my grandfather more than anyone, and I should still tremble, if I saw him [he wrote dramatically later]. My father never suffered us to say a word of criticism against him, but he was a wholly frightening and unlikeable old gentleman, selfish to the finger-tips. He looked like a Frenchman, had perfect manners, which was all except bills that he left my father, was a great sportsman, and wore so many club colours when he played games that my brother once remained unforgiven for a year for telling him he looked like a nigger minstrel.

Since criticism of him was not allowed and he was spoken of as a wonderful man, I used to feel almost wicked at being afraid, and until I was fifteen or more I did not even tell myself that there was any justification for my dislike.

Grandfather Sheppard was Professor of Psychology in the University of London. The Home Office called on him to give decisions on the mental condition of murderers who had been condemned to death, and he had at one time been Governor of Colney Hatch mental asylum, where he had been so powerful a personality that the inmates, however violent, were cowed the moment he came near them. He had opposed the marriage of Dick's parents because his mother came from pure Cornish and Devon stock and was not an heiress.

He knew I was frightened of him, and he delighted in making me feel awkward and unhappy. That terrible day, he started by asking me the meaning of *tempus fugit*, and though I knew, I was too terrified to utter the words. After a dissertation on wasting my father's slender resources, we sailed away on a perfect hurricane of attack and defence around the dreadful business of the wall which Balbus unfortunately built, but instead of having it built in Latin and then having done with it, he insisted on Balbus building other things besides a wall, like tables and ditches and fosses.

I was too young, too prejudiced, and too frightened, to realise that my father's father was really a considerable person — a genius, I think — and a colossal, if to me forbidding, personality.

Dick enjoyed school. He was a good mimic and he had a devilish sense of humour. He was also very good at games, and what he lacked in the classroom, he made up for on the cricket field and was very popular as a result. By the time he was twelve, his father had been given the additional post of a Windsor canonry. Randall Davidson was Dean: today he and Dick are buried side by side, at Dick's request, in the grass at Canterbury. With some scrimping from his parents, who were neither poor nor rich, and with the financial help of the eccentric old German Duke of Cambridge, Dick was sent to Marlborough public school in Wiltshire.

The old Duke was scorned and ridiculed for his obtuse wartime record and his pantomime marriage to an actress. 'Also you will do well,' he said. 'How lucky you are,' Dick's mother told him. 'You must do well.' And if he had misgivings, as he undoubtedly did, he hid them in order to keep up the charade which he could see was very important.

In spite of his prowess as a fast bowler, he hated Marlborough. His mother's natural spontaneity constantly bubbled beneath the surface, at war with the rigid respect for convention implanted by his father. The result was a tension which was later to become the secret of his dazzling sincerity. At Marlborough it only confused him and made him feel awkward and diminished.

He rented a room of his own from his father's allowance, and spent all his spare time alone in it. A fellow schoolboy remembers him, sentimentally, as a saint at twelve, having 'in a complete degree the positive quality of Christian courtesy'. But a carelessly sarcastic master called him a fool.

I can remember now [Dick says], a letter arriving from my mother, in which she stressed as gently as possible the difficulty of affording education for a family of three, and begging me to do all I could out of gratitude to my Father.

Scholarship was never my strong point, but I determined that I would do well to make some recompense for what I was costing my parents, and the real sacrifice they had made for me. I resolved to work with all my might.

The will was eager, but the brain was weak.

That day was one on which Latin translations were required in my form. I was called upon in a loud voice by my form-master to translate a passage from Virgil, and he knocked all the stuffing out of me at the outset by saying 'Let us hear what our little fool has to say.'

As I stood up I was literally blinded with fear, and remained speechless, then—horror of horrors—tears began to trickle down my face. There was a pause, and again the voice of the master: 'I *am* sorry, Sheppard, for your Mother and Father. It must be dreadful for them to have a son like you.'

That torture, inflicted years ago, literally ate into my soul, and for years, and in some respects for ever, gave me what is called an inferiority complex. Even when I made a hundred runs in a cricket match without making a mistake, I could not get any real satisfaction from the innings, feeling that somehow or other, it must have been a thoroughly bad one.

One thing had been burned into me—that the cruel punishment of sarcasm which was inflicted on me as a boy should at least make me try to avoid being sarcastic, and try to go alongside the vast number of people who suffered the torture of sensitiveness.

In a way it was to be the reverse of his father's comment, which he copied down later in a notebook of quotations: 'No soul was ever won by sarcasm.'

Holidays brought temporary respite. Dick and his older brother and sister were sent to Devon, to their mother's parents, and to Dick, the weeks at Instow, half-way between Barnstaple and Bideford, where the Tor meets the sea, were weeks of heaven on earth.

The train journey from Paddington was one long palpitating romance [he said]. At Exeter, we arrived at Enchantment. We used, when young, to travel to Instow in charge of a Nanny, whose towel work on our noses, eyes, and mouth was pre-eminently thorough. There was no accommodation for washing on a train in those days, and no corridor.

Almost the moment we left Exeter, although there were still two hours to go, Nanny would begin cleaning us up so that our Granny might welcome spotless children. Every kind of con-traption was brought down from the rack – soap, towels, and other instruments of torture, and bit by bit, inch by inch, we were scrubbed and flayed until we cried for mercy.

'What would your Granny think if you arrived like this?' was the preface. 'Now sit you still and don't smudge your fingers on the window, or your Granny will think I'm not fit to look after you.'

How we resented it all, and yet we were caught in the romance of the journey, and it was all according to immemorial plan. Gorged on soap and sandwiches, we steamed over the sandhills and approached Instow, first the cricket ground, then the white house where we were to stay.

Undoubtedly the nicest people in the world lived at Instow when I was young. There was our hero, Admiral Chichester, whose deeds of daring were the boast of North Devon. He quarter-decked it about Instow, and Instow sunned itself in consequence. You could hardly walk down the front without stumbling on a colonel who earned a C.B. in India, or who earned one but never got it, and there were majors galore who went to Bideford to shop and even carried a basket for their shopping. We saw them off by the one good train and were there to welcome them back to lunch. And there were ladies of all degrees who ran things in the parish and were kind to children and gave incredible tips.

But most exciting of all were the fishermen who inhabited the quay rather than their boats, and wore ear-rings and chewed tobacco and were the spit of the loyal and disloyal sailors in *Treasure Island*. Long John Silver passed under our windows at night, and that awful blind man with the grip of iron sometimes knocked on our door, and as children, we asked what lay behind his mild request that we should go out in a boat or buy his cockles.

Instow meant freedom, Devonshire cream, cockles for breakfast all fried and lovely, and carefree days with cousins and tea parties at which there was cream and jam in glorious plenitude, and for three weeks nothing could spoil our fun except the awful haunting memory that after the holidays, term began again.

Within eighteen months of going to Marlborough, Dick left.

It had been impossible to talk honestly about his unhappiness because the façade had to be kept up, as it was for the rest of his life. 'I would never have written and signed anything heretical while my beloved Father was alive,' he said later to Laurence Housman. 'I would have been damned for a humbug rather than hurt him.' First he decided to run away, dressing himself in borrowed clothes and walking north, leaving his school clothes in a pile by a lake. When he realised the sorrow his 'death' would bring his parents, he walked back again, and soaked his bedclothes with water night after night instead, in a determined effort to make himself ill. Whether or not it was this that laid the foundations for the asthma which eventually caused his death, is impossible to tell.

Undoubtedly he called himself a coward and a failure, but when he finally caught pneumonia so badly that he could not stay at the school, it was the result of a quiet, intense tenacity.

'Without those times of early unhappiness,' say those who

knew him well, 'he might never have achieved such sympathy with others.'

The relief of telling them was such that the rest of the auto-biography was left unfinished.

2

From Cambridge to Oxford

'THE VIEW OVER Appledore at sunrise and sunset, the gentle noise of hammer on iron that provides Appledore with its sea-faring trade, mellowed as it comes across the water, the peace of the sand-dunes, and the sight of the bar that is crossed to the sea, with its straight line of foam, is a scene enchanting to me beyond description,' Dick had written of Instow, where he went to convalesce.

Comments of similar lyricism and rusticity are almost non-existent in his writing.

In sentimental days, I bargained for a plot of land in Instow churchyard in which my body was one day to be put facing out to sea. But I don't want to lie there now. Beauty does not lie with loneliness, and the vision of nature at her fairest is ghastly when one is unhappy and alone.

I had rather be in Whitechapel when I am sad than in Instow, which would only speak of dreams unrealised.

Dick was fourteen years old when he left Marlborough, and beyond cockles and cream teas, it is hard to know what dreams he entertained. In order to matriculate he was sent to a coach in the

Hertfordshire countryside, where he sang and acted, played cricket and learned how to shoot.

'He had the most delightful sense of fun,' said a fellow pupil who was later to become Dean of Ripon. 'He had the gift of mimicry, and an evident pleasure in anything human, as if the person to whom he was talking was the one person in the whole world who really interested him.'

In 1898, he matriculated. His father, as Sub-Dean of the Chapels Royal, divided his time between London and Windsor, where he and Dick paced the cloisters regularly, in deep conversation. It was the year of Omdurman, and Kitchener shocked the Queen by returning home with an inkpot which turned out to be the skull of the Mahdi, mounted on silver.

Dick indulged his love of the grand gesture by covertly dispensing a full week's pocket-money to a poor family living in the Windsor slums, and gave the butler a shilling to put on a horse because a 'sour-faced old lady kept me in one summer evening while she tiraded against gambling'.

> The Christian is told to love his fellow [he remarked later], and as a child I worried absurdly about this problem. They told me that if I would be a Christian I must love everybody, and when I asked if that entailed liking the arm-twisting bully next door as well as an ancient relation at the other end of the town, I was told that of course it did.
>
> Not for many years did I discover the great and refreshing news that a Christian, when called upon to love his fellows, is asked to do something which often, happily, does include liking them, but does not of necessity involve it.

Under this daunting illusion, he toyed with several careers, the stage, the law, politics or the army like his brother Edgar, but had only one overriding determination: 'Never to become a parson.' Instead, he obtained a commission in the Militia under Lord Salisbury, and in January 1900, at the age of nineteen, he volunteered for service in the Boer War, like most instinctively adventurous young men.

He and his father set out for Waterloo Station and the Imperial

Yeomanry on an icy February day. Before they arrived, one of the horses pulling the hansom slipped against the kerb and fell. Dr. Sheppard and Dick were thrown out of the cab and lay in the snow for more than an hour before help came. One of the cab shafts went through Dick's leg.

Lying in hospital, Dick read of Kimberley, Spion Kop and Ladysmith. He came out of hospital with a limp which he never lost. Later, perhaps due to the influence of university and the East End, he talked of being mobbed in Fleet Street for his pacifist views on the South African War. Entered for Trinity College, Cambridge, with the vague possibility of law or politics the other end, he set off to busk his way round South America with a couple of friends, winning the American Cake Walk prize, and a tango competition in Buenos Aires, and coming home triumphantly with a trophy for tap-dancing.

At Cambridge, 'he was certainly no scholar, nor did he pretend to do any more work than was absolutely necessary,' wrote a fellow undergraduate.

Twenty years later, Dick preached at Cambridge and talked of 'a mis-spent University career in which Fenners, the racquet court, the A.D.C. and The Pitt played parts wholly disproportionate to their real value'.

With a Wooster-like enthusiasm for pranks which perhaps led to his subsequent delight in the stories of P. G. Wodehouse, he earned membership of the Bad Eating Club by eating jelly through his nose. He wore well-tailored suits and had his friends carry him through the streets on a stretcher when his tailor made one that was too tight. He boxed, and he joined the smartest cricket clubs, the M.C.C. and the I Zingari.

What degree he was proposing to take, none of us ever knew, but he was wonderful at snob cricket, and he was the ever-welcome guest at every form of undergraduate frivolity — bump suppers, birthday parties, 'Athenaeum Teas' and May week festivals. His end of the room was always the most cheery and at the same time the least disreputable.

If ever one went into the Pitt Club, one was sure to find Dick entertaining a large circle, constituted of normally diverse

elements, with his views of life in general and Cambridge life
in particular. His generosity was outstanding—no one ever
appealed to him in vain—and it led to the most embarrassing
results.

Once, already late for dinner with a high University dignitary, he remembered he had pawned all his studs and links
and buttons to help a friend in need. For years, the high
dignitary entertained his guests with an account of the mis-
cellaneous outfit in which Dick eventually arrived.

It was the first time he had been called Dick. Towards the end
of his time at University he began spending his vacations working
with other undergraduates at Oxford House, a settlement in
Bethnal Green in the East End of London. Lawrie was considered
childish and Hugh effeminate, so it was Dick again.

'You can't preach Christ to empty bellies,' he was to say
cynically later. 'Sympathy doesn't prevent children from getting
rickets. It doesn't put boots on their feet.'

Oxford House and Toynbee Hall, both pioneering settlements in
the East End, had first been sold to undergraduates in 1884 as
'religious in motive while secular in working'. 'The strongest
force on earth is love,' said Canon Barnett, who started Toynbee
Hall. 'Our settlement will rest on a secure foundation only as
far as it is based on love—love strong enough to stand the strain
of working with little or no apparent results, broad enough to sink
differences in one common purpose.'

Oxford House began in the old day school of St. Andrew's
church, with three beds and room for a club, a library and a lecture
room. By 1889, when funds were being sought for the building of a
new house, over a thousand men belonged to the club where they
could play billiards, bagatelle and cards, and learn free-hand
drawing, shorthand, book-keeping and English composition. A
boys' club with an expectation of twenty to thirty boys had a membership of four hundred.

Scattered in a variety of premises, there was a workshop for
tailoresses, a boot shop, a cabinet-maker's shop and a dispensary,
a Mutual Loan Society, a medical Provident Society, and a Co-op
attended by a thousand customers every Saturday.

Seventy boys were attending Bible classes on Sundays, and two hundred men communicating in the House chapel every Saturday evening.

'We have heard much of the needs and wants of East London,' said Henry Scott Holland, the social-reformer canon of St. Paul's, in a witty period piece supporting the rebuilding fund appeal at a glittering Mansion House meeting.

But there is another social problem. There is the problem of the surplus of educated gentlemen. What is to be done with them?

They sit idly in their clubs, or moon and cadge up and down Piccadilly, and many of them are wholly unemployed, having to fill up their time with horse-racing. General Booth classes them with people who throw whole legs of mutton into their wastepaper baskets.

So it is partly with a view to dealing with this problem, that shelters for congested gentlemen have been set up in the East End. It is most delightful [he said] to see the haughty depression that hangs about people in the West End disappear from the faces of these poor gentlemen, when put to work in the East. It brightens up the whole man. They gain good heart and great hope in finding that they are really of use, and when they go back to their melancholy and ignorant people in the West End, they dissipate many false impressions and stories of pigmies and cannibals. They tell them that what they found in the East End were men very like themselves; some were wise and some were foolish; and some had good methods of curing the ill, and some bad.

These gentlemen [he concluded] only ask for a house to be built in which it is possible for them to do the proposed work. The houses on the spot were never built in view of these new needs. They want rooms, halls, classrooms, and rooms, too, to live in themselves, because they don't pretend to be monks, sacrificing their own condition in order to be very poor with the poor.

No. The intention is to bring them, in their character as Piccadilly cadgers, to the East. The East wants them just as they are, with all their delicious quaintness and pretty clothes. They have no idea how interesting they are thought to be, down in Bethnal Green!

When Dick first went there, the new red-brick Oxford House in Mape Street, off the main Bethnal Green Road, topped the tenement houses that surrounded it, and was pointed out as a landmark. The aims of the House were set out on a leaflet:

> The Oxford House in Bethnal Green is established in order that men may take part in the Social and Religious work of the church in East London; that they may learn something of the life of the poor; may try to better the conditions of the working classes as regards health and recreation, mental culture, and spiritual teaching; and may offer an example, as far as in them lies, of a simple religious life.

The secretary was a young Oxford man from Queen's, called William Temple.

Dick graduated unremarkably in 1904, and decided to go, like so many other young men, to live full-time in the East End. 'At Cambridge,' he said, 'I had accepted the estimate of Jesus Christ given to me by a layman of vast intelligence. He was so clever and sure, and I was so foolish and uncertain. It was a considerable time before I awoke to realise that he was as inexpert in the subject on which he loved to dogmatize as I was on higher mathematics.' Years later, the memory was to haunt him of 'the easy confidence with which, under inexpert advice, I was persuaded to let Christ pass me by, and of what it cost to attempt to catch him up again.' Provocatively Cambridge, he applied to Oxford House, and arrived there on Michaelmas Day.

'I am a sinner—are you?' he wrote years later to Laurence Housman. 'By that I mean, do you acknowledge that there is such a thing as sin, and if you don't, how do you account for the fact that you can't pick up a paper or spend a night in east or south London without coming across something that looks terribly like sin?'

He dressed as prettily as the best of Scott Holland's Piccadilly cadgers, and was on the committee of the fashionable Bath Club, but because of his alarming generosity, he was not always so well accoutred as the majority. In the middle of a magnificent dinner to launch a friend on his way to India, Dick disappeared and pawned his watch to cover the costs.

Similarly he had no intention of being poor with the poor, which would have smacked of hypocrisy and done nobody any good. He dressed smartly and well, even meticulously, and behaved with his usual immediacy to anyone who came his way. He was a good enough mimic and wonderful at charades at Christmas time, but when it came to real life, he was quite incapable of pretence. Under the gay, extrovert exterior, he guarded a fierce longing for reciprocal affection, and an immense, almost childish desire to please. Known as Brother Dick, he still insisted he would never become a parson, in spite of hearing Dr. Winnington-Ingram's often repeated and surprisingly successful sermon, 'Why Should I Not Be Ordained?', two years earlier.

'Have been to hear the Bishop of London preach,' he wrote in his diary. 'He hit me between the eyes. I must be ordained.' But he was passionate and impetuous and changeable as a weather-cock, and he set his heart instead on doing all he could from outside the confines of the Established Church.

'It is strange what little things will choke a youngster off religion,' he said some years later. 'As an undergraduate I lost for a time what little faith I had because I saw a Bishop unable to take a beating at tennis like a gentleman. A poor faith mine, you say. Yes, undoubtedly, but if Christianity does not prevent one of its leading exponents from behaving like a cad when he loses a game, it is a bad look out for the rest of us.'

Oxford House had taken him on as manager of a new club for boys too old for the existing 'Repton' Club backed by Repton School and catering for the neighbourhood tearaways. The premises of the new club were a dismal old Co-operative grocery, and when the club opened, there were billiards and bagatelle, a penny bank and a library.

'We were a pretty tough mob,' one of the original members wrote in the *Oxford House Magazine* later. 'An exceptional man was needed, and that man was forthcoming in Dick Sheppard.

To see the face of any Old Rep light up at the mention of his name shows how strong a bond of love there was between him and every member.'

Before long, boys had caught the university habit of shaking hands with Dick and with each other, and Oxford House was being sniped at for catering for well-mannered better-off boys, instead of roughs and toughs, because the roughs and toughs were smartening up.

One day one of the boys told Dick his father had burned his hand at work, and the blisters were hurting. The next morning, Dick got up before four in the morning to meet the man and give him a soft, strong glove. The usual belligerence knocked out of him, he turned the glove over in his hands as if it was a miracle. 'You got this for me?' he said at last. 'You turned out at four o'clock in the morning to give this to me?' Dick didn't say much and the man shook his head. 'You've got me beat, Mister,' he said.

Later Dick wrote an article for would-be club managers, and it is worth reading what he said.

It is the Manager alone who can build up and maintain a system of real Club religion, practical and brotherly, touching the heartstrings of every member of the Club [he wrote]. There is no need to ask whether his system be 'compulsory' or 'voluntary' so long as he himself loves his boys, is in close touch with Jesus and prays for his boys by their Christian names night after night and morning after morning.

The Manager must be the hero of the Club. Everything will be a trifle cold when he is not there. He must be the first to hurry off to the Fever Hospital when a member is ill. He must stand on the touch line and shout at his boys until they kick the deciding goal. He must go to the Club because he can't stay away, and because he finds it the most certain cure of depression, and he must laugh so naturally that the boys must laugh too. No favourite can be allowed: a genuine smile must welcome every boy as he enters the Club, tired after his day's work, and yet with it all, the boys must know that they have seen this same odd creature pick up a boy by the seat of his breeches and the scruff of his neck and literally hurl him outside into the streets, simply for an extra bit of impertinence.

Poor man [he said], who would become the ideal Club Manager, for you have a deal to learn! Keep cool, whatever thrilling situation you may encounter. Never lose your temper, but pick out the ringleader and talk to him slowly, deliberately, and alone. If you say you will do a thing by a certain day, you must do it, or you will run the terrible risk of being for ever called a 'Swanker', (a Manager is either 'Alright' or a 'Swanker', and there is nothing below the 'Swanker'). If you propose to hold a Committee on Wednesday you must be in your place on Wednesday, and not try to hold it on Thursday. Have short and business-like Committees, and make the boys grouse in your presence and not behind your back. It is essential that you should trust your boys, and they you.

Last, and most important of all, look all your boys straight in the face when you shake hands with them and give them a genuine smile. If you cannot, leave Boys' Clubs alone.

On Maundy Thursday 1905, Dr. Sheppard wrote to the Bishop of Stepney, Cosmo Gordon Lang, to ask advice about his son's future. Lang, one of the youngest and most attractive Church of England bishops of that time, had already noticed Dick. He had been looking for a lay secretary, and according to his biographer, he read Dr. Sheppard's letter and pounced.

'When your letter came,' he wrote back, 'I had myself decided that I should like to try the experiment of a resident lay secretary if I could get the kind of man I want.

'I have been much attracted to your son, and I think he would be just the sort of companion who could lighten my load.'

In the summer of 1905, persistently refusing to be ordained, Dick went to work at No. 2, Amen Court, where Lang stayed as a canon of St. Paul's. One over-emotional, the other constantly holding his emotions in check, they understood each other from the start. Lang had also vowed never to go into the Church: he had studied Law instead, and then abandoned it. He called Dick a layman-secretary-companion who delighted me by his wilful, wayward, whimsical ways, and whom I tried gently to steer towards Ordination.

Dick Sheppard was to me almost as a son [he wrote after Dick's death]. He lived with me during the difficult years when he left Cambridge and was perplexed about his future. I like to think that it may have been largely due to me that he decided to be ordained.

Ever since, although sometimes his ardent spirit impelled him to take ways along which I could not travel with him, my love for him was constant: and although I know I must have disappointed him, I know also that his love for me remained full and generous to the end.

Dick's presence did a lot to lighten the red-brick sobriety of Amen Court. Once, in order to despatch a workmen's delegation so that the Bishop could prepare for an evening engagement, he rushed in wrapped in a bath towel shouting, 'The geyser's blown up and the house is on fire!'

His duties as a secretary were not heavy, and much of his time was still spent in Bethnal Green, coming back in the evening and delighting the reserved Scotsman with his exuberance and impetuosity, 'declaring one evening that the East End working man was a hero, and the next that he was a swine'.

'I told him to say it again and I'd knock him down,' Dick related, after a man cursed the Bible in a public house where he was having a drink. 'They said he was a prize-fighter, but I'd boxed a bit at Cambridge, and I'd never prayed so hard in my life . . .' he said, explaining how he laid the man flat on his back.

Through his new friends in the East End, Dick was making the sudden, astonishing discovery that genuine love could work miracles. He really did love and long to please, and the result was proving to be irresistibly attractive. It was the exciting manifestation of what another Bishop of Stepney, Joost de Blank, would have called the sacrament of personality, and he revelled in the slow sense of rapport which was beginning to develop with people, whatever their class, character, or intellect, simply because he behaved openly and talked to them without pretence.

There came a day in that East End life [he wrote later] when a boy said to me, 'Do you know, last night my Dad said to Mum and me, "Good God, Mother, what should we do without 'im?" ' That 'im was me, and I had really done nothing for Dad and Mum save take Dad a glove for his blistered hand which his work was making worse.

Here was a hard-pressed family who had no pal in the world who could stand by them except me, and I was wanted. How wonderful to be needed when for years it had seemed as if it could never be possible.

Of course I knew I had many a friend who wanted me to dine or dance, but there was no one—at least so it seemed to me—who felt that I had staked down a claim in their heart, and that circumstances would be less happy if I were not at hand.

The political career that I had contemplated was all forgotten in the wonder whether after all I might not be allowed to be of some service by just walking around when humanity was hard put to it: by learning its lessons, and respecting its suffering, and enjoying its humour.

Beneath a characteristic sense of drama, there was a genuine relief that he had found his way at last. As Scott Holland had shrewdly observed, the East End experiment sometimes proved to be a surprisingly mutual affair.

'I pray that God may lead and guide you into the work He has in store for you in the greatest service in the world,' Lang said, when Dick wrote to tell him that he had decided to be ordained. 'Your letter was the best Christmas present I have received.'

3

The Happiest Man
in Europe

WHEN DICK WENT to Cuddesdon, he left a message for his
successor at Amen Court: 'You'll find him clean about the house.'
As always, the slick, sophisticated humour hid the depths of
delighted understanding which had drawn two very different men
together.

At Cuddesdon, friends said that Dick emanated the gaiety of
holiness.

Attempting to tackle the job with proper application, he made a
reading list in a magnificent leather-bound notebook with a brass
clasp:

Oxford House Papers (3 vols.)
St. Francis of Assisi (Oliphant)
Mohammed (Margoliouth)
Pastor Pastorum
Gore's *Sermon on the Mount*
Church: *Oxford Movement*
Farrar: *Life of St. Paul*

Later he added Benson, Ruskin and Emerson's Essays. The first
quotation he noted down as worth remembering was from
Emerson:

'Be yourself, never imitate. Remember that you can present
your own gift at any moment with the cumulative force of a life's

cultivation, while of the adopted talent of another, you have only an extemporaneous half-possession.'

Refusing, as always, to fit into the format, he knocked a colleague down and rolled him in the mud when he refused to talk during a silent retreat. Shot through with a disarming sincerity, he sensed a snobbishness in the Cuddesdon air, and condemned the place at the outset as irksome and disappointing.

Just what I expected [wrote Lang]. I well remember a young barrister seventeen years ago, on his second day at Cuddesdon, saying 'How long?' Now the same person never thinks of Cuddesdon without a deep yearning that he could be there again, and a thanksgiving to God that he was ever there at all. And his room was far worse than yours, and his knowledge far less, and the strangeness of the whole thing far greater.

Make an offering of your time there [he said]. And don't in thought take your offering back.

By the following September, Dick had learned something of the value of discipline, silence and the Holy Communion. He had even made some sense out of Church Law. 'But he had little patience with theorisers or with those who think in order to reach a conclusion and not in order to act,' Dean Matthews said of him later. 'Knowledge divorced from activity had little interest for him. He would probably have ploughed in the General Ordination Examination at any period of his life.'

The Rev. Charles Matthews visited the college, recruiting for the Brotherhood of the Good Shepherd, a society of priests and laymen working in the Australian outback.

After addressing the students, I asked any one who was prepared to consider the possibility of going out to work in the bush to come and see me privately [he said]. I was disappointed when only one man responded to my invitation.

I remember expressing my disappointment to the then principal, Canon Johnston. 'Who is your one volunteer?' he asked. When I told him it was a man called Sheppard, he said,

'Well, at all events you have got by far the best man in the college.'

Whether Dick volunteered out of kindness or impetuosity, nobody knows. Perhaps so far as his health was to be concerned it was a pity that he promptly threw himself into work in London, and never went to be a missionary in Australia.

A week before his ordination, Lang wrote again.

> I must send a word to greet you in this momentous week [he said]. I want you to know how much my heart goes out to you and goes up for you in prayer.
>
> I try to put myself back 17 years to the time when I was preparing for the great venture; and set myself at your side as an older comrade in the service, conscious, alas!, of many failures, defeats and surrenders, knowing something of the toils and trials of the long campaign, seeking to recover his own early faith and ardour at the side of the young knight waiting for the first call. So, in spirit, I kneel at your side, and pray both for you and with you, as I remember kneeling at the altar of Cuddesdon Church those 17 years ago alone in the stillness and darkness of that sacred place, on the eve of my ordination.
>
> Recalling those days, then, what I would say to you is just this—during this week, *let yourself go*. Let yourself go in a simple, sustained, trustful surrender of yourself to the great Captain and offer all your services. Don't let any doubts or apprehensions enter your mind now. The time for them is over.
>
> Probably you have already made your last and full confession of all your sins and poverty and weakness. When that is done, then, I repeat, let yourself go. Let the thought of the great Love which has chosen you, called you, enter into you—open yourself out to it as arid sand lies open to the inflowing tide— realise all it means to be thus chosen by the Infinite Love to go out and witness to it and fight for it, and let all your manhood welcome it and give itself over to it.
>
>   O Love I give myself to Thee
>   Thine ever, only Thine to be.

Those simple words of the hymn I repeated so often to myself just before ordination that they always come back to me bearing the association of that happy time with them, recalling me from the dryness and dullness of work to the freshness and fullness of the first consecration. Bathe yourself now in the spirit of them.

By God's grace you know something — more than many — of what love, and loving, means. Try to think of all you can conceive of Love, at its highest, fullest perfection and reality giving Itself to you now — the Love which is seen in the Life and Passion of Jesus giving Itself in all its promise of strength and inspiration for the years and the work that are to come — giving Itself in the very call of your ordination — and give yourself over to It.

> O Love I give myself to Thee
> Thine ever, only Thine to be.

Don't *now* check your emotions and the words in which they clothe themselves; don't stop to question and test their reality. The time for that, as I said, is over; and there will be plenty of time for it again. But for this week let yourself go. Then the memory of these days of Love, welcomed and accepted and given, will often come back in later years, to rebuke sometimes, but also to cheer and refresh.

And, lastly, if sometimes during these days, you feel tired and the fount of feeling does not run quickly, don't be distressed, and don't attempt to work up your emotions. You can quietly say, 'Lord, Thou knowest all things. Thou knowest — even if I cannot feel — Thou knowest that I love Thee.'

And may God the Holy Spirit be with you to prepare and then to empower you.

Forgive these words. As you know, I don't often let *myself* go: perhaps I ought to oftener than I do: but this perhaps may make my words more real — let yourself go now.

The following Saturday, Dick visited Lang at Amen Court, and came away with a scribbled note: 'Don't worry any more,' it said — and Dick read it again and again. 'You have prepared yourself as carefully as you can. Now lean back on a Father's love and say over and over in St. Paul's Cathedral just these words:

> O Love I give myself to Thee
> Thine ever, only Thine to be.'

The next day, Sunday, October 6th, 1907, Dick was ordained.

Ideally [he was to say later], there is no job so humble or inconspicuous, or so apparently secular that a parson may not tackle it, if by so doing it he can serve his neighbour in the spirit of Jesus Christ.

He should light fires in dark rooms, and go on lighting them all his life.

The parson is a man who is travelling hopefully. He is within the crowd, and not outside it; he is a pilgrim with all other pilgrims on the road, and not a cocksure and confident little guide going on and disappearing in the distance. He is one who has every social evil—war, unemployment, slums—permanently on his conscience; he should condemn injustice and exploitation passionately and fiercely, and without compromise—even to the emptying of his church.

He must be a supremely human man, unshockable, and yet hating sin. Above all, he must be a man of prayer, and yet the world need not know how often, or how hard, he prays.

On the bus to Bethnal Green after the ordination, a drunk swore at him. 'Don't blame 'im, George,' said his pal. 'It ain't 'is fault. It's 'ard luck.'

'Of course I laughed,' said Dick later. 'Who wouldn't? But I didn't laugh deep down, for I knew then that no words could have explained better than that homely backchat, just what the world thinks about the minister of religion.'

'It is delightful to see Mr. Sheppard in the Club again,' said the *Oxford House Chronicle* for November. 'His entry in his new clerical attire was great. But to Par(s)s-on to the older members . . .'

According to Dick, his practical business as the House chaplain was 'to try to interpret not so much the Church as Christ. The difficulty of Oxford House,' he said, 'is that you might as well expect a boy to thrive in his local church as expect a new baby to thrive on an iceberg.'

He began monthly services—not very well attended—at the dimly-lit Excelsior Hall down the road and in a house chapel, took boys to holiday camps, and gave lantern lectures with titles like 'The Christian Knight'. 'The rock bottom truth about St. Francis,' he said, 'was not that he was poor, but that having nothing, he possessed all things.'

Sometimes he went out early in the mornings with men in search of work, and came back shocked at the brutality of terse refusals. On Sundays, he stood on a tub in Victoria Park, defending Christianity. When an unconfirmed boy was seriously ill, he caused an uproar among conventional church people by administering Holy Communion, but according to the doctor, the boy began to recover from the moment he received the sacrament, and criticism seemed irrelevant.

Contemptuous of those who tried to be what they manifestly were not, he continued to patronise West End tailors and to wear hand-made braces. When he visited his Bond Street barber, he was turned away because he had head-lice.

In his own estimation, the most Christian deed he ever performed was to use the hairpin an old lady took from her hair to prise out the winkles she served him for tea.

Despising insincere heartiness—what locals called a sea breeze off a winkle stall—he came also to distrust as well as rejoice in the power of personality. A man who had been a drunkard told him, 'When the vicar called it seemed as though Jesus Christ was in the room, and I knew I could never get drunk again.' And Dick had thought the vicar an old parsonical duffer.

On Fridays and Saturdays he lived in a hired room where the streets were marked on Booth's map as 'perpetual crime and destitution'. Policemen patrolled in twos, and Dick slept in a hammock and lived on bananas, staying out late in the public houses to try and stop men getting drunk.

Although he bought large rounds of soft drinks to compensate, the takings began to go down, and thugs came to his lodgings at night and pulled him out of bed for a fight in the street.

'If there were only two or three, I took them on,' he said. 'If there were more, I cleared out.' Once he was kicked in the groin and knocked unconscious, but he insisted on going back again the next week.

'I was in such a funk I daren't *not* go back,' he admitted. 'I knew if I didn't, I would never show up in the place again.'

Later when he left Oxford House, one of his most treasured possessions was a document from the police giving him authority to keep order in that area.

Friends warned him to take things slowly, but he was congenitally incapable of following anything but the inspiration of the moment. When a colleague was unable to take a boxing lesson at a particularly tough boys' club, Dick took the keys and went off to do the job himself. The next morning his bed had not been slept in and there was no sign of him at the breakfast table.

A search party set off and found him marooned high up in a hay loft, dirty, tired, and extremely cross.

He had arrived at the club full of jokes, goodwill, and jollity, and the boys took one resentful look and thought: 'What the hell does he think we are—kids?'

They put up a convincing show of co-operation, and Dick glowed with satisfaction. They fetched a long ladder and showed him where the boxing balls were kept in a high loft at the far end of the hall, and when he climbed up, they took the ladder away, put out the lights, locked up the hall and went home.

After a bath and a sleep and a good meal, Dick laughed a lot. Later, when they knew him better, the boys laughed too.

'He was the most loving and lovable friend,' said the Rev. Harry Woollcombe, Oxford House head at that time. 'That love gave him easy access to the hearts of the warm-hearted cockneys of the East End. He was always welcome in their homes, where they regaled him with winkle teas and other dainties.'

One of the daughters of the superintendent of a nearby private asylum famous for having housed George the Third in a strait jacket of white linen with frilled cuffs, remembers him as

a small, kindly man, always laughing and doing the wrong things; always being told to pull himself together and look after himself more.

I remember him [she says] sitting on the floor eating a large tea, listening to my mother giving him good advice, and full of stories of his hair-raising adventures. He wasn't like a clergyman. He was more like a layman. But he had a very, very deep religious belief, as if he lived so close to God that it brushed off on you.

His bed was never made and his socks always needed darning, and he often only had a sandwich to eat all day, but he loved life, and he didn't know the meaning of the word pompous.

One night Mr. Woollcombe was woken by shouts and crashes and bangs as a resident, in from a late-night dance, walked into a booby trap. Dick had strung up every fire-iron in the house and tied the threads across the staircase.

Dick's personality was unique [he said]. He was brim full of fun and mischief, but behind it all, and above all, he was deeply religious.

The power of love within him came as the fruit of an intense love of God revealed in Christ, and an implicit trust in the Divine Saviour of Mankind, and that was the real secret of his abounding light-heartedness in the midst of poverty and conditions of life which his soul abhorred.

The only possible way to face these evils without breaking one's heart was to put one's whole force into attacking the evil conditions and trying to alleviate the suffering.

I think the seed of his future was sown in Bethnal Green, at Oxford House.

Gradually the big leather notebook — 'the best tonic against pessimism that I know' — was filling with the words of people less eminent than Gore and Emerson. Scribbled reminders of incidents provided the background for fund-raising sermons in smart West End churches, and gave an indication of the impact the East End was having.

'Boys who whipped round to get money together to give pal bath.

'Boys who offered to come in rough clothes to O.H. Sunday confirmation classes to keep their pal company.

'Boy who stole coat and gave himself up in order to get home after being discharged from the army.

'Boy who couldn't say prayers because fell asleep after hearing brothers and sisters say theirs.'

And snatches of recorded conversation:

' "Did God make the moon and the stars and the Bethnal Green Road? And if he did, didn't he make a mistake with the Bethnal Green Road?"

'Boy who pinched money from mother's gas meter: "What did you do with it?" "Bought pears and apples and rode up and down the Mile End Road in a bus." '

And the rare touches of comedy:

' "Things aren't settled yet: Father's in chapel praying for guidance and mother's packing." '

Rich people disgusted him by sending bundles of old clothes for the poor which, he said, made a mockery of charity, and an undergraduate from Balliol came to 'uplift the East End'. 'He was only able to lift between tea and dinner twice a week,' said Dick bitingly, 'and he was profoundly disappointed with the impression he made—so,' he added, 'were we.'

In 1908, Cosmo Lang was appointed Archbishop of York. According to one of Dick's characteristically extravagant letters, he went taking nearly all of the younger man's heart with him.

I expect even Archbishops need human love at times [Dick wrote]. And since you can never realise what East London is to me without you, I must tell you that I shall never cease to pray for God to give you the greatest power and the biggest guts in Europe, and the knowledge, in times of depression, that a young freak of a deacon, who owes the intensest joys of his life to you, and who finds he loves you even more than he loves the East End boy, is often on his knees trying to switch on a little light and love to penetrate the loneliness of His Grace's study at York.

That year, Dick suffered his first attack of pleurisy. He was working all day and most of the night and not eating properly.

He was not a man of boisterous health or hearty appetite [said Woollcombe]. One of my chief anxieties, especially in camp, was the fear that he would not eat enough to keep him in good health. The sight of food in the mass repelled him, and in camp he existed on chocolate.

Like many devoted people, he refused seriously to consider his own needs or his health, though he never forgot the needs of others.

Often his light was on during the night, writing little notes to insignificant people, commenting on a shared moment in the day. It was the start of a lifetime habit.

When he was unable to sleep, he was reading Peabody, and noting down the sentences which struck him:

'A man does not own his wealth, he owes it . . . is not the alleviating service of Christian charity rightly described by the modern revolutionist as an anaesthetic administered to the poor to keep them from realising their position?'

He had also started another habit of a lifetime. After a man attacked him in his room, he kept a gun in his drawer. It gave him a sense of security, although he would probably have thought twice about using it.

In June 1909, he was priested, and appointed deputy priest-in-ordinary to King Edward.

'I fear I am a little prejudiced when thinking about Ordination,' he wrote to Alan Don, later to become Dean of Westminster Abbey, who was thinking of coming to Oxford House to test his vocation. 'It turned me into the happiest man in Europe.'

In July, he succeeded Woollcombe as head of Oxford House and Alan Don joined the staff.

Dick threw himself into everything with whole-hearted enthusiasm [he said]. Needless to say, he never spared himself. He was at the disposal of anyone who needed him, and if constant interruptions prevented him from getting on with his job during the day, he would work into the small hours of the morning after all the rest of us had gone to sleep. There were nights, I suspect, when he never went to bed at all.

Not surprisingly, by October 1909, Dick was taking an enforced rest at Instow, recuperating from neglected illness and lack of sleep. As head of Oxford House, quite apart from an increasing amount of work carried out locally, there was administration, university lectures calling for recruits, and speaking and preaching engagements to raise money and enthusiasm.

> And yet [says Alan Don] Dick's time at Oxford House was, I believe, one of the happiest periods of his career.
>
> What is more, he had an extraordinary power of infecting others with his happiness.
>
> His natural gaiety, inherited perhaps from his French ancestors, his irrepressible sense of humour, his uncanny instinct of knowing how to poke fun at the pompous or self-important without giving offence, made him at all times a most entertaining companion. But his friends derived more than mere entertainment from his company. They learned something of the secret of that more abiding joy which is the reward of those who in singleness of heart 'seek first the Kingdom of God and his righteousness'.
>
> As I look back [he said] the thing that strikes me as most remarkable is the unifying influence that Dick exerted on the heterogeneous collection of young men who passed through his hands. He took us as he found us, diffident, tiresome, uncouth, angular creatures that we were, and by merely living with us, transformed us into a happy family, a band of brothers.
>
> Individually, we all adored the Head, and that being so, we simply could not be other than friendly with one another.

By Christmas, the *Oxford House Magazine* was still playing to a West End gallery, writing of 'sweet little cripple boys' and recording the banquet of beef, goose and plum pudding given to 'poor inmates of the common lodging houses', who responded by playing musical chairs and 'singing about the joys of a night in Trafalgar Square'.

'Kiddie caught fire and burned to death calling up chimney to Father Xmas to send food down,' Dick jotted more realistically in his notebook.

'Midnight service in Bethnal Green, St. James-the-Great: "What I says is vote for Tariff Reform".'

The weather was bad, cold and slushy, and he missed the blazing fires and the Christmas festivity at home. His parents were hurt, but he was determined to slog out the holiday in the East End, otherwise the brotherhood of man would have been an empty phrase. People had at last ceased to regard him suspiciously as a plain-clothes detective, probably since he had made his attitude towards crime and the reasons for it abundantly clear. Now they regarded him with tolerant affection.

Calling on a man who was ill, out of work, and very poor, he noticed the branch of a tree stuck in a pot with paper parcels hanging from it. 'How nice!' he said, relieved to find the picture less black than it was painted. 'Presents for the children.'

'I like them to have something to undo,' said the man's wife. 'It's make-believe. There's nothing in them but stones.'

'God's shadow is strangely shaped,' said a schoolteacher who spent his Christmas vacation at the house. After several nights wandering among down-and-outs in the City and the East End, he took away with him the memory of the sun rising behind St. Paul's, shedding a flood of light on the river, and a cockney voice saying, 'Shall we put out to sea?'

> This life and vision refreshes a tired schoolmaster [he wrote in a letter of thanks later]. As some small mountain stream that, tumbling headlong down from rock to rock, finds rest awhile in silent pools that mirror heavenward reflections of the flowers that burgeon upon their banks.
>
> Such a pool is Oxford House. I speak metaphorically, for silence is the last infinity of any place where Mr. Sheppard may be found.

By 1910, nearly fifty men were attending monthly services at the Excelsior Hall, where clergy preached on subjects like 'The Moral Demands of Socialism', 'Straight Talks on Purity', 'Some lessons from the London Police Courts', and 'What are the Odds against Betting?' One old man raised his hat every time he passed the dilapidated front door.

'I'll be damned if I'll come,' grumbled another.

'You won't be, if you do,' was Dick's reply.

Nevertheless, it wasn't easy. 'That Excelsior Hall Service has led many to go to church, and to bravely face the cost,' reported an article in the *Chronicle*, and factory boys were literally fighting for their faith.

At the Easter service, Dick used two verses of a poem he had come across, and they held within them much of his own basic faith:

> If Jesus Christ is a man—
> And only a man, I say
> That of all mankind I'll cleave to him,
> And to him I'll cleave alway.

> If Jesus Christ be a God
> And the only God, I swear
> I'll follow him through Heaven and Hell,
> The earth, the sea and the air.

The words held much of the abandonment and totality of his faith. By October, because of that utter abandon, Dick was away again, resting. Close friends said he was physically and mentally destitute. Sitting in bed, he wrote two letters. 'I am getting on,' he wrote in one of them, 'but they are making me chuck Oxford House, and I am almost heartbroken.'

'I've had to resign O.H.,' he wrote in another. 'I can hardly hold my head up. It is very good to fall on your bottom sometimes, but it hurts a lot.'

The *Oxford House Magazine* for January 1911 carries a stunned editorial from Luke Paget, the Bishop of Stepney at that time, written from his home at Clapton Common.

> Yes, I know it, hold ye your peace [he begins]. That is what we are inclined to say when people remind us of our loss, and condole with us over the removal of our Head. We are not averse from sympathy; but just for the present we do not want to say very much.
>
> He had found his way to our inmost hearts; we had come to

love and trust him without reserve; we were rejoicing every day as more and more we discovered the depths of strengths and goodness that underlay his extraordinary attractiveness. We looked forward to almost any amount of happy advance and prosperity under an ideal leader.

Deo aliter visum! and we can only acquiesce; assuring our Head that our hearts are with him, that we count on his restoration to real health and strength, and that the life of the House will go on as he would have it.

Later, he wrote more fully, and the unrestrained affection and admiration in what he wrote gave some intimation of the feeling which Dick left behind him:

We are not in a mood to conceal the greatness of our loss [he said]. We are not going to compare it with the losses of the past —for such comparisons are impossible, and fortunately they are quite unnecessary. But it is extra hard that he should have won all our confidence, all our admiration, all our love, and then, so quickly, have to leave us.

In attempting to write about him one naturally begins with the lighter aspects of his work and character; one speaks of the irresistible humour, the boyish high spirits, the love of merriment and laughter. One thinks of the wonderful versatility, the perfect social charm. All our best stories came from him, and we told them all over the place, yet half-ashamed of telling so badly what he told so well.

One goes a bit deeper, and thinks of his entire courage, never more clearly shown than in his times of suffering and bad health. He leaves the House, and Bethnal Green and the men and boys he loved, the example of a moral and physical fearlessness that never failed him or us. It is impossible to picture him as shirking or refusing a hard duty or an irksome bit of work.

One naturally shrinks from going further and deeper than this, from penetrating the innermost of a man's heart and life. But here you must, for apart from it, you will never know the Head as we learnt to know him.

4

You could not be long with him before there came to you the surprise of finding yourself at close quarters with a spiritual influence of extraordinary directness and strength. Keen as he was about everything; vivid, eager, enthusiastic in all the countless things he touched and uplifted; intensely interested in all that interested you, none of these things were final or supreme. His highest gift was neither his humour, nor his courage. It was his intense power of love.

I dare not speak of how he loves God. I only say that if any of us ever doubt God's power to win and keep and gladden a man's heart; doubt whether God really can be loved with the full strength of human affection, we doubt no longer when we remember the Head.

But the other, the kindred love of the brethren, of us! Was it not the most wonderful thing in the world? What made the men and boys of Bethnal Green his very slaves? What made a word, a letter, a line from him such an extraordinary pleasant thing to get? What made us all want to meet, to see him? What made it so awfully hard for him to leave us; for us to surrender him? What kept him, when soul and spirit should have been taking their needed rest, thinking and thinking over someone who was sick, or sorry, or disappointed, or downcast?

We are accustomed to high qualities in those who, one after another, have served as Head of Oxford House. We have never felt our loss more grievous than we feel it in wishing farewell and Godspeed and good health to one who gave us many things, but, still, gave us his best in giving us his love.

*   *   *

In 1936, the telephone bell rang at Oxford House. A policeman wanted to know if there was anyone at the House called H. R. L. Sheppard. A man had been found dead on the embankment, and his only possession was a letter he had kept for twenty-five years headed Oxford House and signed by Dick Sheppard.

'The love Dick so lavishly bestowed on us, and in bestowing, called forth,' said Alan Don, 'was the nearest approximation to the love of Christ that any of us are likely to see on this side of the grave.' Other equally extravagant statements came from people who were neither sentimental nor excessive.

Leaving on a wave of adulation, popularity and success, Dick showed the strange diffidence with which he was always to face what seemed to him to be utter failure. Years later, he said he was still haunted by what he had seen, still burdened by the horror of poverty.

4

East End to West End

'SAVE FOR THE Blackwall tunnel,' Dick wrote to the Bishop of Burnley in his usual extreme way, 'I have never seen anything that reminded me so much of hell.'

The letter came from the north of England, from Bishopsthorpe, Lang's home in York, where Dick had gone to recuperate and work as a temporary secretary, a job he called pure charity.

'I can imagine simply loving every inch of Sheffield and Hull if one was really working there,' he went on, 'but just to go and talk and then retire is more than depressing.

'When I get back here it is like coming up from the bowels of the earth in a basket and feeling that one did no good in the bowels of the earth.'

He and Lang went on holiday together to Iona, and when they returned, Dick enlivened the place by blackmailing Cosmo into letting him play golf with the butler.

'If you don't say yes,' he threatened one day in York Minster as he led the Archbishop's procession into Matins, carrying the primatial cross, 'I shall take you all round the Minster and down into the Crypt . . .'

By spring, he was 'pining to be in touch with souls again'.

For a few months he went to a dilapidated vicarage in Middlesbrough and came back demanding to work he didn't care where so long as it was among unconverted miners. Ex-Oxford House colleagues, receiving ecstatic letters from him, queued up to come as curates.

'I am like poor old Bishop Montgomery,' Dick said, 'seeing lovely visions with no dog's chance of ever making them any more tangible than air.'

With twenty-eight past members of the Oxford House community, he presided over a group called The Clique, who went on wild holidays together and pledged themselves idealistically to evangelise the world. 'As I prayed this morning,' Dick wrote ingenuously to Alan Don, 'a sudden vision came to me of The Clique going in a solid body in three years' time to some distant part of the Empire to plant the Church of Christ.

'Is there anything in this idea?'

Lang was no fool, and such diverse enthusiasms had to be suspect. He knew, and so did Dick, that there was only one place for which Dick was entirely suited, but Dick, like Jonah, was turning his back on Nineveh. In April 1911, he went to see his London doctors. He stayed with his parents near St. James's Palace and entertained at the Bath Club. Dry lectures in Christian ethics ground on at All Saints, Margaret Street; Dean Ryle lectured on the Old Testament at the Abbey. Pioneering priests were blazing spectacular trails in industrial areas and in the East End slums, but for the most part, complacency and doldrums dominated the churches of the rich.

'I am sweating with horror,' Dick wrote to Alan Don, when his doctors pronounced him fit. 'Cosmo's brain is at work, and I believe it is pointing to West London.'

Within a week, the decision was made. 'I have tried so hard to quiet my conscience and allow myself the glorious battle in the north,' he admitted, 'but this FILTHY West London keeps on calling softly but horribly persistently.'

On April 19th, he wrote to Alan Don to say he had 'closed with Old Thick'.

Old Thick—Archdeacon Thicknesse—was himself new to his Mayfair parish of St. George's, Hanover Square, a drab barn of a place which he was stripping of varnish and painting white. Incorporated within the parish were two smaller churches: the Grosvenor Chapel in South Audley Street, which was being renovated and redecorated, and a pretty little imitation country church called St. Mary's, built in red brick in Bourdon Street mews for the use of the coachmen.

A few people attended St. George's, and nobody attended St. Mary's, where rows of hard-backed chairs filled the plain interior.

'It will probably be worse than anything I have yet encountered,' Dick grumbled pessimistically. 'As far as I can make out, my parishioners will be Rosebery and Bob Siever, Hugh Cecil and Sol Joel, and a few chauffeurs, who will be much better dressed than I could ever hope to be.'

First impressions led him to call the place wondrously stiff and pauperised. 'I've got the pleasant job of telling all the classes they're not going to get any more buns served up to make the Gospel more palatable,' he said. 'I don't see how I can possibly get any sort of congregation together for a year at least.'

Cards were placed on each chair with a prayer by John Oxenham printed on them: 'Father, we pray thee to send into our hearts and into the hearts of all people everywhere, the spirit of our Lord Jesus Christ.' Later, Hugo Johnston, one of Dick's closest friends, and a curate at St. Martin's, called the words the key to Dick's character.

Services were straight Church of England; sermons pure gospel and an immense effort. 'I'm no good in the wood,' Dick always insisted.

He simply preached St. Matthew, St. Mark, St. Luke and St. John [says Archbishop Thicknesse's daughter]. I was young, and there were tremendously learned people in London who talked a lot. Dick was very direct, and he didn't go in for frills. If he disapproved of something, he was very outspoken about it. If you said something stupid, he let you know that you had. He never said things just to please, and yet he had a kind of magnetism.

A lot of clergy were saying, 'What about this man Sheppard?'

Soon, the doors of the church had to be shut five minutes before the service began, because the place was full. 'My little

St. Mary's is getting along quite nicely,' Dick wrote to a friend.
'It has proved to me that Mayfair is just as hungry for the Gospel
as Poplar or Bethnal Green.'

He roped in aristocratic amateurs to sing at parish parties, and
started a typically pre-Great War club called The Cavendish,
backed by the Duke of Devonshire, which aimed to encourage
ex-public-school men into social work and Christian commitment.

'Half the peerage has joined,' Dick wrote, soon after the Club
began in 1911, and membership rocketed to two hundred and
fifty in the first ten days. 'It's the rummiest collection of members
you ever saw. Public schoolboys and undergrads, cranks and
doctors and lawyers and soldiers. I don't suppose such a gang
ever entered the same building before.'

Every week, a hundred of them gave up their weekend in the
country to sing in the church choir and overflow the choirstalls.

> He was like a breath of fresh air [says Thicknesse's daughter].
> He had a pale face, and he had bad health. He was nothing to
> look at, and yet he was wonderful. He should have been in
> Music Hall: he could be George Formby at a moment's
> notice, or turn up his collar and be a nun.
>
> My father was rather serious-minded towards his children,
> and Dick had a mission to make our lives less solemn. He'd
> appear round the door with three minutes to spare, and he'd
> spend every one of those three minutes totally with us. He never
> said 'I must go soon' or 'I'm in a hurry', or 'I've only got a
> second'. He sat down and talked, and then he got up and went,
> and you saw him rush down the road waving his umbrella for a
> taxi.
>
> He always had piles of correspondence which he brought
> back to our house to dictate in the bedroom. Often he was up
> all night, rushing off because someone far away needed com-
> fort and it never occurred to him to refuse. He never seemed to
> sleep, and he was always reading books on railway journeys.
>
> The tango was just coming in, and he beat all the other young
> men at it. Then you'd come in and find him dead asleep in a
> chair.

In the spring of 1912, Dick's old leg wound was worrying him, and he had to go into hospital for an operation. When he came out, he was forced to rest. Archdeacon Thicknesse was a tower of strength, visiting and encouraging and calling Dick one of the best organising brains of the generation, but it was a problematic time of success tempered with recurrent exhaustion, of joy and questioning: 'I hate everything,' he claimed sweepingly, 'the rich and the poor.'

But the rich and the poor were devoted to him, and only complained that there was not room enough for them all to fit comfortably into St. Mary's. 'Much as I dislike West London,' Dick admitted grudgingly, 'I quite see the importance of it.'

Two months later, he was impetuously contemplating the offer of the living of Windsor.

> I cannot see how what we both accepted as God's purpose for you in February can be regarded as no longer His purpose in April [was Lang's pained reply]. Decisions of this kind are very responsible things and they ought not to be set aside so quickly.
>
> I admit the attractions of Windsor: I don't see the call. I do see, so do you, so at least you did two months ago, the call of West London. You felt the attractions also. But that is a secondary matter. And if the attractions ought not to weigh too much, still less [he added shrewdly] ought apprehensions.

By 1913, preparations were going ahead for the re-opening of the colonial-style eighteenth-century Grosvenor Chapel. Since the previous priest-in-charge had remarked grudgingly that he supposed there were uglier churches to be found, Ninian Comper, famous for his designs at St. Cypriot's in Baker Street, had been brought in to transform the dark little galleried hall into a gleaming temple of bright, white light, with golden angels and an ornate rood screen which was immediately condemned as High Church.

Trevelyan, an Anglo-Catholic famous for his work in the Westminster slums and at Liddon House, where he was Warden, had been invited to come as priest-in-charge. Before he could take up the appointment, he fell seriously ill, and Thicknesse asked Dick to take his place. Cornered for the moment on his uncomfortable West End cross, Dick accepted.

He turned down an offer of a living in Pretoria—'with a heart that is almost broken in two'—and quixotically offered to give up what he was calling the finest site in London, to help Lang by taking the post of chaplain at Bishopsthorpe. Instead, they went on holiday together again, and Dick nearly collapsed with fatigue.

'I don't know what we are going to do with him,' Lang wrote despairingly to his chaplain. 'He can't go on like this, and is impervious to reason, yet he is doing great work.'

In November, he went as curate-in-charge to the Grosvenor Chapel, and was relieved to find that his congregation at St. Mary's did not follow him. Numbers there hardly dropped, and the Cavendish Club choir sang on regularly. In many ways it was, and was always to be, a greater tribute to him than the fact that so many people had come in the first place.

At the Grosvenor Chapel, it was to be a repeat performance. He preached a sermon on owing money, and asked his congregation to think what they would look like if all the clothes they had not paid for were suddenly stripped off their backs. 'In Mayfair,' he said on another occasion, 'there is a curious tendency to believe that a talk with the vicar in the school holidays will counteract the influence of years of home neglect and indifferent Christian example.'

When ladies made too much noise with their fans on a warm summer day, he tartly suggested sending round the verger with iced drinks.

One member of the congregation left the church, 'because I ventured to suggest that that part of Matins which had reference to Og, the King of Basan, was not, as I thought, of paramount importance,' and Lady Meresia Nevill, his childhood astonishment, called him a socialist and a bolshevist.

'He's the best chap I ever met,' wrote a parishioner. 'Today the church was packed for the three hours' service. He has the power of getting at one's heart-strings in a way no other parson has. The worst of it is, one never can get hold of him, he is so busy.'

When two little girls crept into the Devonshires' pew, and only discovered their mistake during the service, when the Devonshires crowded in on top of them, Dick chuckled with delight, and they never forgot him for it.

'Your prayers are worth all in the world to me,' said a young man facing illness, madness and death.

To Dick, it seemed that the church filled in spite of, rather than because of, himself. He didn't disclaim his success, but his personality was like a separate entity. At times he used it shamelessly, almost unwittingly. At others, he appeared to regard the results of it with an apologetic humility, as if to say, 'I'm terribly sorry. These things happen, and there's nothing I can do about it.'

The fact that he was becoming one of the most eligible, fashionable young professionals in London largely passed him by, because in his own mind, he had done nothing to earn success, and it was therefore irrelevant. He had a knack of knowing the best people as well as the worst: of being as at home in the back parlour as he was on the stands at Lords. Surrounded by people, longing to share their comedy and their tragedy, his nature was such that he could do nothing but respond.

He was learning to know himself: his limitations and his potential. Every time he passed by the open-air pulpit outside St. James's in Piccadilly, he felt a sense of envy.

With the Church's aptitude for getting things wrong, William Temple was offered a Westminster canonry, only to have the offer hastily retracted when it was discovered that he was not eligible for it. The Bishop of London then intimated to Dick that he might be offered St. James's at the same time as Haldane, the Lord Chancellor, made a similar offer to Temple.

Since it turned out to be the Lord Chancellor's turn to nominate the living, it went to Temple, and Dick continued 'waiting for something big'. Across the road from the Grosvenor Chapel at St. Mark's, North Audley Street, the celebrated Cronshaw emanated jealousy.

For most of Dick's life, what he called personal failure dogged his spectacular public success. He had already suffered one broken engagement. Now he was disappointed again when the girl to

whom he was engaged realised she could face neither the demands
of marriage to him, nor the demands made on a vicar's wife. In
spite of Dick's reassurances she said she was not good enough and
left him.

Before he had fully recovered, a strangely good-looking girl,
tall and blonde, with perceptive blue eyes, came to hear him
preach. 'I'm going to marry that man,' she said to the friend who
was with her as they left the church.

Alison Carver came from Cranage Hall in Cheshire. Her parents
were wealthy cotton-mill owners and she had four older brothers
who adored her. She was the idol of Cheshire, and it was well
known there that one young man had shot himself when she
refused to marry him.

Alison had been taught by a dull German governess who bored
her. She had always been given everything she wanted, which, in
its way, was becoming boring too. She had been sent to London
by her mother, an ardent temperance worker, to help out in the
East End, and she was fascinated by psychic research and
spiritualism. Shy, sensitive, spoiled and very beautiful, she had
an extraordinary magnetism, and as soon as she saw Dick, she
knew that there was some kind of spiritual tie which had to be
shared between them.

She asked Dick if she could come to him for guidance, and
when she did, he was attracted to her. He admired her childlike
directness, her boldness, and the grace of her straight back and
easy movement. And because Dick interested her more than anyone she had ever met, an impetuous vivacity overcame her boredom.

Dick felt the magnetism. Those who knew them both called
them two bright stars. 'Dick,' said a friend, 'was a person who
always had to respond.'

In July 1914, he was offered the post of Vicar of St. Martin-
in-the-Fields. Dyed-in-the-wool clergy quibbled, and criticised
the Bishop of London for offering a two-thousand-pounds-a-year
living to a thirty-four-year-old curate. When he considered
accepting, his friends were astonished. 'You mustn't go there,'
they said. 'You'll be buried alive.'

5

Three Months
on Calvary

CHARLES THE SECOND was baptised at St. Martin-in-the-Fields. George the First was a churchwarden. It was known as a church with a great past and no future. New road schemes had swept away half the parish, which was considered little more than a comfortable sinecure for elderly clergy.

On his first visit, Dick found one thing that attracted him. 'I sat in the empty church for a long time,' he said, 'and the only sound I could hear—to me a strangely hopeful one—was the noise of the busy world outside, punctuated by children's voices in the churchyard.'

The church was dark, with dark varnish and dark pillars. There was no cross on the altar and no candlesticks. The St. Martin's *Monthly Messenger* announced that during the week, the doors would be shut at four o'clock in the afternoon.

I did not find the atmosphere stimulating [Dick said].

The church struck me as cold and rather depressing, and rightly or wrongly, it seemed to me to say, 'Remember, young man, I am decidedly low, even a little flat.'

I loathe and detest ecclesiastical labels, but I must own I would rather smell incense than varnish in the House of God.

That altar, on which stood no cross, seemed to me lacking

and unlovely, and as for that high pulpit—well! if I ever got into it, I should be as remote as Nelson in the Square.

I came away thinking it would be hard for me to feel at home at St. Martin-in-the-Fields.

According to one friend to whom he wrote for advice, he could run the place easily with the help of a part-time curate. The following Sunday, he paid a second visit which was even less encouraging.

The service was conducted by a little man with an amazingly powerful voice. I have never heard a voice boom and thunder through a church in the same way. He roared at us as if he were a sergeant-major shouting against the wind, and my friend, who, like myself, suffers from a tendency to laugh when laughter is out of place, caught my eye and for the rest of the service we sat almost back to back for fear of disgracing ourselves.

Every time an extra powerful blast swept down from the reading-desk, Dick ostentatiously gripped the front of the pew. He was not, he admitted, in any mood to benefit.

The sermon—the longest I think I have ever sat through—seemed to urge us to give all we possessed to a certain church society that had long outlived its usefulness, and for which I had a peculiar dislike.

In the gallery which runs round three sides of the church were a few children very insufficiently policed, and one small boy created great diversion by popping his head up over the pew near the preacher, to make faces at a friend below, and then with incredible speed racing round to repeat his antics on the opposite side of the gallery.

The amazing rate of his progress from one side to the other so fascinated me that I found myself watching him with the deepest interest. Indeed, I was sorely tempted to time his venture by the minute hand of my watch.

Later, he explored the parish, 'talking to all who would talk
to me'. He spoke with patients in the casualty department of
Charing Cross Hospital, and to the people who lived in the
tenement buildings of Bedfordbury. He visited the public
houses and the shops and the hostels, and when night came,
he carried on visiting. The only people still out on the streets
in Piccadilly and by the river were the hurt and the sad and the
people with no home to go to, and he sat on benches with them
and talked until he ended up in the early morning with coffee
and a bun from a stall by the church, sitting on the parapet of the
National Gallery watching the dawn break.

'That night's impressions,' he said, 'persuaded me that no
square mile could provide a more thrilling or adventurous
pitch.'

Within a month, he had decided to accept the living. It was
what he had been looking for; something big and run-down,
with room for manœuvre. Nevertheless, 'St. Martin's is a very
old-fashioned church,' he wrote to a friend. 'I do not think I
should be justified in playing Old Harry there as I have done at
the Grosvenor Chapel.'

It was summer 1914, hot and sunny. By August, the courtyard
of St. Martin's was crowded with boys waiting to enlist. The
majority were young, and many had walked all the way in from
the country.

'Your duty cannot be done unless your health is sound,'
Lord Kitchener warned them as they left on the troop-ships
for France and Belgium. 'Be constantly on your guard against
any excesses. In this new experience you may find temptations,
both in wine and women. You must entirely resist both temptations.'

Dick was to be instituted at St. Martin's-tide in November.
For the three intervening months, he agreed to serve as chaplain
with the Australian Hospital, run by Lady Dudley, one of his
Grosvenor Chapel parishioners. Lang disapproved, but held
his peace, and King George the Fifth, according to a distressed
Dr. Sheppard, 'got quite fierce and told me to say he was dead
against your going'.

On Waterloo Station, a Roman Catholic soldier who was dying

gave him a tiny splintered piece of wood which was framed and said to be a relic from the true cross. Dick called it 'my little bit of the Cross' and kept it all his life. While he was in France, the blast of a shell sent it flying, but he searched in the black mud and disorder of the battlefield until he had it again: 'finding it makes me think it may even be genuine . . .'

In spite of Lord Kitchener's stirring message, the first sight greeting soldiers on their arrival in the French towns and villages were the red lamps of the brothels and long queues of men waiting outside.

Some of us [Dick said] were foolish enough to believe that this ordeal through which the nations were passing would deepen and intensify spiritual values and arouse us to a new apprehension of the things of God.

We learned as the time passed that men who live constantly in the shadow of sudden death are more apt to turn to the Devil than to God.

He celebrated his thirty-fourth birthday kneeling by a dying soldier.

I had just arrived in France [he said] and he was the first soldier I saw die.

As I bent to catch his painfully-spoken words, I discovered that he had had little need of my ministry. He was thinking of a life that was still unborn. His wife was expecting a baby at Christmas, and he died thanking God that if the child was a boy, he would never have to go through the hell of war.

That man believed what he had been told—that he was fighting in the war to end war. Innumerable others also believed it and died, as he did, at least happy in the thought that their sons would be spared Calvary.

Later, he took part in his first infantry attack, praying and running towards the enemy with his eyes shut. 'I've sat in a dug-out expecting the Germans at any moment all through the night,' he wrote to Lang. 'I've held a leg and several other limbs while the surgeon amputated them. I've fought a drunken Tommy and protected several German prisoners from a French mob. I've missed a thousand opportunities and lived through a life's experience in five weeks.'

Your letter made me feel that after all, you were right to go [Lang wrote back]. You are learning lessons which will inspire years of teaching. You are seeing war as it is, apart from its pomp and circumstance and the thrill of the fray. Things that seem give place to things that are.

I don't wonder that war brings the Cross of Christ nearer to you. It is itself a great Immense Calvary, and surely in some mysterious and true sense the Son of Man is there on the old abiding Cross of his suffering and love.

One night, a sergeant, 'as noble a Christian as I ever met', stopped to joke with Dick while his hand was bandaged. Immediately the job was done, he returned to the Front. 'I remember at the time, in the confused way in which we thought in France, seeing in that muddy soldier something of what pain meant to our Lord,' Dick said later.

'His hand hurt like hell, but it never once occurred to him that it should hold him back from his purpose.'

A bishop was seen in a front-line trench wearing gaiters and a tin hat, 'his head moving with the times and his legs firmly rooted in the past,' Dick recounted grimly afterwards, 'like the true reformer!' Sudden exploding shells reminded him of a twenty-stone canon of his Windsor youth, whose laugh went off like a bomb.

'I remember as yesterday seeing German prisoners getting out of a train with tortured bodies and tortured faces,' he was to say over twenty years later. 'The extenuating circumstances given at the time were that some Gordon Highlanders had been put into the train with the Germans immediately after the battalion had been cut to ribbons. They had a great deal to drink and no officer in command.'

Chaplains of different denominations who dropped their

official barriers and worked together were accused of suffering
from shell-shock when they returned to England with a new
vision of Christian unity, and Dick invited soldiers to Holy
Communion only to find that they had always understood it to
be an officers' service.

'Men had been the victims of a veritable caricature of God,'
he said. 'A caricature which the Prayer Book, in certain places,
does a good deal to encourage. The war did not produce this
false God. It brought him into the open.'

Soldiers, exchanging uncharitable remarks about each other
quite openly when they were with him, stopped several times in a
sentence to apologise for swearing.

'Here are men who make use of a silly word or two of slang
about which there is nothing in the smallest degree unchristian,
yet who apologise to the parson, and repeat the apology, for what
they have said,' he said. 'They then proceed to utter sentiments
wholly unchristian and anti-christian. Sentiments which deny
most of everything which the name of Christ stands for, and it
never begins to enter their heads to apologise for it.

'What a give-away for us parsons. What a revelation of the
futility and failure of the ministers of Christ.'

It was, as Lang said, a chaotic seminar, where things that had
seemed gave place shatteringly to the things that were. Dick
dreamed of liberty, and a new life within the Church. It began
with a new creed:

I believe that I—

> Must love God,
> And my neighbour as myself;
> Must love my enemies,
> Bless them that curse me,
> Be good to them that hate me,
> Pray for them that despitefully use me;
> Must judge not,
> Condemn not,
> Forgive, and despair not;
> As I believe in Jesus Christ my Lord.

By October, his health had broken down and he was ordered home.

> He identified himself with every dying man, and in conse-
> quence nearly killed himself [said an Army doctor]. He would
> sit up all night with some soldier, unconscious, kept alive
> only by natural strength and youth, unable to see or whisper
> or make any sign, except, as death came closer, to grip
> Sheppard's hand. Sit there, just because he had promised the
> dying man that he would.
> He had no right to be so reckless, so stupidly careless of the
> elementary rules which govern fatigue and strain.

'I think the memory of those months haunted him all his
life,' said someone who knew him later. 'When he was well,
he never talked about it, but when he was ill, he always remembered Mons. It went deep inside him and he never really
got it out of his system.'

It was while he crouched in the trenches during the weary
retreat from Mons, that he suddenly knew what he was meant to
do with the church that was waiting for him at home in Trafalgar
Square.

6

Two Words Only

LAMP POSTS IN Trafalgar Square bore the insignia of St. Martin wrapping half his cloak round a beggar. The same insignia was on the handles of the doors of the church. Seizing the idea with characteristic impetuosity, Dick had his stipend reduced by half when he arrived at St. Martin's.

If the congregation was not prepared to be what he thought a group of Christians in central London ought to be, and to shoulder the financial responsibilities themselves, their new vicar was not going to fulfil their obligations for them.

The church was dark and unlovely. A glorious Ascension window backed a drab, bare altar. Pews were no longer rented, but they were locked and numbered and unlocked ceremoniously for their owners by official pew-openers on a Sunday morning. Guides met downstairs in the crypt and spent dimly lighted evenings among the tombs. An average of seven attended Matins, and twelve Evensong.

Rich people came to church in carriages with liveried footmen. Poor people who lived in the Peabody tenement buildings of Bedfordbury had their own mission chapel, the church of the Good Shepherd, which was famous because Mr. Gladstone frequented it. Boys helped to pump the old-fashioned organ and the church had a font, but it was not licensed for marriages, funerals, or Holy Communion.

Previous vicars had been old: Prebendary Kitto, with his cooks and his carriages and his children for whom a new floor had been built on top of the vicarage, and Prebendary Shelford who had died at St. Martin's. Sidesmen included a Harley Street specialist and a lord. One of the churchwardens was a publican who spent more of Sunday in his pub than at church, and the other, McMaster, was 'a pompous old devil' who made cavalry boots and wore a skull cap.

By the time Dick came, McMaster had already had his fill of charity work. Trying to help Francis Thompson the poet to give up laudanum by offering him a job, he had been rewarded with *The Hound of Heaven*, but no boots.

According to the editor of the *Church of England Newspaper*, Dick came back from France 'a prophet aflame for God', and his new parish regarded him with justifiable trepidation.

Eleven people came to his Induction on a foggy November morning. 'As long as I live, I shall never forget that day,' he said later. Awaiting the Commission he longed to escape from the sanctuary, crying in his heart, 'Please don't look at me—for God's sake pray for me!'

To those eleven people, he told the vision that had come to him in the trenches.

I saw a great church standing in the greatest square in the greatest city of the world [he said]. And I stood on the west steps and I saw what this church would be to the life of the people.

There passed me into its warm inside, hundreds and hundreds of all sorts of people, going up to the temple of their Lord, with all their difficulties, trials and sorrows. I saw it full of people, dropping in at all hours of the day and night. It was never dark, it was lighted all night and all day, and often and often tired bits of humanity swept in.

And I said to them as they passed: 'Where are you going?' And they said only one thing: 'This is our home. This is where we are going to learn of the love of Jesus Christ. This is the altar of our Lord, where all our peace lies. This is St. Martin's.'

It was all reverent and full of love and they never pushed me behind a pillar because I was poor. And day by day they told me the dear Lord's Supper was there on his altar waiting to be given. They spoke to me two words only. One was the word 'home' and the other was 'love'.

And I left that wonderful church then and I looked on the thousand thousand that streamed by, and I recognised that into them were going all the great flood of those who loved their Lord. They were mixing with the crowd and telling them: 'We know the Lord and love the Lord'.

Will you give a hand? [he asked his small, surprised congregation]. Will you give a hand in trying, even if we fail, to build up this church, in the greatest city in the world? Will you come next Sunday morning at half past eight, those of you who mean to try and help, just in all simplicity to receive in reverence the Body and Blood of Christ, to pledge ourselves, there, God being with us, to have absolute reverence in this church, and absolute love, and to go out from the church to take the story of our Lord into the streets outside?

There may be someone of you who has little to offer [he said]. One who is thinking to himself or herself, 'It is a great scheme, can it be done? Have I anything to offer?' To you, most of all, I would say that you have wonderful things to offer.

The gospel of the day had already been read: a favourite of Dick's, about the miraculous feeding of the five thousand.

There was not enough to go round [he said, recalling it]. And suddenly one of the disciples went to our Lord, almost apologetically, and said, 'There is a small boy here with five loaves and two fishes'.

So small a gift as that! You remember our Lord asked just for those small pieces of bread and the fishes, and you remember that he took them and used them, and everyone had enough. That is the way with our efforts, which to us seem so very small.

But if we offer just the little we have, in love, to our Lord, he will use it. He will say: 'Make the crowd sit down'. He will take our gift.

It was an astonishing vision. Astonishing, because Dick was
a man of his time. He called himself one of the young Victorians,
and only a very reluctant revolutionary. For all her cumbersome
stupidity and short-sightedness, he loved the Church of England,
because he saw in her all the potential for saving a sad world.

The task of a vicar, he said, was nothing less than to present
every man within his district perfect in Christ. It was an awesome thought: one that overwhelmed him throughout the
ceremony.

'Who,' he asked, 'is sufficient for these things?'

St. Martin's Lane led north from the church and it was much
like Soho today. Pick-pockets made a living from the courts
opposite Bedfordbury. Crowds gathered at the weekends in
Trafalgar Square, and in Leicester Square, to sit on the benches
where Dick had sat with his grandfather. Charing Cross Hospital
and Charing Cross Station were two minutes' walk from the
vicarage.

Wounded soldiers waved to girls in the streets below from the
hospital windows, and when they threw down bandages, the
girls tied fruit and chocolates and cigarettes to them for the
soldiers to haul up again. Crowded troop-trains arrived and
left in the early morning, and throughout the night there were
soldiers sleeping on the church steps, or keeping dubious rendez-
vous in the dark.

When I first arrived at my new home, it was still in the
hands of the decorators and threatened to remain so for ever
[Dick said later]. My first night there was not propitious. The
handles were not on the doors and the rooms were practically
unfurnished. I arrived more to get the workmen out than to
enjoy myself. Rather rashly I had invited a friend to dine,
and I was so tired that I told him I should go to bed at ten
whatever happened.

We talked, oh how we talked! But ten came, and true to my
word I said good night and stumbled to the study door. But
man proposes . . . the study door was shut and there was no
handle to turn, and no bell to summon the kindly aid on the
top floor.

We tried to climb over the area railings outside the window, and I even called the police to our aid, but all was in vain. (Subsequent history has proved it easier to break into than out of the Vicarage.) There we were all through what the hymn calls the livelong night, with no coal for the fire on a bitter night, and only one rug on the floor in which in the end we wrapped ourselves and lay down, he to continue talking, I to groan till the blessed morning broke, and with it the hope of release.

Oh, the cold and misery of that first night in the Vicarage!

When it was evident that the back room of the ground floor was the haunt of footballs and cricket balls from the courtyard—using it as a study, Dick found that the boy who landed a ball on his desk scored six—he moved to the front room instead, chain-smoking and holding court from one of the red-cushioned seats beside the high fireguard. Tall windows looked out across the Square.

'No one can realise how ominous it became at sunset,' he said. 'It seemed that besides revellers, all the most undesirable people in London were washed up into our darkened parish.'

When he wasn't still up and around, he spent the night reading and sleeping badly, waking in time to watch from his window as the sun came up, as he had watched it the first time he visited the parish.

'I loved to be awake then, and to go to my window and look across the Square,' he said, spellbound by 'the haunting stillness of that one quarter of an hour in the whole twenty-four when as if by magic, Trafalgar Square empties and becomes completely still and silent.

'It seemed to me that it was then more than at any other time, that the needs and longings of those who lived in the shadow of the church could, so to speak, be held up before God.'

By Christmas, there was a plain cross and two candlesticks on the altar. A meeting of the church vestry had been called before the decision could be made. 'I think they add dignity and reverence to our morning worship,' Dick commented carefully. 'The present ones are only temporary . . .'

Like a tactician, picking his generals and deploying them strategically, he planned work for six curates, two part-time and four full-time. 'I feel very strongly that a church like ours, which belongs to London as well as to the parish, should have a large staff of responsible clergy,' he said, 'some of whom are giving themselves to the parish and some of whom are being given by the parish to the big problems that are not limited by parochial boundaries.'

Oliver Quick, one of the original members of The Clique, gave up the vice-principalship of the Leeds Clergy School to come and write theological books under St. Martin's aegis. Utterly different from Dick, Oliver said working with him had been one of the hopes of his life.

Hugh Matthews, 'who carries the joy of his faith in his face', came from the East End, where he had been serving his title, and Wilfred Parker gave up a parish in Johannesburg: 'I think I am the luckiest man in the world to have you,' Dick wrote.

Claude Jenkins, a part-time member of the staff for the previous ten years, agreed to stay. Professor of Ecclesiastical History at King's College, London, he was to write later in the *National Dictionary of Biography* of Dick's 'great organising ability, intuitive sympathy, and simple, kindly, often humorous direct-ness of speech. Sheppard united an irresistible desire to make others happier and to enlist them in a fellowship of service,' he said.

His curates called Monday morning staff meetings thrilling occasions. Full of exuberance one day and down in the dumps the next, indignantly condemning and outrageously tolerant, demand-ing criticism and acquiescing with an eager humility, he involved them in his own excitements and disappointments, discussing new ideas and sharing encouraging encounters.

'He loved to make people feel at home, and to feel at home with them himself,' said Pat McCormick later, succeeding Dick as Vicar of St. Martin's. 'He made his congregation feel not that they were members of a team, but of a family.

'He was like the men in the trenches. He could turn from gay to grave in a moment, and you would find that the humour was often the stepping-stone to a glorious and profound truth. To

meet him you would think he hadn't a care in the world, and
then you would find a sense of humour so profound that it often
shocked people.'

A painfully tactful letter in the January issue of the St. Martin's
Monthly Messenger displayed diplomatic determination. To most
of the old-guard, it looked like the thin end of the wedge.

Dear People, I want you to be patient with me [he began,
asking those who had hitherto received the magazine free to
pay twopence for it]. I am going to ask you to forgive me if I
make some alterations in the times and forms of our services,
and to believe that the only motive that prompts these altera-
tions is that our church may, by the extension of her arms,
gather more into her embrace.

However beautiful Evensong is to those who love our church,
we must be obliged reluctantly to confess that there are thousands among us who need catering for with something that
is a little more simple and more warm and loving in its appeal
for men and women at the beginning of their search for
Christianity.

Blandly self-confident, he went on by suggesting a voluntary
choir of one hundred and fifty to sing at mission services, and a
large parish room where people could meet.

Quite soon, I am afraid you will be receiving an appeal
from me asking all who worship in the church and care for it,
to contribute to its upkeep and its spiritual requirements.

Please remember [he ended tactfully], I have no wish to do
away with all that has been done at St. Martin's for so many
years. Rather, just because it has been done, it has made it
possible for me to suggest that we should make additions
which I am certain will not be out of place on the foundations which have already been laid by those faithful clergy
and laity who have gone before.

That, he hoped would stop the mouths of those who said that

nothing could ever be done that had not been done before, and the remainder, who insisted that what had been done before must continue to be done. Of course, it did nothing of the kind.

For one who was being pilloried as an upstart and a revolutionary, he published a surprisingly weighty list of establishment preachers. They included the Archbishops of York and Armagh, eleven bishops, the Archdeacon of London and Dean Inge. When Bishop Gore came to preach, Dick was furious with two sidesmen who chatted at the back of the church throughout the sermon. Disappointed and disillusioned, he found such rudeness and apathy almost impossible to understand.

He was thirty-four years old, with dark hair, pointed ears, and quizzically arched eyebrows. Many old St. Martin's people were automatically prejudiced against him because he was young. Throughout Bedfordbury, where his presence was a surprise, he was known as The Boy.

By Easter, there were rich-coloured hangings on the altar, and a ten-fifteen Choral Communion, which was Dick's favourite service. One of the sidesmen wrote to say he had never seen such absurd ceremonial since visiting a Shinto temple in Japan. On Easter Sunday, the churchwarden walked in from his public house in time to receive communion, turned away from the altar, and walked out of the church before the service ended, as he always did, to return to his pub.

Dick stalked down from the altar and through the church catching up with him on the portico. Hardly able to speak for anger, he told the man that he would not be welcome at the altar again. When the publican wrote through his lawyer threatening to take the case to court, Dick said he would be delighted—and heard no more.

By April, after working non-stop since he came home from France, he was ill again. 'You are a religious genius,' said Oliver Quick. 'My hope and prayer is that you will understand your physical limitations sufficiently to give your genius a fair chance.' Recuperating at the Carvers' home in Cheshire, where a wing of Cranage Hall had been turned into a convalescent home for officers, Dick and Alison were aware again of the strange animal magnetism that drew them together.

In need of the very things neither of them could satisfy, they became engaged.

It had been expected that Alison would marry the local clergyman, a man strong enough and sure enough to dominate her. Dick, ingenuous, secretive and never wholly self-sufficient, idealised women and romanticised the idea of marriage.

If God permits me to win her love [he wrote years later in a newspaper fantasy], may he protect me from ever killing her romance or ever dragging her out of the fair land in which she lives, and in which she is even now seeking for a fairy prince.

I suppose if I loved her as a man should love, I would wish her to meet that prince and to love him, and the measure of my sorrow is that I love her so much that I would fain act the prince and deceive her, even while my whole soul tells me that I am not great enough either to take or to sustain the part.

One day Alison made herself look foolish playing tennis, reaching dramatically for a ball and throwing her racket at it so that it flew out of her hand and hit her on the head. When she rushed from the court and shut herself in her bedroom, reproaching Dick for hitting her and sobbing that the engagement was broken, he smiled patiently and blamed his own stupidity.

'She rides like the wind,' he wrote to Wilfred Parker. 'She loves Christ more than anyone I have ever met, and she is as beautiful as she is good.'

The wedding took place in June, overshadowed by mourning for men lost at Gallipoli and Ypres. Archbishop Lang took the service, and talked of it as 'a day sent to cheer us in our sadness'. The village was hung with flags and Boy Scouts formed a guard of honour. Afterwards, Dick and Alison rode to Cranage Hall standing on the seat of the car, waving to the villagers of Holmes Chapel. A band played in the grounds, and there were gifts from the Prince of Wales among the presents on show.

You, my dear brother in Christ, you who are so specially

endowed with the gifts of sympathy, love and kindly feeling towards your fellow creatures [said Lang], you must realise that you need a gentle and restraining hand to guard you from spending yourself too freely for them. You will always obey this restraining hand, because it is one you love.

You, dear bride, who are called to help him in his work for God—for his life is set apart for God's service—must realise the honour of your call. You know that he needs a gentle influence in his life, which must ever guide and aid him in his important work.

I would like to say to you both that you must guard your home life from being sacrificed to this work for God. Let love always be present there. God wishes this, for God is love.

When they returned to St. Martin's, bell-ringers rang a special peal of bells, but Alison asked them to stop because she had a headache. Dick was determined that a vicar's wife should never become an unpaid curate.

He treated her young, like a sister [says a Bedfordbury parishioner who still remembers today]. He brought her to introduce her to us, and she was just like a girl. She had a girlish dress—just below the knee, but girlish for that period. It was pale blue, with a brim hat and a lovely wide sash with a big bow at the back.

She'd come to meetings with him and sit at the side of him like a sidesman, or jump in his chair and share it with him. I can see her now, if it was cold in the vestry, with his overcoat round her shoulders.

He had no rest, though, even in his early married life. He was in the church because he was wanted there, and he'd be out all hours of the night, like as if he preferred to live always and not to have any rest.

She had a lot to bear, being young. He was torn between her and the people but I suppose she understood.

At Christmastime they entertained parishioners to dinner in the vicarage; a banquet of roast beef and plum pudding, followed by cigars and sweets and fruit. Dick was thirty-five and Alison was twenty-three, younger, and so much in love that she would have done anything for him. She was childlike, direct and imaginative. She enjoyed making the enormous old vicarage warm and comfy, and when Dick came home tired, she had a magical way of lifting his spirits and taking him out of himself.

As the months went on, he became more and more involved with the parish, out all day and up half the night, calling St. Martin's the little drawing-room of God. His aim, perhaps a mistaken one, was to shield Alison from anything she might find tedious or difficult or tough. When the vicarage was finished, and he sensed she was becoming bored, he blamed himself, and sent her away on holiday.

Instead of going with her, he found a companion for her, and began planning how to play Old Harry with St. Martin-in-the-Fields.

7

Playing Old Harry

I AM QUITE certain that where possible, big central churches like St. Martin-in-the-Fields ought to be entirely free and open, and no seats should be reserved [Dick wrote in the December *Messenger*]. Everyone, poor and rich alike, should sit wherever they choose.

I am afraid that is asking a good deal of some of you who have had seats for some time, yet I think you will realise what a great benefit it will be for the worship of the church. I would also like to point out that there will never be any difficulty in people sitting in their present seats or in any seats which they would prefer, provided they would come a few minutes before the service begins.

Therefore on December 16th I am going to propose at the Vestry meeting that the church shall be free and open and that allotment of seats be rescinded, and I can only ask those who will feel hurt if this resolution passes, to forgive me and believe that I am only considering what I feel to be best for the welfare of the church we all love.

To the intense displeasure of one old lady who had installed all kinds of contraptions for her comfort, including an umbrella stand, the motion was passed. The doors of the high-backed pews were taken off their hinges, and all through Lent Dick led open-air Mission services in Bedfordbury to try to attract people to their parish church.

'I hope we left some impression behind us, but I cannot say we had a large and enthusiastic audience,' he reported. 'We spoke mainly to heads behind windows at the top of the buildings, and to the wall opposite.' Whenever he could, he went from door to door along the echoing stone corridors of Bedfordbury, telling the people there that St. Martin's was their church and they could come when they wanted and sit where they liked.

He put it to us [remember the old people]. He came and said that St. Martin's was our church and he wanted us to feel welcome there. He said he wanted his own people from his own parish in his own church. He told the Mayfair people that they had their own churches, and St. Martin's belonged to the people of St. Martin's. He said it from the pulpit, but it didn't make any difference. They still came, and it didn't matter who they were, they were put in the pews the same as other people, even if there was someone out on the pavement holding the horses of their carriage for them.

Soon the figure of the vicar with the slight limp became well known in the streets behind the church. Where once doors had been opened with infrequent ceremony to wise and elderly gentlemen, they were now opened with pleasure to a man many of them still regarded as a student.

'We used to play cricket in the yards with a stick and a ball of newspaper,' remember the men today. 'Whenever he passed, he'd stop and take off his jacket and hang it on the railings and roll up his sleeves and join in.' The next afternoon he could equally well be in the stands at Lords, or playing for the I Zingari.

1916 was the year of the National Mission, when Church leaders made a concerted effort to cash in on the intense emotionalism of the time. Studdert Kennedy, dishing out Bibles and packets of Woodbines at the River Gauche Siding *en route* for Ypres, called it a run on the bank of God. Off the main cobbled street at Poperinghe, Tubby Clayton opened Talbot House—Toc H—'a home for Jesus Christ in Flanders', where troops were told 'If you are in the habit of spitting on the carpet at home, please spit here' and invited to 'come upstairs and risk meeting the Chaplain'. Up a ladder in the hoploft, corps commanders knelt by corporals and 'prayed as they'd never prayed before'.

Betrayed by the horror and the duration of the war, Dick called the phrase 'Dearly beloved brethren' nothing more than an occasion for parody. 'The Magnificat,' he said, 'is as much more revolutionary as it is more beautiful than "The Red Flag", and it is only because we sing it without thought that we fail to realise the fact.'

Adapting to what he saw as the need of the moment, he began simplifying services, cutting the long litany, the Exhortation, and the psalms, many of which he thought wholly pagan, and maintaining that if a parson couldn't do what he wanted to do in an hour, there was something wrong. At the same time, he preached on the tortuous Athanasian Creed, admitting he could not understand it, but calling it the enthralling song of the love of Jesus.

He backed the National Mission to the hilt, but it was out of loyalty rather than realism: a desperate, illogical hope that for once, actions might accompany the welter of words.

'The world is so evidently waiting either for chaos or Christ,' he said, 'and the Lord have pity on the Church if she fail to recognise that she must fight now as she never fought before, and with weapons that are forged for a modern warfare, that chaos may not win the day.'

He loved the Church and despaired of it, and set to work to coax and bludgeon and shame his own small patch of it into shape. When he opened a bookstall in the porch, newspapers called it 'an ultra-modern institution'. When he decided to keep the church doors open all night and invite the soldiers in out of the cold, they were up in arms.

The troops arrived in London at half-past two in the morning, when even the Y.M.C.A. and the cafés were closed [remembers a member of the congregation]. Troop-trains didn't leave London until the early morning, so Dick said they must come to St. Martin's.

There was an uproar. People thought they'd bring bugs into the church. There was an enormous row, but nothing happened. The troops went on coming, and people gradually accepted that they should come. People did accept things with Dick. He was doing what he knew was right, and in the end, they were proud of him.

Audaciously sentimental, he had a red lamp hung from the door of the church, glowing all night in the darkness, reminiscent of those other red lamps that drew the crowds so heartlessly in France.

They had passed me, some dozen of them, tramping across Trafalgar Square [wrote a reporter from *The Globe*]. It was so dark, for it was long past midnight, that I only just escaped cannoning against the impediments that soldiers returning from the Front hang round them. Their pockets, stuffed to bursting, swelled their forms outwards, even the rifles were bandaged round the trigger guard, and in the dim light they looked less like men than moving heaps of parcels. The darkness swallowed them, and only their steady tramp echoed across the deserted Square.

A small red light, glowing under the portico of St. Martin's, attracted me, and I felt my way up the steps of the church. On reaching the pavement of the portico I found that the light was illuminating a board on which a notice read: 'This church is open day and night for soldiers.' Wondering if the invitation was accepted, I pushed the swing doors and entered the church.

The air struck warm inside and gave a feeling of great repose. The place was strangely silent. Two or three electric lights twinkled beneath the galleries which surround the nave, and the little light they shed made the interior of the building vaster than it is. The capitals of the pillars were lost in the darkness of the roof, and not a line could be seen of the tracery of the ceiling.

The altar, lit by candles, alone glowed out of the blue-greys and darkness of the chancel. It was almost dazzling in its white-ness. A gold cross glinted on the table, some gold needlework on the altar-cloth sparkled, and two vases of white lilies shone in the rays of the candles.

Coming from without, with the rumble of London traffic still

in my ears, the stillness was so profound that it seemed to me
I was the only thing alive in the building. But as my eyes grew
accustomed to the darkness I noticed a bowed head, and the
kneeling figure of a Scots soldier at the further end of the pew
into which I had sunk. So still was he that he might have been
cut from wood. Then I discovered other bowed heads and
kneeling figures, no two together, but scattered in separate
pews, and piled on the seats beside them were their bundles.

There was no music from the organ. No singing of choir, no
exhortation being given from the great pulpit. No talking of any
kind. Possibly there has been too much talking, too much
sermonising, too many exhortations.

I tiptoed out of the church, and standing by one of the great
pillars of the portico, I looked down on the shining black
surface of the Square. There was a swish of rain, overhead the
broken clouds flying fast, and Nelson's Column, silhouetted
against the night sky, from where I stood, looked like an
enormous cross held up high in the heavens.

Behind me the swing doors parted and an Australian trooper
passed under the red light. Again there was a tramp, tramp of
feet crossing the Square. The man swung his rifle on top of the
haversack, and putting both hands to his mouth gave a shrill
Coo-ee.

'Coo-ee' echoed back from the darkness of the Square, and
the tramp, tramp stopped. 'Half a mo', I'm coming!' was
shouted, and the soldier ran down the steps of the church and
the blackness swallowed him.

Dick preached a blunt sermon on the money needed to support
such a venture, in addition to staff salaries, printing, postage,
bell-ringing, flowers, altar hangings, choir and organist. 'I sometimes think I must needs file a petition as a bankrupt before this
neighbourhood will appreciate that the money at the Vicar's
disposal is not inexhaustible,' he said.

People who worked with him were learning a new scale of
priorities: 'Never mind whether we have the money. Is it right
that we should do this? Decide that, and talk about the money
afterwards.'

'The financial policy at St. Martin's was not a very complicated one,' said Harold Anson. 'It consisted in seeking first the Kingdom of God and his righteousness, in the security that "All these things shall be added unto you".' Girl Guides, accepting the challenge, held frequent jumble sales, taking the Scouts' trek cart to Carlton House Terrace and trundling it back along Pall Mall *à la* Toulouse-Lautrec, topped with upper-class cast-offs: a bird-cage and a pair of black stays.

'Only one thing now stands between us and the development of an aggressive policy of Christian adventure, and that is our need of money,' he said, begging shamelessly whenever he could. Even *Punch* magazine chided him gently for financial opportunism:

> St. Martin-in-the-Fields,
> St. Martin-in-the-Fields,
> Considering the barley
> To find out what it yields;
> If the yield is scanty
> He's going to plant oats,
> And sell the crop for lambs' wool
> To make beggars' coats.

Again, as always, it was the thin end of the wedge. All kinds of people began coming to the church at night, the lonely and the destitute as well as soldiers and people sheltering from air-raids. Helpers guided women to one side and men to the other. 'That church is a most curious place,' said a young Army doctor, invalided home from Mesopotamia, tired out after a fruitless search for lodgings. 'People kept on coming in to say their prayers. Some stayed, some went to sleep, some went away, and yet it was as still as anything all the time. Something in the church itself seemed to get hold of you . . .'

When an Admiralty official's wife slept the night in the church, to see what was going on, Dick told her to keep her shoes on if she didn't want them to disappear, and to treat every blasphemous word as a cry for help. She calls him the most practical Christian she has ever known. Others commented on his extraordinary love for the spiritually down and out.

A girl came with lilies in her arms to lay them on the altar when her lover was killed in France, and Tubby Clayton, slipping in to the church on short leave, went back to Poperinghe and renamed his Upper Room the Chapel of St. Martin-in-the-Fields. Dick recorded a scrap of conversation overheard between two commercial travellers in Wales.

'What church do you go to when you're in London?'

'St. Martin-in-the-Fields.'

'What's the name of the vicar there?'

'I haven't the slightest idea. All I know is that it's open all night and all day, and that's good enough for me.'

A shrewd observer commented that the St. Martin's congregation was beginning to display a smug familiarity as its numbers grew and the posters proliferated on its railings. 'I am now able to tell you that the Churchwardens and I have been able to instruct the architect to go ahead with our hall,' Dick announced at Christmas. 'We are proposing to convert the vaults . . .'

'What with air-raids outside the church and you inside, there seems nothing but explosions,' sighed an old lady.

The new year of 1917 opened with St. Martin's being heralded as a little Sorbonne by John Garrett Leigh of *The Treasury*. Quoting a forthcoming list of lay speakers from Irving to Lansbury, he said:

As I understand it, the church of St. Martin's is to become a little university, a place where something is to be done in the direction of helping ordinary men and women to understand something of the relationship of religion to everything in life around them.

There is to be no realm of human life which is not to be brought to the touchstone of the Cross. St. Martin's is a challenge in stone. It protests to all the materialism and self-seeking that it has its own special message. The Gospel is for the solution of problems; the weary and distressed may find in the Gospel the true balm for all earth's questioning and wonder.

For this, St. Martin's stands today.

Dick was a realist as well as a sentimentalist: it was another tripwire in his deceptively un-complex make-up. 'I am bound to say,' he admitted cheerfully, 'that though many addresses have been instructive and very intelligent, only one layman has preached the Gospel, and he was once a carpenter in Bethnal Green!'

In January, a Guild of Fellowship was started, over a hundred joining from all the different church organisations, pledged to help with parish work and with social work within the community.

In February, the first Parish Conference was held, when subjects like 'Improvement or Deletion of Existing Services', 'Means of Strengthening the Fellowship of the Congregation' and 'Means of Counteracting Evil Influences in the Neighbourhood' were discussed freely between clergy—those who had not been commandeered for war service—and laity.

In the summer, a new Girls' Club was opened at the top of No. 449, Strand, a tall building like a lighthouse, with neon lighting round its high circular rooms. Catering for chorus girls and struggling young actresses, it soon grew into a hostel run by Lady Mabelle Egerton, who had come back from a canteen at the River Gauche Siding, where Studdert Kennedy had drunk mugs of tea and absent-mindedly eaten left-overs after the troop-trains had gone.

In the summer, too, the Bedfordbury Mission church closed. 'Everyone trusted him,' say old people from the Buildings now. 'Even before he got married, people would say if they could only stretch their hand through a group and have a grip of his hand, so much as to say "I know—I understand," they'd be satisfied. He seemed to reach your thoughts. He'd look at a face through a crowd of faces and say "How's he getting on?" and that helped us and lifted us up.'

Twelve hundred people were coming to church for the Sunday morning service, and parishioners were finding that even what Dick called a little judicial umbrella work did not always secure a good seat. 'It may be hard for a rich man to enter the Kingdom of Heaven,' said one of them, 'but it is easier for the camel to go through the eye of a needle than for a parishioner of St. Martin's to get into his own church.' Children ran out into the street, hanging on to his hands and begging him to stop for a game. Once a week, Lady Egerton's daughter came to him for confirmation lessons. She calls him a plain man, pale, pudgy and pug-faced, with a marvellous sense of the *risqué* and the ridiculous.

He always called me Miss Joan [she says], and yet he was the sort of person one could say anything to. I was a shy, gauche teenager, and I had a big hate against the Bible and religion, but even if you'd committed the most ghastly crime, he would have said 'Oh yes'.

He told me riveting stories about his ambition to break the bank of Monte Carlo, and he never asked me any catechism, but he put over the whole idea of religion all the time.

He was so in touch with it that he seemed to be not quite human.

Before I talked to him, I knew you were supposed to go to church, and if you didn't you'd be burned up in hell. This companionship with God was new to me.

Tentatively announcing a popular Sunday afternoon service especially for sailors and soldiers, with hymns and a short address, he suggested parishioners should sit in the galleries until they knew how many men from the forces would come. Seats were reserved for the wounded, and provision made for wheelchairs, and when over one thousand three hundred people came to the second service, St. Martin's people were crowded out, the church full of troops with their wives and sisters and girlfriends, and the choirstalls filled with the unfamiliar red and gold of the Guards' band.

Over the next months, the service became so popular that King George and Queen Mary attended, and Dick left his notes— 'Loyal and sincere gratitude to His Majesty, but no soap'—lying beside the service paper in the King's pew.

By the autumn, parishioners were considering bringing camp-stools to church with them, and men with poles were stationed at the doors to control the crowds. By winter, the vaults were open, transformed into a hall and five big rooms. The dampness was dried and the darkness made bright with lights, and everyone came to shelter from the Zeppelins and the shrapnel or just from the cold, and no one was turned away.

'Would it not be glorious if in a few years' time we are able within our parish not only to baptise, marry and bury our parishioners, but to keep them instructed, happy and cared for—yes, and entertained from their childhood days,' Dick was able to write joyfully in a magazine which more and more reflected a communal sense of astonished enthusiasm as the dry bones of what had been condemned as a moribund parish came rattling to life again.

'You ought to have insisted on reform,' he said, delivering his usual blend of autocratic democracy in clipped, plaintive tones.

But you have been so lethargic and conservative that you have consented to a system which is indefensible, and to a Church that is saying almost nothing to the problems of human life.

To me it seems clear that the next revival of religion will not run through the channels of any one denomination, but that each Christian church will be used in proportion as it can respond to a gospel of upheaval which must surely be the first characteristic of the gale of God.

The first stage towards that goal is to cease to be bitter about Roman Catholics and snobbish about Nonconformity, and even to be tolerant towards the extreme ends of our own church.

At night, wherever he had been during the evening, Dick went to walk through the church and the crypt to see who was there and what he could do for them, and what he did, he did on impulse. When a soldier fell asleep during a service, he interrupted his sermon to stop an over-zealous sidesman from waking him. When a man began smoking in church, he led him politely to the door, explaining how heavy the air would be if everyone smoked. A tramp, complaining that he wasn't allowed to hang his shirt over the front pew to dry after washing it in the crypt, learned, perhaps to his surprise, that the church was primarily a church and not a wash-house.

'I suppose it's too much to hope that I shall find a Book of Common Prayer in this church,' said Hensley Henson, the acid Dean of Durham, when he came to preach.

'We take our religion too seriously,' Dick insisted. 'It is not adapted for argument. It is at its worst in defence. It is only when the risen Christ in us breaks through to the world that Christianity can live in tears and laughter. Christianity needs presenting, not protecting.'

Later he called his first year at St. Martin's 'just hell'; the first three years, especially difficult. By the end of them, he knew that his vision of the place had a chance of coming true. If he doubted it, a holiday-maker's description must have reassured him:

I have been present at the Sunday services with their crowded congregations. Every day of the week I have been there too. I have seen two or three gather together in the morning and a score or so faithful souls at noon, turning aside from the bustling world to kneel in intercession for their country. I have been present at the quiet evensong. But most strange of all, sometimes in the long night watches, I have entered in. In the dark hours of the night or cheerless early morning, when I suppose the doors of every other church in the great city are bolted and locked and barred, I have climbed the steps of St. Martin's and the doors have swung free upon their hinges, and inside I have found the lighted candles gleaming on the altar and in the pews other wandering pilgrims like myself, resting, praying, perhaps even not afraid to weep; nor any prying inquisitor there to question us or say us nay.

And as I have come and gone, these are the voices that in this wonderful church I have seemed to hear. Chiefly I have seemed to catch the sound of this refrain echoing there: 'Christ's religion is Reality, Christ's religion is Love'. And then sometimes I have thought that I could hear something after this sort: 'Welcome here, ye children of men, be ye nobles or commoners, rich or poor, be ye learned or ignorant, good or bad, be ye High Church or Low Church or no Church, be ye fighters or pacifists. Welcome here, if only ye have some poor love for Christ and your fellows burning in your hearts.'

Have I heard aright? Surely I have, for I go forth from my stay in London a braver man, with a new hope surging up in me that, in spite of the passion and hatred and sadness that has possessed the world today, out of the wreck of his religion our Saviour Christ may yet be born again.

Four thousand people came to the church during the course of St. Martin's day, taking Communion together and breakfasting afterwards in the rooms downstairs where there had been musical chairs and Sir Roger de Coverley the night before. 'At last we are gathered in Fellowship,' Dick said to them. 'Nothing is yet accomplished, but the prospect of what may be is full of hope. We have got to pray and think and plan, but it will be our fault in future if the neighbourhood does not fraternise under the very spire of St. Martin's church.'

People who worked in the area called St. Martin's bells a *Sursum Corda*, as they played 'Oranges and Lemons' and the hymn for Absent Friends. Over four hundred girls joined the Club in the Strand, over a hundred using it every day, and Dick was elected Chairman of the Charing Cross Association, which undertook 'rescue and preventive work' in the area.

In January 1918, after being confined to bed with pneumonia, he presided over the Parish Conference and preached three times on Sundays. 'In spite of this, or because of it,' reported the *Messenger*, 'the doctor flatly refused to allow him to repeat the performance for some weeks, and refused to fall in with Mr. Sheppard's ideas of what is possible for a patient recovering from overstrain complicated by pneumonia'.

Letters were coming to him from all over Europe: there were five St. Martin-in-the-Fields on land and two at sea. 'I am pinning my hopes on a simply sung Communion service which I want to be as much like the 10.15 at St. Martin's as possible,' wrote Hugh Matthews from a battleship of the Grand Fleet. 'I believe that service alone will give the men power to live up to the standard they would like.'

In Italy, engineers built a little St. Martin's chapel for Wilfred Parker with an Italian style floor of black, white and red tiles.

Dick called the world a whispering gallery, and let fly at Lang in his monthly sounding-board 'The Casual Correspondence of a London Vicar', a column which he put to all sorts of subversive uses. In what he said lay the seeds of his later bitterness towards the man he loved so much.

> I am convinced [he said], that for more than three years now the leaders of the Church have displayed complete incapacity for effectual and vigorous leadership, and a disastrous inability to realise that heroic days need and welcome heroic action.
>
> Does Authority realise that there are thousands who are standing aloof from organised religion not because of what is worst in them but because of what is best, because a Church that is content to referee the game of Civilisation as the world chooses to play it, instead of boldly attempting in the name of Christ to change the rules of the game itself, has no power to excite their loyal enthusiasm.
>
> Has anything that has come from our Anglican Vatican quickened the pulse by one single beat, or are there any signs that we who boast that the Holy Spirit guides us are to be led to cleanse our own life to-day that we may summon men to-morrow to save the soul of the nation? I had rather see the Church reduced again to eleven faithful and vigorous disciples than continue to excite the mild regard of the docile, and the sorrowful contempt of all who dream nobly of the Kingdom of God.

The maroons went off at eleven o'clock on St. Martin's day, November 11th, 1918. In the High Courts, a judge announcing peace added solemnly, 'If I may venture to say so, thank God.'

'Most of us did venture to say so,' said Dick, 'and with no uncertain voice.'

Services were held all through the day and into the night, while rockets exploded and car horns blared in the Square outside. On the following Sunday, Walford Davies came to conduct hymn-singing in the courtyard outside, and queues stretched to the National Gallery. Three times the church was filled to over-flowing, and those who were unable to get inside the doors stood outside on the steps.

Newspapers called St. Martin's the national tabernacle of peace.

'I tell you that by now, the Church ought to have been brought

out into the open,' said Dick savagely, 'bearing in one hand her
charter of freedom, won at I care not what loss of pomp and
worldly circumstance, and in the other an unfettered gospel of
new values for the needs of a world of heroic men.'

8

Gawdsakery

As THE LAST German offensive against the French petered out, and the British moved in for the final attack at Amiens, a Movement appropriately called Life and Liberty was celebrating its first anniversary.

Dick called it the Gale of God, and it was prompted by shame for an inadequate Church, disillusion in the National Mission, and a conviction that the Day of the Lord had dawned, when Christians should come forward boldly wearing their hearts on their sleeves.

In the spring of 1917, he had been chatting with William Temple in the study of St. James's Rectory. 'Don't you think,' he had suggested suddenly, 'there ought to be a ginger group in the Church?'

Freddie Iremonger, vice-chairman of Life and Liberty, called it Dick's 'gawdsakery': for God's sake do something. 'Dick's gawdsakery,' he said, 'was an impelling force in his life and work, and that the Church should get a move on was his passionate desire.'

Temple was thirty-six, Dick thirty-seven. 'We are *not* too young,' Temple wrote. 'Our youth is both our excuse and our attraction.' Later, he said 'Dick *was* the Movement. Apart from him, there would have been no Movement at all.'

The first meeting was held in March at St. Martin's Vicarage in the room where committees had once met to plan the Revised Version of the Bible. Forty people attended, charmingly press-ganged by Dick, 'who,' said Iremonger, 'attracted the most mixed body of church people that could be found in any spiritual movement of that time.' Temple's careful wisdom balanced Dick's practical enthusiasm, and by the end of the afternoon, although a course of action had been decided, Dick was probably thoroughly depressed.

Dissatisfaction with the Church was enormous. Later, a scandal sheet was produced.

It is a scandal that the right to appoint a man to the cure of souls should be bought and sold.

It is a scandal that parishioners should have no right to determine who their priests should be, no power to prevent him imposing his theories of worship and ritual on an unwilling congregation, and no power to eject him except for gross immorality.

It is a scandal that there should be no place for women in the councils of the Church.

It is a scandal that the Church should have no power to alter her forms of service according to need, and it is a scandal that the Church should be unable to re-adjust her finances, which too often permit a great inequality of payment for services rendered, and allow some of the most important offices to be only eligible to men of private means.

In two bordering parishes, one priest ministered to eight hundred and fifty people for an annual income of over six thousand pounds, while the other, with a parish of nineteen thousand, received only four hundred pounds. As things stood, the only way to put things right was through Parliament, and even in peacetime it had taken nine sessions to settle the salary of the Archdeacon of Cornwall.

In order to begin reforming itself, the Church had to achieve some kind of autonomy from Parliament, which was the conclusion which had already been reached by a report prepared by Lord Selborne on the Church and the State. But the Report, once issued, had not been implemented, and any attempts to do so had been condemned as hustling. At the inaugural meeting of the Life and Liberty Movement, it was decided that the first objective should be to implement an Enabling Act, by which the Church would be empowered to handle her own affairs.

'Dick had conceived a Movement for a great quickening of religion in the Church,' said Temple later. 'It rather irked him that our objective should be the passing of an Act of Parliament.'

Dick was not the only one.

To some members, all this seemed utterly unheroic [wrote Iremonger later]. At the first and subsequent meetings, and in personal correspondence, chaplains who had been working in the Army and the Grand Fleet pleaded that nothing short of a crusade would find any widespread support among the men who were serving, and what sort of a crusade would it be that had 'Pensions for Parsons' as its slogan, and quicker legislation as its end?

Temple replied that it had never been imagined, at least by those responsible for initiating the Movement, that Church reform was to be the 'end' of their efforts. The end was that the Church should be able, through a cleansing of its life, to preach the Gospel to the nation with a clear conscience.

Within a month there was a Life and Liberty office, Life and Liberty literature, and a Council with a membership restriction summed up by Dick as 'no gaiters'.

Those who were in the Movement from the beginning have found it difficult to describe the thrill of those early days [continued Iremonger, who was among them]. One conviction was common to them all. They could hold out a hope to be found in no human institution. They had an answer to the question 'who will show us any good?' which was being put on every side, as a disillusioned people groped its apparently aimless way through a darkness unlit by any ray of hope except the shining courage of the fighting services.

Politicians were discredited, unpleasant tales were abroad of contractors, commissions, and profits. Public and private morals had touched a new low level. The cold grip of fatalism was fastening on the mind and heart of the nation. Was this not the time, if ever, when the Church of the living God was summoned to cast off its worldliness and sloth, and rise up once more to lead and inspire? Here lay the hope—and the response was immediate.

Defeatism was killed outright. The depression that had hung over the Church suddenly lifted, and gave place to a faith and fervour that mounted as the Movement spread and was carried forward with a momentum that surprised even its promoters.

'I feel immensely cheered,' wrote Maude Royden, the pioneering feminist and Congregational minister who professed to love Dick 'just this side of idolatry'. 'Having discovered that there really is one whole person willing to go ahead, besides myself, I immediately feel that we are an army.

'If you and I, why not others? Thousands of others? Now I feel full of hope.'

Hensley Henson, Dean of Durham, condemned Life and Liberty as a few shell-shocked chaplains and a collection of young men in a hurry, and Dick wrote a pamphlet headed *Without Delay*.

Ask the chaplains and churchmen on the battle front if they desire the Church to wait until they return [he said]. They are maintaining—and it is not wise or true to call them shell-shocked prophets who need rest for recovery—that the Church is too timid to face her real problems. Those of us who are in the parochial groove know this to be true.

'Henson and Co. may sneer at youth,' commented Temple. 'Lots of people think it the one hope.'

On June 20th, 1917, a letter was published in *The Times* under the heading MOVEMENT FOR REFORM:

Amid the ruins of the old world, the new world is already being born [it said]. In the ideas of reconstruction now being

formed there is hope of a new and better era. The Church
has felt, and to some extent imparted, the new impulse in the
National Mission. It has in altogether new ways realised its
responsibilities and its impotence at the present time to dis-
charge them. The Archbishops have appointed five committees of inquiry to consider where reforms are needed and
what the nature of the reforms should be. That this should
have happened at all is evidence of recognised need for
change.

A vigorous forward movement just now may revive waning
enthusiasm and hopes, retain for the service of the Church
the eager souls who now doubtfully watch it, and, by com-
bining these together, exert such pressure on the official bodies
as may result in real reform.

But as soon as we consider the changes that are needed to
make the Church a living force in the nation, we find ourselves hampered at every turn by an antiquated machinery
which we are powerless to change except by a series of Acts of
Parliament. Everyone sees that the House of Commons is a
highly unsuitable place for the settlement of questions affect-
ing the Church's life and work; and even if it were suitable
in its composition, it has no time. Whatever else may be
thought of the scheme suggested by the Archbishops' Committee on Church and State, it has at least this advantage,
that under its provisions it would be necessary to find time
to stop legislation for Church reform from taking effect instead
of its being necessary, as it is now, to find time to pass it.

If the Church is to have new life, even if it is to maintain
the life which it has, it must have liberty. Those who are
promoting this movement are convinced that we must win
for the Church full power to control its own life, even at the
cost, if necessary, of disestablishment and of whatever conse-
quences that may possibly involve.

It is proposed to hold a meeting at Queen's Hall on the
evening of Monday, 16th July, when these principles will be
enforced and support for them enlisted. All information and
reserved tickets can be obtained from the Hon. Secretaries,
Life and Liberty Movement, 6 St. Martin's Place, W.C.2, or

from the Rev. W. Temple, St. James's Rectory, Piccadilly, W.1.

We propose to do whatever can be done by constitutional channels; we wish to arouse the Church to a sense of its vital need, and to call on all who love it to demand for it the liberty which is essential to its life. We believe that the leaders of the Church are ready to advance along the path of progress if they are assured of an earnest and widespread desire to go forward. But with them or without them we are constrained by love of our Church and country to raise the standard of advance and call to it those who share our anxiety and our hope.

The letter, which was sent from St. Martin's Vicarage, was signed by Louise Creighton, A. A. David, A. Mansbridge, J. B. Seaton, A. L. Smith, W. Temple (Chairman), A. P. Charles, F. A. Iremonger and H. R. L. Sheppard (Hon. Secretaries).

In spite of idyllic summer weather, the famous promenade hall was packed on July 16th. Dr. David, headmaster of Rugby School, said the opening prayers, and William Temple, still suffering from an attack of gout the night before, made a speech which lucidly clarified the aims of the Movement, while at the same time appealing to emotion and imagination.

Maude Royden spoke for the women of the Church; Walter Carey pulverised the bishops. When it was Dick's turn—'You simply *must* speak,' Temple had insisted, 'no one can say these things as well as you'—he spoke of the inarticulate mass of church people, most of them communicants, who took no part or interest in Church affairs, and of the need to show them the romance, the adventure, the love and the courtesy of Christianity.

I am so glad [he said] that those who came here tonight expecting to hear abuse hurled at the heads of our opponents have been sadly disappointed.

Maybe the reason why the bulk of our manhood is now so astonishingly unmoved by all we say is that so far it cannot reconcile the timid summons of the Church with its own large ideas of brotherhood, equality, and service, which represent for the average man his ideals of Christianity.

7

Only once in recent years has the Church shown her capacity for genuine enthusiasm [he said] and that was when she was defending one part of her endowments. Our own people are bored with our negotiations. Those outside are not interested in our trivialities. There is a new demand, a new need for religion, but for a religion that is concerned with great causes and big issues, that is not bounded by the parish magazine.

The days are ripe for heroic things.

If men saw us caring for the large things and understood that we are prepared, however chilly the outlook, to launch out into the deep at our Lord's command, I am sure we should take and hold many willing captives for Christ and his Kingdom. I believe if we were to care above everything for Truth and Righteousness and Justice amongst men, we should soon have the world kneeling before the Throne of God.

It is, I am certain, because we are hugging the shore and fearing the dangers of the sea, because we are caring too much for our own possessions, because we are fighting over things that are not mentioned in the New Testament, that we remain so extraordinarily powerless in these days.

It would be great and glorious epoch making tonight if we could provide the spectacle of three thousand sane and healthy citizens inaugurating with deep-throated acclamation a movement within the Church which stands for risk and danger and service and sacrifice—but also, I am sure, for life and liberty and for the glory of God and the extension of his Kingdom.

The meeting ended with a resolution:

That whereas the present conditions under which the Church lives and works constitute an intolerable hindrance to its spiritual activity, this Meeting instructs the Council, as a first step, to approach the Archbishops in order to urge upon them that they should ascertain without delay, and make known to the Church at large, whether and on what terms Parliament is prepared to give freedom to the Church in the sense of full power to manage its own life, that so it may the better fulfil its duty to God and to the nation and its mission to the world.

Only one hand, that of the Dean of Durham, was raised in dissent.

Temple wrote to Dick from the country, setting out carefully in black spidery handwriting the exact turn of his conversation with the two Archbishops:

> Our Lambeth visit was, I think, very successful. I gave a sort of summary of what I said at Queen's Hall, adding that by 'without delay' we did not mean 'without the proper preliminaries' but 'without delay', and that as Selborne's Report was published nearly eight months ago and the Church Council had not yet met to discuss it, we were justified in holding that at present there is delay.
>
> Garbett was excellent—on the expectancy among clergy and laity alike, and the psychological moment. Mansbridge [founder of the Workers' Educational Association], was also very effective from the Labour end.
>
> Then Cantuar replied: 1. The Archbishops have done a great deal to get reforms carried out; 2. What is the chief obstacle? Not the opponent but the indifferent folk of the Church; 3. We need spade-work to get these men to see that the thing is urgent; 4. But they will be converted from apathy to opposition if they are once persuaded that there is a conspiracy to rush things; 5. None the less, the course of procedure recommended in the Report is too tardy; 6. He would vote for Disestablishment with both hands if he did not sincerely hope to get our faults remedied otherwise.
>
> York's points were: 1. He could not say how much he rejoiced at the emergence of this new and strong movement(!); 2. There is general unrest, give it the light of hope and do not let it settle down into discontent; 3. At the Front, everyone interested in the Church is keener on self-government than anything else; 4. We cannot wait. We must at once get our plans ready; 5. It will be a great mistake to go to Parliament while still uncertain what we want; it would only irritate. We

should meet with a rebuff, and then (a) the more conservative would cry off for fear of Disestablishment, (b) those who want this would say the State would not meet the Church's demands and would go straight for Disestablishment without giving the other plan a fair run; 6. What is the way of co-operation between Life and Liberty and Archbishops? Let Life and Liberty go on rousing the Church while the Arch-bishops put the official machinery in motion; 7. At meetings, frame a resolution less open to criticism through misunder-standing.

In thanking the two Archbishops, I said that we should feel able now to go ahead with the sense that we were calling men to back them up: and both nodded.

Altogether very promising, I think.

At a Council retreat at Cuddesdon in the autumn, Temple agreed to resign his living at St. James's and 'launch out into the deep' to lead the Movement on a third of his income. He was a Proctor in Convocation and editor of the radically brilliant paper *The Challenge*, not only in the centre of Church affairs, but fifteen months married, and he called it a turning point in his career. Later he was to say that his leadership accounted for much of Dick's disappointment with the Movement.

Within the next year, adherents were nick-named the Lovely Libertines, and Temple wrote a prayer asking that they might know when by impatience as well as by patience they might serve best. Dick issued yellow-press pamphlets in heavy black print, setting out boldly and sensationally the scandals of the Church and the grievances of the Church people. On the first anniversary, less than a month before peace, Freddie Iremonger called Life and Liberty's policy, 'not a leap in the dark, as some have termed it, but a leap into the light of freedom'.

During the first week in May both Convocations passed the scheme, with only twelve voting against it in all four Houses. The Enabling Bill was given its first reading in the House of Lords on May 13th. While Dick set out the exact terms of the Bill in the *Messenger* — 'we venture to think that it will be gravely discreditable to anyone who professes to care that the Church should be able to do its work efficiently if he or she is not able to answer the question what is the Enabling Bill for and why is it necessary?'—Temple spent his time writing defensively controversial letters to the Press.

'While we deliberate, He reigns,' he said. 'When we decide wisely, He reigns. When we decide foolishly, He reigns. When we serve him in humble loyalty, He reigns. When we serve Him self-assertively, He reigns. When we rebel and seek to withhold our service, He reigns.'

The second reading of the Bill in the Lords was carried on June 3rd; the third on July 21st. Temple had been in Knutsford, where prospective clergy trained in a disused gaol.

> I gather that after hearing you they nearly chucked it [he wrote], as they also did for totally different reasons after hearing the Archbishop of York.
>
> Your pessimism about the present condition of the Church and His Grace's complacency were tending towards very much the same practical result. Anyhow your visit was obviously one of the most glorious things they have had, and resulted in an even heartier welcome than they would otherwise have given for Life and Liberty as a channel through which to agitate for improvements.

On November 7th, as the crucial second reading took place in the Commons, Life and Liberty was in Congress. Proceedings were adjourned from twelve thirty until five p.m. so that members could pray together in St. Martin's, and when the reading was carried overwhelmingly by three hundred and four votes to sixteen, an M.P. said the work had been done by those who prayed. Dick was sad that our Lord's name had not been mentioned once throughout the debate, but when Temple hurried in to the Congress with the news, members leaped to their feet and sang the Doxology.

'Cheer up, Robert!' Dick called to a gloomy policeman in Trafalgar Square, as he was on his way to a great Thanksgiving meeting that evening. 'The Enabling Bill's through!'

Royal Assent was given two days before Christmas, and Lang

preached at a service of Prayer and Dedication in the Abbey.

> For the first time, at least since almost primitive ages, the
> laity in every parish throughout the land are offered vote and
> voice in the management of their Church, [he said]. This is
> not merely as parishioners or as citizens of the nation, but as
> citizens of the Church; and not merely by the favour of this
> or that incumbent, but as a right conferred by the whole
> Church with the concurrence and recognition of the State.
> In a degree never before possible, every man or woman
> who professes allegiance to the Church is now invested with
> a personal responsibility for its welfare, for the success or
> failure of its divine mission. All depends upon the spirit, the
> motive, the purpose, the outlook, with which church people
> enter the new era.

The first meeting of a Parochial Church Council at St. Martin's
took place in May 1920, with forty members representative of
all the activities and groups within the parish, from Bedfordbury
to Carlton House Terrace. An Electoral Roll was set up, as it
was throughout the country, producing results—one hundred
and twenty-two thousand and seventy out of a London population of nearly four million—which the Bishop of London was to
call astonishing and alarming.

The first sittings of the National Assembly of the Church of
England took place in June 1920, and as far as Dick was concerned, wasted most of the time on trivia. Subsequent sittings
did nothing to sweeten that first bitter disappointment. 'Clergy
are like manure,' he said, making light of it. 'Spread about the
earth they do a lot of good. Gathered together in a mass they are
apt to be offensive.'

Life and Liberty voted to continue for two years at least.
'Remember,' it was said, 'work is only beginning.' But having
achieved its great objective, the incentive was gone, and the
emotional advantage of so much enthusiasm and so much goodwill
was never really harnessed.

'Dick fully assented to our policy, but he always looked beyond
it,' said Temple later, referring to Dick's shrewd practical judge-

ment which sometimes bewildered by its contempt for logic
and then delighted with its vindication in practice. 'Life and
Liberty was his creation, and yet it was never quite what he
wanted it to be.'

Aching for the Church to be what he wanted it to be, Dick
wrote to Iremonger, begging for reassurance about truth and
tradition. 'Maybe I think too much of the Church and you find
all you want in the Gospel,' Iremonger replied.

Dick's familiar blue notepaper came by return post, dated
four in the morning from Bristol Station waiting-room: 'Without
the Church I would have lost heart long ago . . .'

9

The Stirring of a Great Crowd

IN THE SUMMER of 1919, the Peace Treaty was signed at Versailles.

I never realised war was over [Dick said lightly] until I sat on a June day in the Pavilion at Lords and heard all the old familiar sounds again: the bell ringing for the leisurely umpires in their white coats to move out to the wicket, the sound of eleven young men with nailed boots clattering down the Pavilion steps to take the field, and the voices of gallant old gentlemen, most of them ennobled by the loss of at least one son, talking the old stuff, for once so welcome, about how cricket wasn't played now as it was in their young day.

During the war, there were men who had found a mission and a meaning to life. After the war, they came, as if by instinct, to St. Martin's.

Studdert Kennedy came to preach: Dick called him 'an ugly little man with wonderful eyes, wearing an immense collar'. In spite of Studdert's unnerving habit of thinking his eloquent, inflammatory thoughts aloud in the pulpit, Dick took him on to the part-time staff, where he spat and sparkled with nervous Irish zeal.

'The result of Studdert,' Dick said, 'is to send me away thanking God for him, but trying to think as he thought, and tending towards despair at the immensibility of all he has put before me.' King George the Fifth had appointed both Dick and Studdert as his chaplains, which meant they wore scarlet cassocks, and soldiers on leave chased them round the Square calling them bloody lobsters, until they went to ground in the crypt.

Tubby Clayton, 'bitter, chilled and disappointed', touting his 'dreams and absurdities' before disinterested London clergy, put on the crumpled suit which he called his best, and decided as a last resort to try 'the busiest man in London'.

'Dick rose and came to me,' he said later. 'He took me by both hands, made me sit down, and then broke in upon my opening sentence: "Before we start to talk, I want to tell you that I have prayed for you and for Talbot House day after day since I first heard of it".'

Then, in the way which so confounded those critics who said he was all heart and no head, Dick swept Tubby along, ironing out the absurdities in his great dream.

You want a house in London, in the centre. Also you need a good round sum to start with. Now let us think. The simplest thing is that you should take over this large Vicarage, it's much too big for us. But then, Church lawyers—they'd object. I will try to doublecross them, but if they repudiate the whole idea, then we must get another house for you.

And some money. How much will you need? Of course, I can't say how it will come, but I am quite sure it will. The work is God's, and no one can tell what happens in St. Martin's. Remember, Tubby, that everything happens which God means, and I am quite sure he means Talbot House.

When would you like to come and tell my people? Do write something for the *Messenger*. And if you want me, let me come and help on your committee till you have things started. Then I step overboard.

That was the way Dick treated me [said Tubby]. I had arrived crestfallen, almost beaten. I left St. Martin's Vicarage that night, having been kept to tea and then to supper, supremely conscious that here was a friend hitherto unsuspected.

The result was above all that I could ask or think. The first £10,000 which founded Talbot House in London came through St. Martin's from two worshippers. Within a year from that first interview, Talbot House was Toc H in two big houses: the dream came true.

Young men like Ronald Sinclair, back from the war with a Military Cross and bar, came straight to St. Martin's from theological college, preaching what they called the gospel of the Christ of the common man, whose supper they had seen celebrated from tin mugs and ration boxes.

The Christ we had thought confined to church or to institutional Christianity had escaped these bonds and become real [he said]. This was a crucial experience for us. As real as wounds or death.

On the strength of this, and this alone, we had decided to be ordained if we survived the war.

Against tough opposition from those who disliked doss-houses, the crypt remained open, and relief work, begun among soldiers who wanted messages taken to their families, continued. Soon there were the same soldiers, queuing for meal tickets, out of work, disillusioned and penniless.

The Sunday afternoon services for sailors and soldiers turned into popular People's Services, attracting tourists, tramps, and aristocracy. People who scorned conventional church services came in from the suburbs to attend, and so did the King and Queen and the Prince of Wales. Guards' bands continued to play, and Dick was accused of humanism, of stunting, popularising religion, and attracting people to church with a band and making them laugh when they got there. Unabashed, he organised a People's Service Outing, with donkey races by the sea. Once there was a pound note in the collection with writing on it: two people, in love and unable to marry, had felt peace and contentment, and they put in all the money they had.

Dick could be maddeningly, genuinely humble; bitingly, sarcastically shrewd. Besieged by doubts about almost everything he did, a basic, overriding certainty carried his P.C.C. staunchly with him; sometimes they even had ideas of their own. At a time when religion, against a background of poverty and increasing disillusion, appeared unreal and ridiculous, the religion of St. Martin's was real. Its vicar was a man who could say without a shadow of doubt that the one thing he was prepared to die at the stake for was his passionate belief in the presence of Christ at Holy Communion, and he had working with him men who could make religion as real in the immediate misery of hunger and unemployment as it had been in the comfort before the war or in the hope that lay ahead during the war.

> Pray! [wrote Studdert] Have I prayed! When I'm worn with all my praying!
> When I've bored the blessed angels with my battery of prayer!
> It's the proper thing to say, but it's only saying, saying,
> And I cannot get to Jesus for the glory of her hair.

A clergyman who believed with all his heart and yet spent nights wrestling with doubt and temptation was a new kind of clergyman, and he made sense.

The *Mail* called St. Martin's a non-stop church, with practical Christianity and a practical parson. An 'Impenitent Presbyterian' called it his night-and-day-kirk. George Lansbury, bearded and grandfatherly, refusing to wear a top-hat to the Palace, came to speak on Industrial Unrest. Shaw came to talk about religion. An East End Mayor came to tell of 'houses fit for slaves' which had been condemned long before the war, and as a result, Bethnal Green housing was at the top of the agenda of the newly elected London County Council and the Mayor spent half an hour with the Queen.

Dick invited speakers from the League of Nations and set up a special League of Nations Committee. He was still Chairman of the Charing Cross Association, with St. Martin's people elected under him, and he was on the Executive Council of Westminster's Social Services Committee.

He wrote to *The Times* begging people to pray about the Rail
Strike, he talked to the Secretary of the National Union of
Railwaymen, who would say little but that bloody revolution lay
ahead, and he invited controversial people like peace campaigner
Arthur Ponsonby to speak on controversial issues like pacifism.

Lord Ponsonby, whose sister Maggie helped Dick at St.
Martin's, was puzzled 'that a man so amusing, so ready to laugh,
so entertained by trivialities,' should command such attention.
'I had come across many ecclesiastics in my time,' he said. 'Some
were learned, some mystic, and all rather alarming, perched on
pedestals beyond reach.

'Here was a man who had none of these characteristics, and
did not even appear to be an ecclesiastic at all—just an ordinary
man trying to help people.'

When Ponsonby confessed his exasperation with what he
called Church Christianity, Dick invited him to the vicarage
to talk to the clergy. Ponsonby called it a formidable group.

What sort of man was this [he asked], who, without flinching
from his own position, was ready to encourage someone who
wanted to undermine it? But I found he detested the views
of theologians and formalists far more than he did mine.

His faith was rock which needed no examination or in-
vestigation. It was the mainspring of his action, and works
not words had become his way of life. His influence covered
politicians, admirals, generals, the old and the young, the
bewildered, the down-and-out, the boss and the workman, the
fool and the knave and the drunkard, and his method of
approach was based not on reproof, admonition, or ecstatic
prayer, but on pure friendship and indestructible love.

He had long kicked any pedestal from under his feet.

Ramsay MacDonald wrote on House of Commons notepaper
headed PRIVATE AND CONFIDENTIAL: 'I would do almost anything
on your prompting . . .'

Maude Royden—'a better Christian than I can ever hope to
be'—sent people for counsel and Holy Communion: '. . . she
wants to be assured of forgiveness, and was relieved to learn that

others beside High Church people went to confession . . .' Hearing the phrase 'devoted to social service' used of Dick, she said it jarred: mere philanthropy had nothing to do with love.

Viscount Byng of Vimy sent warm, flippant notes calling himself a scrap-heap general: 'Hark the herald angels sing! Here's a card from Julian Byng!' 'Dear Parson,' he said, leaving for Canada in 1921, 'I will take you out in any capacity you name.'

Herbert Asquith requested 'a few minutes' for Lady Tree, 'who wishes very much to see you.' 'Is it possible to get in to your church?' wrote his wife, Lady Margot Oxford. 'I stood from 11.00 until 11.30 last Sunday, and then sat on a hassock.'

> Dick crystallised for me and for many what we had seen but had been unable to formulate in France and in Flanders [said Ronald Sinclair]. He brought the living Jesus, whom we had been vaguely conscious of on active service, right into the heart of London.
>
> No doubt he laid himself open to criticism. No doubt he was impatient of much organised Christianity. Doubtless he shocked many cautious people. But he knew Jesus, preached Jesus, lived Jesus, and made him real. He let Jesus walk the pavements of central London and made him the very centre of all our life.

Outside Dick's study window, the statue of Nurse Edith Cavell was brought for erection under dust sheets. Overcome with curiosity, he ventured out one night in his pyjamas to look underneath. A passing policeman, astonished to see the covered statue billowing frantically, discovered the Vicar of St. Martin's trying to get out.

When the statue was unveiled, Dick thought it an artistic abomination, and joined a four-year battle to have the words 'Patriotism is not enough—I must have no hatred or bitterness for anyone' cut into the plinth. At odds with the mood of the country's leadership, he wrote to the papers asking for a National Day of Remembrance, Humiliation and Prayer, only to find himself opposed by the Archbishop of Canterbury, who, he said bitterly, was representing the wishes of the Government and not of Almighty God.

In the House of Commons there were angry clashes over Ireland.

It is idle to ask for Days of National Humiliation, Prayer, etc., when the Church is as indifferent as it is to the Government policy in Ireland [wrote Lady Oxford]. The Church has occasional letters by occasional bishops, and is as dead as it was through the war. In every village, every town, and on all the street corners, men should ask where Christ is today.

He won't come to us while we shirk action and take refuge in kneeling when we should all be fighting.

At St. Martin's, Dick, according to his curates, 'followed where love led'. He heard confessions and yet sometimes he cut the creed from his services. He maintained the rigid, and to many people, old-fashioned, discipline of saying the morning and evening Offices, calling it the best way he knew to be alert and responsive to the leadings of the Spirit, and yet in church on Sundays he slashed the psalms to pieces and gathered his congregations together in silent and extempore prayer.

He prayed publicly for Roman Catholics, Anglicans, and Non-Conformists, and said if the Quakers' Meeting House along the road was to burn down, he would give them a home, as he hoped they would do for him.

'The only service which meant everything to him was the daily eucharist,' said Sinclair. 'No Anglo-Catholic ever ordained, however devoted, could value it more than Dick, and he broke down the fences that so often make it a service for the pious few only, so that it became the service of the common people.'

Crowds came to the Choral Communion on Sundays. Often twenty or more would come in during the week on dark, foggy winter mornings. Dick celebrated in his own way, as if he was entertaining to tea, helping people up as they turned to leave the rail.

'What do you imagine the word "incarnate" means to them?' he asked a young deacon who had just preached his first sermon.

Astringent, for all his gentleness, he was liable to stop hymns half-way through to tell the congregation to sing better, and sometimes he did unforgivable things like sending the collection round a second time.

'My dears,' he said, stopping a hymn and leaning over the pulpit to address some ladies singing about the army of the living God, 'you may think you are the army of the living God, but you don't look it. If you were, you'd be radiant.'

Often in the summer he took the entire congregation outside into the courtyard as an act of witness.

'Our sermons will not be comfortable,' he said. 'How can they be? They will be aflame with the burning, passionate love of God. They will come from our own daily prayer and study and Christian adventure, and they will go we know not where. About that we need not worry.'

An irate lady, swept off her feet in the crush to get in, wrote to ask reimbursement for her hat and her umbrella, and a boy told to take off his cap because he was entering a church answered in astonishment, 'This ain't a church. This is St. Martin's.' Dick told with glee of the day a man just out of Charing Cross Hospital after an appendicitis operation came straight to a service at St. Martin's, burst his stitches laughing, and had to be taken back to hospital again.

'Now I am going to say "A very happy Christmas to you all",' he said one Christmas Day. 'And will you, if you really feel like it—but not if you don't feel like it—answer back "the same to all of you".'

I owe more than I can say to the spirit of audacity with which I was inoculated during a brief sojourn at St. Martin's [wrote an ex-curate]. It was there I learned to 'go ahead', and when, as often, I am challenged by friends of a more cautious turn and asked if it is really necessary to break forth in these unexpected directions, I disarm them by saying that the question is not one I can answer. I must refer them to the Vicar of St. Martin-in-the-Fields.

An outer London vicar suggested holding annual Dismissal

services. 'Send back missionaries to all the stuffy, sleepy churches that you have taken the living people from,' he said. 'We would gladly send you fresh patients to be inoculated in their place.'

Late every night, after he and Alison had come home from a dinner party, or early in the morning when he was unable to sleep, Dick went down to the crypt. Members of the congregation took it in turns to help the women auxiliary police, encouraging men to sleep in pews instead of on the floor, and to keep their coats and boots on. Sometimes it was so dark in the mornings that they gave them tea to shave in instead of water.

There were those who had missed the last train out of London, and mothers and children in search of a home. Dick kept confidences, and only worked with the police when he wanted to. He was immensely practical, aware that a stiff drink and prompt action could sometimes do more good than piety and Christian counselling in the study. Finding a girl who had run away from her home in Scotland, he caught the night train back with her to make sure her parents gave her a welcome. Another girl who was expecting a baby, he put in a taxi to the Lansburys who took care of her and the baby when it was born: 'Isn't it wonderful to have friends you can rely on in a crisis? I knew George wouldn't fail me!' Action always accompanied talk, and often involved inconvenience.

A drunk in top-hat and evening dress clattered down the stairs early one morning, looked round at the men lying flat out on benches, and said 'Good God! Passed out already? What a party!' Suddenly confronted by the big cross on the crypt altar, he took off his hat and looked around again. Then he sat on a pew with his head in his hands until the morning, when he left after writing out a cheque for ten pounds.

Night after night, an old flowerwoman came to kneel behind the altar rail in the dazzling warmth of the candles, linking arms with Dick afterwards and urging him to 'Say one yourself, Guv'nor.'

Of course there were those who laughed: those to whom the whole thing was a great and glorious beanfeast. For the majority of St. Martin's people, though, it was a serious effort to accompany Dick, groping together along an unlit path, trying to understand.

'He who possesses the power to love,' he said, preaching at William Temple's consecration as Bishop of Birmingham, 'loves because he cannot help loving: he can do nothing else.'

'The most exhilarating experience to men in my profession,' he said, lecturing at Cambridge, 'is the ever-increasing proof that what they dared to hope on the eve of their ordination is actually and gloriously true, namely that Jesus, the Master of the art of life, is indeed the satisfaction of a world of men and women.

'Year by year this certainty increases.'

To his staff, Dick spoke of Jesus just ahead, leading on, always out of reach. 'He never misses fire,' he said. 'He baffles often. He eludes often. He goes on. Yet for those who ask and seek, he is not only the Way, but he is with them on the way.'

November 1921, as well as celebrating Armistice and St. Martin's day, was the two hundredth anniversary of the dedication of the present church of St. Martin-in-the-Fields. Dick commissioned novelist-dramatist Laurence Housman, to write a Pageant for the occasion and sparked off a life-long attachment between the two. Housman was a contradiction: conservative and radical, romantically and reluctantly agnostic, believing in Shaw rather than the Church, and calling men the eyes of God.

'Odd as you may think it,' said Dick, 'I count you a real Christian, though you say you are not one, and I count you as one who has sermons to preach to me, not as one to whom I shall ever be called upon to preach.'

Leonine and impressive in his mild Victorian way, Housman came up from the New Forest to look Dick over. Dick and Alison played demon patience while Housman looked on, and Dick teased a bit.

'Mr. Housman,' he said without looking up from the cards, 'Do you like us? We want to know, because we like you.'

Housman referred to Dick as the Shoving Leopard. 'Well, you amuse me,' he said.

The Pageant played for five full nights at Church House, and Dick wished he had booked the Albert Hall.

I had protested my disqualifications [said Housman]. The

8

Church of England and I were no longer on friendly terms. We had parted. That, I was assured, was almost an additional reason why I should write the play. I might say anything I liked about the Church and its past behaviour, so long as I did not attack Christianity.

Finding the distinction easy, I accepted the commission and said just what I thought, with Christianity to the fore and the Church making a bad second all down the ages, and the Pageant found rather a puzzled audience for itself.

Dick indulged himself shamelessly by writing a bad poem to celebrate the occasion:

> Just to shield a soul forlorn
> Martin's cloak in two was torn,
> And I need the warmth that may
> Wrap me round on Martin's Day,

and re-wrote the end of Housman's play to feature Trafalgar Square: Housman, not surprisingly, called it 'a horrid excrescence —artistically'. Alison produced the Pageant and Dick played the Beggar, in an un-named cast. Both were in their element. Shaw met Dick for the first time and said he had the technique and the passion for saving the souls of the public. Father Jim Adderley, Dick's neighbour at St. Paul's Covent Garden, talked of St. Martin's as the cathedral of central London, and Dick as its ideal Dean.

> There is no other church in London which could cheerfully engage two or three large halls in which to keep its two hundredth anniversary and expect to fill them [he said].
>
> Reality is the mark of it. It will not chatter about Reunion and Peace and Toleration and Christian Socialism without showing some practical attempt to realise such ideals. It is determined to give modern Anglicanism a very good trial, to see what can be done with it. It may fail a hundred times, but it will go on, because it has faith.
>
> The beggars to whom this modern St. Martin gives his

cloak are of many kinds, from the ragged person who sleeps in church at night, to the aristocrat or plutocrat who sleeps in church by day when the Guards' band is not playing and some funny old dignitary is preaching.

And if you ask, 'Why ask the old dignitary to preach?' the answer is that he belongs to the Church of England: even deans and canons must have a chance in the great experiment.'

On Remembrance Day, half-way through the week of rejoicing, the Central Hall was filled, and four times too many people applied for tickets for the final service of thanksgiving at the Coliseum.

We sometimes dream of greater things beyond this week of ours [wrote Dick].

We have dreamed that Someone took a people by the hand, and telling them to be humble, led them to a hill-top, whence He showed them a world all gone astray for lack of love and ready to be told, simply, about Him, not about His status.

We saw a look of longing on His countenance.

There were faces around Him we knew quite well by sight, and many a stranger beside. The hour of decision was at hand.

Then we awoke with just the memory of the stirring of a great crowd which haunts us still. We have been wondering ever since . . .

Festivities on such a grand scale had meant more work than usual, staying up through the night and accepting without question the exhaustion that followed. At the final meeting, Dick talked about Jesus washing the disciples' feet. 'We have been too ready to interpret the life of Jesus as a series of moral lessons,' he told the tiers of people listening. 'Jesus didn't merely wish to teach them a lesson in humility. He loved them.'

As he finished speaking, he faltered and staggered, and the next few weeks were spent in a nursing-home. From then on, he was never really well.

★   ★   ★

Over the next few years, as well as the phrases 'break-down', 'pneumonia', and 'nervous exhaustion', the word asthma began to gain prevalence as the reason for what Dick called his foolishness in being ill. It was never to be really clear whether the root cause was his adolescent fall in the snow, the harrowing months in France, when he came home with pneumonia, or the tension which had built up as a child, and was now being exacerbated, between things as they should have been, and things as they were.

All his life, Dick played charades. Not the gay, extrovert rough and tumble which so delighted him at Christmas, but a more secretive invention. Dreams had to be held on to. Success so often seemed like glaring failure, and failure had at all costs to be distorted into success, the cracks papered over with a great big smile.

Dick and Alison's first daughter, Peggie, was five years old. Rosemary, their younger daughter, a few months. Alison was marvellous at coping with never knowing how many people Dick would invite in for breakfast, but she had a nanny to look after the children and felt at a loss with Dick when he was ill. Escaping home or to the country, she felt justified and yet full of remorse.

When she was in London, she took the children for walks along dull Edwardian terraces, transforming the houses into fairy castles where princesses lived, so that they expected Cinderella's coach around the corner. At night, when they woke with nightmares, she was warm and comforting, picking them up and taking them to bed with her. Otherwise she was 'a beautiful person who came in to say good night'.

She rarely went to church: religion was an impulse and an emotion, stirring music, beautiful words, and telling fortunes with cards. She wrote romantic stories for the *Messenger* — the philosopher who had never learned that you must receive as well as give — and found People's Services anathema.

Dick took Peggie for cream cakes on Saturdays and played bears with Rosemary, crawling round the floor until he had no breath left. At mealtimes he performed outrageous practical jokes, turning bowls of rice pudding upside down on his head and playing unforgivable games with food on the plate of a blind aunt.

If he felt like it, he brought the house down by describing Mrs. Baldwin's hats and her cricketing conversations, or suddenly standing up and acting a three-part drama, taking all the parts himself.

He wore good clothes—which he justified by saying it gave him an entrée to good company—hand-sewn kid-skin I Zingari braces, Lobb shoes which he passed on to the verger, and perfumed hair cream.

There were always queues of people waiting to see him. On Sundays the children counted the different coloured hats from the top nursery window, as crowds stretched beyond the Coliseum, hoping for a seat in church.

'I grew up knowing he was famous,' says Peggie. 'He was special and removed and I adored him. But he was always ill, and we were always being kept away from him. Growing up was the sound of coughing and gasping for breath behind closed doors.'

In the autumn, Dick's father died, and Dick reproached himself for being too busy to visit him the Sunday before. Bishop Ryle told of Dr. Sheppard's contribution to a theological discussion—'That must be wrong, my son Dick does not agree'—and a friend of Dick's wrote to say that 'his eyes glistened when one spoke of you to him'. Christmas was a time of ferocious enjoyment. Dick called it a Gothic ruin and rushed about wearing paper hats and telling everyone to enjoy themselves. 'I say,' he said to one of his curates, 'I saw this marvellous-looking woman in Leicester Square just now, and when I'd walked past her, I realised it was Alison!'

A Relief Fund he called 'a little money to spend just as I like on Christmas fare for poor folks' sent a boy to school and a mother out to see her son's grave in France, and provided 'Aunt' Maggie Ponsonby with toys which she took to Covent Garden on Christmas morning, her whispy grey hair escaping from an unsuccessfully secured bun, her glasses on the end of her long nose.

Dick and Studdert went to Princess Mary's wedding carrying

one white glove between them and wearing Alison's silk stockings. Dick swore he had football shorts beneath his frock coat and his buckled shoes were too big for him. He was working all the time: Ronald Sinclair drew a cartoon of him on the golf course dictating to his secretary, surrounded by portable typewriters, radios and dictaphones.

Charles Ritchie joined the staff, tall, thin, and good-looking, preaching the gospel of the Cross. Just out of the Navy, he came as senior curate, to deputise when Dick was away. Harold Anson arrived at the same time, known—and suspect—for his leadership of the Guild of Health. 'Dick was one of the first people I ever met who believed that I had a gospel,' he said. 'He understood what most of my friends never could understand: why I should give up a desirable parish to be a curate and run about preaching an unfashionable and incomprehensible cult.'

Preaching at the Abbey, Dick recognised a woman in the congregation and remembered that it was the anniversary of the day her son was killed in 1914: he purposely used words and references which she understood, and which touched her deeply. Letters and notes, sometimes a hundred a day, were often headed four a.m. or five a.m., many of them nothing more than thanks for an interesting idea or a passing favour, their unexpectedness giving a quite disproportionate delight. 'Dick couldn't do things by halves,' said Anson. 'He couldn't touch anything into which he was unable to throw himself with all his force.

'He once told me that he knew almost at once when he saw a person, whether they had a burden on their heart, and he couldn't rest until he had taken their burden on himself. He couldn't just be very sympathetic like an ordinary friend. He had to actually bear the burden and be hurt by its weight.'

There is nothing so distressing to watch, or indeed to receive, as that kind of official love which is sometimes bestowed by the clergy, and more often still by church-workers, on their people—and especially on the poor [Dick maintained, at some risk]. They seem to have determined that it is part of their professional duty to love, and so they love because they must.

Professional heartiness that is supposed to be love is a

terrible thing. Those who give it are like people who are keeping a resolution, made that morning, that whether they feel like it or not the people shall be loved that day, and that resolution is being kept against all comers. And they do love, too! It is painful to see.

May we for ever be preserved from loving officially. But love in its highest manifestation is the richest, most persuasive, loveliest, most powerful thing that God has to offer — it is the only weapon we need. It is the only weapon God uses, I think. I believe the Kingdom of God is but a matter of loving as sanely and as wisely as Our Lord loved.

Whether it was love — sane or insane — or a crash course in compensation, by the middle of November, Dick was in hospital again, this time on the critical list with acute appendicitis. 'Who is this Dick Sheppard, that the whole of London should be waiting to know if he is better or worse?' asked a friend of Maude Royden's, landing off a boat from India.

Housman read the news in the papers, and found himself surprisingly moved.

There are so few people in the world about whom I care whether they live or die that it was somehow good for me to discover that you are one whom I want to live [he said]. You are quite a ridiculous person. But probably the people who have the courage to be ridiculous are also the most valuable.

It is, for instance, so beautifully ridiculous of you to remain a priest of the Established Church, the very Establishment of which makes it so difficult for it to be a Christian! Yet there you are, and as a consequence I found the other day that there exists an 'incumbent' who — knowingly — would be prepared to receive me as a communicant. And, as a consequence you did in fact in a way communicate me there and then, and make me a bit nearer to the possibility of some day being a communicant once more.

That, of course, means that you make a ridiculous blend between institutionalism and anarchy. But as I think Christ was very much an anarchist — and that institutionalism has been the great let and hindrance to the fulfilment of His gospel, I don't think you are a worse Christian for that, only a rather incongruous official of ecclesiastical order.

And perhaps it is because I want 'ecclesiastical order' to be thrown into a good deal of disorder—or what you, I suppose, would call 'life and liberty'—that I find you valuable, commendable, and altogether lovable.

On the way to convalesce with Alison in New York, invited to take over the parish of St. George's, Dick contemplated the League of Nations and came to the conclusion that he regarded it much as he regarded the Church, his own life, and mankind in general: 'I am a passionate believer in the League of Nations—not exactly as it is, but as it can become . . .'

When they arrived in New York, which he called a pantomime city, there were reporters and photographers and people who had queued in London for a seat at St. Martin's. Journalists wrote about the celebrated Mr. Sheppard who was Chaplain to Queen Victoria for thirty years—'It is thought I am wearing remarkably well'—and an American bishop felt sure he would feel at home with a gimmicky down-town vicar who had flames leaping from a trap-door in the nave of his church whenever he mentioned hell.

When he returned, it was to a protracted Law Court fight against the Council to retain the Public Library in St. Martin's Lane, and to a summer Bank Holiday Beano in the courtyard for the crowds milling round London with nothing to do.

'What is a Beano?' asked Lord Curzon, pronouncing the word like 'piano'. His high-handed manner irritated Dick, and the pronounciation stuck.

It was also a return to the organisation of a National Call to Righteousness to be held in the Square on Armistice and St. Martin's Day, 1923.

Dick threw himself into the preparations, ordering loudspeakers and arranging simultaneous broadcasting from the eight radio stations in Great Britain. He believed passionately in what he was doing, and tempted by his unanswerable enthusiasm and the promise of a bigger audience than ever before, Prime

Minister Stanley Baldwin, and elder statesman Viscount Grey agreed to come and speak. Following their lead, colonial Prime Ministers accepted the invitation as well.

At the last minute Baldwin withdrew, and so did Grey, whose retrospective fame encompassed books on birds and fly-fishing and the prophecy at the start of the war that the lamps were going out all over Europe. Apparently neither he nor Baldwin wished to see them lit again in their lifetime—at least not if there was any personal risk entailed—and Dick veered violently between profound gloom and energetic condemnation. In the end, he cancelled the remaining speakers and decided to address the meeting himself. From the windows of the study where he prayed with his staff beforehand, it was possible to see and hear the crowds that waited in the Square.

We are sorry for you, and sorry for ourselves [he said to them]. But we are not a bit repentant for refusing to abandon the meeting. Two leading English statesmen, the Prime Minister and Viscount Grey, whose moral rectitude and high conception of service well qualify them to speak to the mind and conscience of England, had promised to come here and issue a summons to righteousness in honour of the dead. The power of such an act of service would have been incalculable. No one knows better than those two men the need of such a summons. They have not been immersed in world politics these last years without realising that peace is a spiritual thing, and that our realest difficulties are not economic but moral.

It was a great opportunity. They would have spoken to a million people at a time when they are peculiarly sensitive to the appeal of idealism, and their speeches might have made history. They might have given a people baffled by the failure of their hopes the fresh courage they need to hold to their ideals. They might even have started the trek of a nation back to God, for the want of which the world waits in the wilderness.

The opportunity has not been taken. I prefer to think it was lack of imagination and not courage that is the cause of failure. I cannot help pleading that someone in high office will one day, before it is too late, plead in public for a policy that is frankly based on the principle of Christianity. We shall remain where we are until this happens.

Never slow to point a moral, he preached in church on breaking promises: 'If, as I firmly believe, our Sunday promises are known to our Father who is in Heaven, then Monday must be for him a fairly depressing day . . .' 'I have no brain,' he wrote cheerfully to Housman. 'All my arguments can be riddled by the astute.'

It was winter: months he was beginning to dread, fighting for breath and battling against pneumonia. Night after night the light was on under his door long after everyone else was in bed, and he jokingly blamed insomnia for having read and re-read books which his curates said they had no time to read. Whenever he was ill, the church was besieged with people wanting to pray for him.

You who are saying that your religion does not save you from sorrow and suffering nor dry your tears nor mend your broken hearts [he said in a Sunday sermon], remember that I do not think it was ever meant to.

It was meant to give you power rather than satisfaction. Hope rather than happiness. Courage to face sorrow rather than safeguards against it. Encouragement rather than explanation.

Take hold of suffering where it hurts most, and in rising above it, crush and kill its power to enslave.

Pulled up short for a moment, he paused, 'So easy to say,' he added, 'so hard to do. I know. I know.'

A Rather Startling Experiment

NOTHING DELIGHTED DICK more than turning the world's weapons to the Church's advantage, which he did with a disarmingly ingenuous worldliness. By 1924, he was exploiting two powerful instruments of propaganda. One—broadcasting—was considered blasphemous. The other—the parish magazine—had been written off long ago both by the clergy and by their detractors.

In 1920, the *Messenger* had become the *St. Martin's Review*, and the senior curate bet Dick that he would never sell a thousand copies. 'With this number we launch into the deep,' Dick wrote. 'That is to say, we aspire to become seriously considered as a piece of Christian literature.'

Four years later, monthly sales of his 'beloved *Review*' were averaging nearly six thousand. The *Morning Post* called it a spirited and entertaining production, and the *Spectator*—whose sales the *Review* eventually overtook—said it was 'up to the level of a serious review'. Lord Astor wrote on the liquor trade, Viscount Haldane wrote on character, and after Hilaire Belloc wrote about military control in Germany, the *New Statesman* commented on Mr. Belloc's 'ingenious article in the *St. Martin's Review*'.

Bertine Buxton, a young twenty-one-year-old, was brought

in as Manager. Previously she had run the St. Martin's Guides: 'children who lived in the Waterloo Road and under Charing Cross arches, and yet still saw fairies'. A hard-headed Scot, Euan Mackenzie Hay, editor of the *Statist*, helped with the finances. Bitter and disillusioned after the war, he had met Dick at a house-party. Since then they had breakfasted together: 'Dick had an exceptional business capacity and yet a humility,' he said. 'He would back an opinion given wholeheartedly, sometimes against his own inclinations and often to his own embarrassment.'

Bertine knew nothing about journalism, but she was determined to learn. Later, she and Euan married.

'Dick had a genius for knowing what public feeling was before it crystallised into public expression,' she says. 'When he thought a thing needed saying, or a topic airing, he didn't mind how unpopular it was or how much criticism or abuse it brought down on his paper.' There were those who condemned the *Review* as arrogant, Communist, and a Marxist travesty. 'If people cancelled their subscription as a result, he was delighted. He felt it had got home, and he said for every one who cancelled, we would get two new readers. He had no thought of playing for safety: once he was really disappointed when a big newspaper didn't bring a libel action he expected.'

Dick used his own journalistic style: short, shot-gun paragraphs, staccato sentences, direct, simple words. There was an immediacy about the topics covered, and a breathless quality of professional reportage:

A member of our staff had a talk with Arthur Benson at the Athenaeum Club the other afternoon, and put to him some questions on Religion and Literature, and has set down here for the benefit of our readers Mr. Benson's replies . . .

Mr. Middleton Murry, Editor of *The Adelphi*, has recently expressed opinions which seem to offer a direct challenge to accepted beliefs. A member of our staff approached Mr. Murry and asked if he would be willing to answer certain questions on points he had raised . . .

Following previous talks with literary men, a member of our staff called the other day on Mr. Stephen Graham at his flat in Soho, and has set down here the conversation. Mr. Graham left London within an hour or two for a remote part of Finland where letters will not easily find him. He was, however, good enough to consent to the publication of this account without first seeing it . . .

With an almost naive, go-getting enthusiasm, Dick went all out for scoops. To Bernard Shaw's postcard, 'I shall not send an article for your bloody *Review*, GBS', he replied, 'Dear Mr. Shaw, thank you so much for your postcard which will be printed in full in the next number,' and received an article by return. He published a shock drug report and a controversial article by the German Chancellor, asking Britain for money. He asked Maude Royden to write about women's rights and printed Ramsay MacDonald's speech on the social implications of Christianity: 'The *St. Martin's Review* is extremely fortunate in being privileged to publish . . .'

Christian responsibility was taken seriously: in one issue there were articles on industrial relations, modern psychology, social services for children, Trades Unions, and the Workers' Educational Association. In another there was a fifteen-page London County Council manifesto.

An article about the Miners' Federation and the coal-owners ended: 'We write thus seriously about the situation in the mining industry because we believe that . . . public understanding of the position before the trouble comes may be the determining factor.' 'It may be asked what this has to do with religion and the *Review* published by St. Martin-in-the-Fields,' commented another writer on the miners' dispute. 'I answer, everything that makes for more life for the people is a matter of religion, and is something to strive for.'

Bertine worked in a cramped little office up above the Royal Box, with her terrier dog Billy. Temple delivered his own articles, three thousand words dashed off in long-hand without a correction. Shaw conducted volatile discussions over tea in the vicarage study. Dick insisted on paying professional writers for the articles they wrote—he disapproved of cadging for Christ—and H. E. Bates wrote to ask for an advance because his wife was having a baby. Masefield and Housman sent in erratic despatches from the country; Professor L. P. Jacks, Dick's hero, wrote prophetically of increasing leisure and how to use it wisely, and Maggie Ponsonby blew in on her way to Palace garden parties wearing an old hat and a wide sash covering the hole in her out-of-date muslin.

The editor of *The Countryman*, with offices along the road, went round local businesses bargaining for advertisements with a brace of pheasants. Bertine followed with Billy on a lead: 'Well,' said advertisement managers when they knew her better, 'you just sat there with your dog until we gave in.'

Review meetings took place in strange settings: railway stations, dentists' waiting rooms and nursing-homes.

Suddenly there'd be a telephone message from Dick to go to him [says Bertine], and there he was, bursting with ideas that had come to him during a sleepless night. Often I'd leave him at seven or eight at night, and the next morning there would be a letter from him posted outside the Vicarage at midnight: 'Put on your best hat, and go along to the House and see what old Lansbury is thinking.' Or it might be Father Groser in the East End or Harold Craxton at the Coliseum, or St. John Ervine or Forbes-Robertson, or Inge, or Galsworthy.

Bertine calls Dick her yardstick. Soon she was editing as well as managing the *Review*, visiting the printers and learning about type-faces and founts. Often late with the proofs, ridiculously short of machinery, the Athenaeum Press, which printed the *Review*, was run by J. E. Francis, an eccentric old man nicknamed Jef, who staffed his antiquated printing press largely from crypt down-and-outs.

He visited St. Martin's twice a day, holding 'porches' at midday and six o'clock, when he dispensed threepenny tickets for a cup of tea or coffee, honoured at a coffee stall in Covent Garden, and bed and food tickets for the Salvation Army and Church Army hostels.

Jef objected to the term 'down-and-out', maintaining that

men were down, but not out unlesss they died in degradation. Dick's philosophy was always, 'If you see anybody fallen by the wayside and lying in the ditch, it isn't much good climbing into the ditch and lying down by their side.'

When Dick asked Jef to join him working in the crypt, Jef asked how much conformity with Church of England practice would be expected of him. 'None at all,' Dick told him. 'I don't know what you are. For all I know, you may be a Muslim. What matters is that you have a flair for the work.'

Both were shrewd and unorthodox. Soft-hearted curates made Jef despair, falling for every easy touch. Dick had his sentimental moments, but he could listen to a tear-jerking rigmarole and then suggest the truth, and he was independent and unpredictable. After pasting a man for using bad language to his secretary he paused and smiled radiantly: 'Now you know my opinion of your behaviour. You wanted to see me in case I could help you. Tell me how.'

Soon—and sometimes against the wishes of the police—Jef and Dick had found work for sixty men, and Jef was negotiating for a run-down house over-looking the Thames where he could open a hostel for twenty-six men. He was so wrapped up in his work that his press was on the verge of bankruptcy, as the old machine ground out copies of the *Review* advertising for beds and tables and chairs and shirts and boots.

'With Dick around, you did things you would never normally have had the cheek to do,' says Bertine, who moved in to manage the printing offices in Breams Buildings, attending night school to learn printing, and buying a completely modern fount with a providential legacy from a forgotten silver mine.

By 1924, the *Review* had subscribers in over forty different countries. 'What a blessed link with home and all that St. Martin's stands for,' wrote a woman from Buenos Aires. 'It happens to be the birthday of my first son, whose name was Martyn. He was killed at Thiepval, but this is the place where he spent a happy childhood. I am so glad to think he knew St. Martin's ...'

'Here am I, staying with a very Christian store-keeper and his delightful wife and children in far-away Winburg, a Dutch dorp at the end of the lines, and lying on their table was *St.*

Martin's Review,' wrote the Bishop of Bloemfontein. 'Beyond us for a hundred miles is no railway, and you look out onto the veldt and nothing more . . .'

A Professor of Oriental Studies found a copy of the *Review* in the lounge of a hotel in Peruggia, with the result that when he was in England a few weeks later, he joined a discussion at St. Martin's on the Moslem World, and Dick wrote in his parish notes, which had succeeded the old-style Vicar's letter, 'We are delighted to announce that in one of the islands of the Pacific, 50 per cent of the white population takes the *St. Martin's Review*. We feel bound, however, to confess that there are only two white men on the island . . .'

Friends were despatched to leave copies discreetly in doctors' waiting-rooms, taxis, hotels and telephone kiosks. Dick dropped a couple of copies at the Palace, and boasted that a burglar had been arrested with a jemmy wrapped up in a copy of the *Review*. 'It's so popular,' he maintained, 'that even burglars can't get along without it.'

At Armistice-tide, special commemoration double-size issues sold over fifteen thousand copies. With the advent of broad-casting, the *Review* was to sell even more.

Broadcasting began in earnest in December 1922. John Reith, at that time Managing Director of the B.B.C., knew of Dick Sheppard as 'the repository of London's schemes and worries', and invited him to join a Religious Advisory Board under Dr. Garbett, who was then Bishop of Southwark.

Broadcast sermons began early the following year, and in July, Dick gave what he called his first 'cry in the dark to over two hundred thousand people', begging them to stop criticising and 'come over and help us'. The response was so great that mailbags had to be emptied into the curate's bath, and the sermon was reprinted in the *Review* and sent off by a band of helpers led by Bertine and Billy, who came in out of the rain and rolled in the stamps.

'My first proper meeting with Dick Sheppard was at lunch at Simpson's on June 14th,' Reith said later. 'It was then that the idea of broadcasting a complete religious service from a church was broached.'

Dick called Reith a man who held tenaciously to his belief that righteousness alone exalteth a nation. Before accepting the offer, he wrote to Westminster Abbey and St. Paul's Cathedral, suggesting they should take up the challenge instead, and the idea was treated indignantly as blasphemy.

'It would have surprised members of the general public if they could have read some of the letters of protest, not a few from Church leaders, that poured into the letter-box of St. Martin's Vicarage,' Dick said later. One churchman suggested that it must have escaped his notice that if a church service was broadcast, a man might listen to it in a pub—with his hat on.

So far as Dick was concerned, this was fine. He asked for an official letter from the B.B.C. to prove to his Parochial Church Council that the idea was no stunt of his own, and later he was able to record with pride that he went forward with their complete approval. Initial suspicion, they had found, should always be tempered with the knowledge that Dick had a nasty knack of turning out to be right.

'The whole nation should remember most gratefully that it was the rugged obstinacy of John Reith that gave us religious services on the wireless,' wrote another famous broadcaster, W. H. Elliott. 'The Church was dead against it. A resolution came before Convocation calling for its prohibition. Dick and I tucked our toes in and said that, whatever the Church might say or do, we would go on. However, it did not come to that, mostly, I believe, because Reith was such a rock that nobody could move him.'

However, 'It was little less than an agony to be treated with such scorn and despising when one was speaking week by week to millions all over the world. Dick felt it, and so did I, though both of us were by instinct rebels enough to feel doubly determined to win through.'

So far as Reith was concerned, there was nothing technically alarming about transmitting a full church service. It was no more difficult than putting out grand opera, which had been done a year earlier. 'But,' he said, 'there were problems and delicacies of another order. The idea was shocking, even sacrilegious, to a number of people. There was a good deal of hostility

9

to it, much apprehension, and doubts as to whether anything of a church atmosphere would get across.'

On the last Sunday of 1923, Dick kept his congregation behind after the evening service, and rehearsed them. On the first Sunday of the new year, January 6th, the first full church service was transmitted, and Reith invited a small party of interested friends to listen to what he was calling a momentous broadcast.

Dick had been reading Wesley's journal: fifty hectic years journeying the length and breadth of the country to preach the word. Five minutes before the service began, a friend commented that it would reach more people than Wesley had reached in the whole of his life, and the immensity of it made Dick physically sick.

'Tonight we begin the happy, if difficult task of attempting to make contact with a great multitude of unseen people which no man can number,' he said in his address. 'It is our ambition that one day this contact may ripen into a friendship.'

There have certainly been great technical developments since then [said Reith afterwards]. More highly sensitive microphones, more knowledge of and attention to acoustical problems. But from what came to our room that night, no one would have realised that this was a first and rather startling experiment.

It was the subject of a great deal of comment afterwards, but I do not remember having heard of anyone who was otherwise than profoundly impressed from start to finish, not merely with the technical perfection of the transmission, but with the sense of having themselves participated in a corporate act of worship as members of the St. Martin's congregation.

As a result of the broadcast, Dick received nearly a thousand letters, twenty pounds for church funds, and a letter from Holland complaining that the sound was 'as of hundreds of kettles with boiling water and thousands of singing birds.'

The Vicar of St. Stephen's, Norbury, wrote:

Dear Sir, I am writing to protest against your action in having your evening service broadcasted last night.

No doubt it was a very interesting thing to do from a purely theatrical point of view, and I expect you will get a great many letters from various people to thank you for permitting such a travesty on Christian worship to take place.

But the harm you have done to true religion, and the thousands of people who you have kept from attending their own place of worship last night cannot of course be estimated.

The practice once started is sure to be continued, and we shall probably have now every Sunday evening a so-called service on the wireless from every kind of denomination to keep people from offering a real act of worship and praise to God in His own House. To you will belong the stigma of having started this sort of thing.

I only hope that a great many more clergy will make their protest, and that the practice, as far as the Church of England is concerned, will be stopped.

A great many other clergy did make their protests. But it wasn't the clergy Dick was speaking to. Invalids wrote in, and old people saying thank you for 'a rare treat'. 'I listened in to the whole of the service,' wrote a man from Fulham. 'First with my pipe in my mouth, until resting back in my chair, I realised that I was one of your congregation worshipping God.'

A woman from Cropton, a hundred miles from London, fixed a loudspeaker outside her house and treated the rest of the village to 'Abide with me', and men in a pub in Lewisham joined in hymns they had not sung since their childhood, and sat around afterwards, drinking beer and discussing the sermon.

As one who has not attended a religious service for many years, and who, I regret to say, must class himself among those you referred to last evening who 'stand outside Christianity and criticise' [wrote a man from Dulwich] I should like to express to you my thanks for the permission given to the B.B.C. to broadcast your service last evening.

Although we do not 'profess and call ourselves Christians',

we still remember at times only, let me confess, our early training, even though we have long ceased to live up to it, and the service broadcast last evening, brought the Church which we have forsaken into our homes.

From then on, services were broadcast regularly at eight fifteen p.m. on the second Sunday of every month, and by October, Dick was able to hold a Listeners-In Social at the Albert Hall. There was community singing—'Swannee River' and 'Three Blind Mice'—and John Reith called it the first great occasion on which a link had been forged between the two parts of the wireless system, 'the owner of the Voice meeting the owners of the Ears'.

Critics called Dick's preaching too easy and emotional and disliked the rising inflection towards the end of each sentence. In fact, what they put down to affectation was partly to overcome breathlessness, and partly to counteract the downbeat pessimism put out by so many parsons. In spite of their criticisms, Dick received three thousand letters after one sermon, and visitors became used to seeing him sitting in his study surrounded by carefully bundled packets of mail.

When he asked for a rocking-horse for a child with no toys, rocking-horses stood in rows in the vicarage and the Vestry Hall, and over fifty years later, there are still those with vivid memories, 'when as a lad I first heard him on the cat's whisker ear phone . . .'

From Hampshire:

I was a schoolgirl at that time, in the lovely little thatched roofed village of Amport St. Mary's in Hampshire, and my dear father with other local men in the village, each Sunday night, would visit the White Hart, our local inn, where the publican possessed a radio set, a great luxury in those days. Father, with his pals, would gather round with their pints in their hand, and join in the singing from St. Martin's . . .

From Bristol:

Sundays for me were one long ritual of church services.

My grandfather was verger of St. Michael's church, Newquay, Cornwall, and so it was church in the morning, church and Sunday school in the afternoon, church again in the evening with granny, when we would wait for grandfather to secure the church before making our way to one of the aunts who lived in the town.

Having arrived and settled down—the wireless was already on—Grandfather would take his Hunter from his waistcoat pocket, the chimes of Big Ben, eight o'clock, and Dick Sheppard was on from St. Martin-in-the-Fields, so yet another hour would be spent joining in the service . . .

From Penge:

It was a broadcast service, and the church was full, but we were conducted right up to join other folk on the altar steps. The subject, and much of the service I have forgotten, but I shall never forget him leaning over the pulpit, arm outstretched, a pointing finger addressing who may, and saying in no un-certain voice, 'Have you ever wanted to run away with your neighbour's wife? If you have not, then do not condemn the man who does—you might have done likewise.'

And from Suffolk:

When I was a girl, my father drank too much, and every Sunday afternoon, my sister and I used to go to tea at my grandparents' house. We looked forward to these outings, as their home was peaceful and yet fun, and we had high tea. After tea we played games with Granny while Grandpa sat by the fire and listened to the radio. I can remember one Sunday hearing Dick Sheppard from St. Martin's saying, 'Never laugh at a drunken man or woman, either in real life or as shown on the stage, because drunkenness causes misery and hardship.'

Those words were a great comfort to me. I thought to myself that Dick Sheppard really understood what it was like.

In order to reply to all the letters he received, Dick sat up answering them throughout two nights every week. 'I must do the job in the only way in which I can do it at all,' he said to anyone who tried to interfere. After a night at his desk he had a bath and went into the church to celebrate Holy Communion. Childhood memories still haunted him: 'Tell them to believe in the God of Jesus Christ not in their Old Testament God of wrath and battles,' he said to his deputy one day when he was too ill to preach.

Labouring up the stairs of the Council offices above the church porch, he blockaded sympathy by making jokes as soon as he had enough breath. By the autumn, doctors were insisting that the only way to cure bronchial asthma was to go abroad for the winter.

'I like pain,' he argued defensively to Housman, who accused him of spiritual masochism. 'It brings me nearer my Master.'

He suggesting resigning, but the Church Council refused to consider the idea. Instead, they persuaded him to take six months away from England, during which time Charles Ritchie would take over, with the help of Dick's dogsbody curate, Hugo Johnston, an ex-Army man who ran a Quest Room in the crypt: 'We have a saying in our family, if anything goes wrong,' Rose Macaulay was to write later, 'let's go and ask Mr. Johnston . . .'

Dick refused to take his stipend, and set off on a desperate search for health. In November, he spent the tenth anniversary of his arrival at St. Martin's in Naples. It was Armistice and St. Martin's-tide, reminiscent of all that had become so important and he wrote as if to a family:

You see the day on which I write, and you can imagine where at this moment we both long to be.

It is very early in the morning and the sun is rising over the Bay of Naples while Vesuvius puffs away in the distance. It is a sight splendid enough to satisfy any man, and no doubt tomorrow I shall revel in it, but today, I confess, I want only to look upon Trafalgar Square, the church, and the home next door.

Tonight as you walk round the Square with the cross to

guide you, my ghost or spirit or whatever that part of me may be called that need not spend St. Martin's Day in Naples will surely be of your company.

You see for just ten years now you have given me great happiness.

We are here until November 23, when the *Orama*—there is a model of her, I am told, in the window of the Orient offices—is due to arrive and carry us off to Melbourne in time for Christmas Day. Our plans in Australia are uncertain. Letters will come and go very irregularly, I fear, after we leave here, and there will be a long stretch of weeks when we shall not be able to hear from you or you from us.

I have with me an address book with some thousand or so of your names in it. I had meant to spend a good deal of time writing to you, but I am not up to it, and I know you will understand if I use the book—as indeed I do daily—only as a Book of Remembrance.

Now as to our journey up to date. After a few days in Paris, where they rob you consistently, but of course in the most charming way, we hurried on to Venice. If you arrive, as we did, at night when the Grand Canal is aglow with lights and music is floating across the water it is like the shock of finding yourself in fairyland. We had only one day of glorious sunshine, but for most of the time it was cold and foggy and I found it hard to breathe there. One night on the Lagoon I was moved to try and sing 'Santa Lucia' but the gondolier thought I was coughing.

Of the wonders of Venice nothing to me quite compared with St. Mark's. I could hardly leave it. It seemed not only more exquisitely beautiful than anything built by man that I had ever seen, but here at last was a cathedral obviously loved of the people. The Venetians stream into it all day long. For hours I watched them. There were countless working girls who before they started work and in the luncheon hour ran in *and without hats*—please note that if there are any of you who would say it is not fitting for a woman to enter the House of God with her head uncovered.

There were tramps, as we should call them, soldiers, sailors and gondoliers, and tourists, all red with Baedekers, arriving noisily but in the end caught and silenced into prayer, and lastly, children by the score who said a prayer and then proceeded to play games quietly and, if you can conceive it, reverently under the two great pulpits with no one to hush them into silence and no stern official voice to warn them how solemn (another word for unnatural) children should always be in the House of God. They were as much at home in their Father's house as were the pigeons in the Piazza outside.

When on my first visit I noticed all this. I felt that—caught under the subtle spell that beauty weaves—I was seeing what I wanted to rather than what actually was. I feared to return lest the illusion should be destroyed, but there it was next time and the time after. Surely St. Mark's is the most homelike as well as the most beautiful church in Christendom.

I went there each morning as soon as the doors were open and passed in and out all day. I shall never forget High Mass one week-day morning when my neighbours in a front pew were a soldier, an old and dirty man, a wizened old lady and next to me a young mother with her baby in her arms. Do you know what actually happened, and during the service too? The mother fed the baby, and two little girls who were kneeling in the pew behind, in the intervals of saying their prayers, were smiling at the baby and stroking one of its hands. And the old priest at the altar, such a kindly-looking old man, looked down and smiled at it all.

I am never likely to be a Roman Catholic, but as I took my small share in that exquisite scene by giving the mother an Anglican smile, I remembered that the late George Tyrrell once said that when the Roman Church died it would be high time for the other churches to order their coffins. If only our English churches could be more like St. Mark's, but I fear many Church officials would think it unseemly if the people 'made free' with them.

We left Venice in a thick fog and bumped for seven hours in an apology for a train into Florence whose beauties I dare not attempt to describe. They must be seen to be believed. You need to read Ruskin in the evenings and walk about without a guide, and give yourself up to wonder. No place so demands surrender. There is probably more beauty crammed into a few square miles here than anywhere in the world.

We happened to spend November 4th, the Italian Armistice Day, there, a noisy day for which the delicate beauty of Florence was a singularly inappropriate background. The walls of the city were plastered with appeals to the Fascisti bidding them grow more fascistier still, which they certainly seemed perfectly willing to do, since they marched about in fours for many hours making incredible noises to the strain of martial music. I wish Mussolini would get them to shave. It is curious how Italy abounds with barbers' shops and yet I have never seen a nation of men so sorely in need of a shave.

From Florence we moved, after a week, to Rome. Maybe we tried to see too much in too short a time, or maybe a severe attack of insomnia was partly the cause, at any rate, treasonable though it will sound, I do not want to go back to the Eternal City. It is impressive beyond words of course, wonderful and tremendous, and lavish in its offering to even the casual visitor. It makes you think, and makes you small, and turns you mentally upside down. But it seemed like a city of perpetual autumn. Its great churches are sights to see rather than places to pray in. If they said anything to me at all it was only 'Aren't we fine?' The pagan monuments at times seemed more spiritual. The Vatican jarred. I could not bear the thought that the successor of St. Peter was condemned for ever to remain behind his own front gate and away from the people, simply because the Vatican had lost its temporal power. What irony it all is, and, if we had not grown accustomed to the idea of a secularised Christianity, how impossible.

I dislike talking about my own health, but since some of you are kind enough to make enquiries, here is a true bulletin as if from the lips of a doctor. 'The patient is decidedly better in general health: the sleep has improved but is not yet as it should be: the asthma is still troublesome, but that was to be expected: he takes his nourishment, with the exception of spaghetti, extremely well: he seems very cheerful and happy and is extraordinarily well looked after': there have been no

signs of real depression except on one foolish occasion when a
band was playing some silly tune called, I am told, 'What'll
I do'.

What a letter. Forgive me, but I have just babbled on. Bless
you all for Christmas. It will be strange to be without you.

From Italy, Dick and Alison went to Australia, where he
observed mildly that the Australians bought books but did not
read them. Having gone to the other end of the earth to seek
out a climate which might do him good, Dick found himself less
able to breathe than ever and he and Alison returned in panic
to the dry air of Naples. On the boat, Dick read Leacock and
wrote to tell Housman that Dr. Johnson blew bubbles down the
spout of his teapot. He was working on a book called *The Impatience of a Parson*, and the title reflected his mood.

On New Year's Eve in London, crowds queued for the Watchnight Service at St. Martin's, and the congregation overflowed
on to the porch and down the steps into the Square. It was the
same at Easter.

Dick was back in England dictating his book in breathless
paragraphs from a country nursing home where he was supposed
to be resting, driving the nurses spare by his refusal to give in
or opt for anything but a normal life.

'I wish I had been in London,' he wrote to Housman. 'But
here I am in a rest-cure for another fortnight and not allowed
to write any letters. This goes to the post via a nurse bribed with
cheap cigarettes.

'I'll be in London from May to for ever, please God, for when
I die I'm to be buried in the crypt of St. Martin's . . .'

He came back to St. Martin's quietly one Sunday morning,
celebrating Communion. Waiting for him in the vicarage was
a book filled with the names of well-wishers, which he said
he could scarcely bear to read, and radio listeners sent in asthma
cures every time they heard him wheeze.

Beloved Dick [wrote Maude Royden], your just being in
the world helps us, and you *are* helping us all the time, whether
you are awake or asleep or working or not working or in Capri

or London—though I'm afraid we like best that it should be in London. Do remember this always.

Just imagine being able to do us more good by just existing than most people can by working and swearing and sweating and making a perfect uproar.

Dick's mother died, 'old and tired and lonely', and he chastised himself because they had drifted apart, but with her went the last nagging loyalties that had restricted him, and he began preparing the manuscript of *The Impatience of a Parson* for publication.

Much of the impatience was within himself, lashing out at those around who did not do what he was proving to be unable to do.

Rosemary's first memory of seeing her father preach in St. Martin's was of people laughing. The next was of seeing him helped down the pulpit steps after collapsing during a sermon. Often his curates found him on his knees in the vestry before a broadcast service, choking and crying with frustration.

Sir Oliver Lodge, the physicist and spiritualist, who called St. Martin's a centre of enlightenment and encouragement, wrote to say that Archdeacon Wilberforce who died in 1916 had named Dick as the new Dean of Westminster, and that the newly deceased Dean Ryle was worried that he would throw open the nave of the Abbey to the homeless at night, much as pre-Reformation abbots had dispensed charity in the form of bread and sack to the poor in the cloisters. When the prediction proved false, Lodge offered to catechise Wilberforce the next time they were in touch.

Housman wrote to say he would like to roll up the Bishop of London in the same dust sheet as Lloyd George and pack them off for burial in the same plague-cart. His letter provided break-fast-time amusement, but Dick's reply had no humour in it.

'The new Armageddon will arrive long before Christianity can take possession,' he said. 'How the poor old Church needs overhauling. I cannot see how I can remain much longer within her as a priest.'

II

No Use to Anyone

1925 WAS a year of coal subsidies, of Nazi reconstitution and Fascism and the Locarno Pact, with T. S. Eliot predicting a world that ended with a whimper.

> Those who have crossed
> With direct eyes, to death's other Kingdom
> Remember us—if at all—not as lost
> Violent souls, but only
> As the hollow men
> The stuffed men . . .

Against a background of greed and unemployment, disillusion and industrial unrest, Charlie Chaplin, a friend of Dick's, made laughter of it in *The Gold Rush*.

Dick's gospel was still Christ or chaos. In October, he wrote to *The Times*: 'A fancy dress ball on a vast scale as a tribute to the Great Deliverance which followed on the unspeakable agony of 1914–1918 seems to me not so much irreligious as indecent . . .'

On the day the letter was printed, the ball was a fixture on the Albert Hall bookings, and tickets were being sold.

'Dear Friend,' wrote Lady Astor, 'I am with you all the way about Armistice. I have been hurt, and cried inside, on Armistice Day, and I am just an ordinary creature who only lost friends. What must mothers and wives feel?'

'To one like myself who has given his whole life to the cause

of our gallant officers and men since 1914, and who knows
better than most the terrible suffering and distress still rampant,
it seems nothing less than an outrage to make Armistice Day
a day of revelry, feasting and dancing,' wrote the celebrated
soldier Sir Alfred Milner, late Colonial Secretary and a Privy
Counsellor, who held yearly services of remembrance at his
home in Maidenhead. 'If only the day could end with the
solemnity with which it begins, it might have a lasting influence on
all classes.'

The dining tables and chairs were laid out before Dick succeeded in having the ball cancelled, and a Service of Remembrance
substituted. The King and Queen accepted invitations to attend,
and so did the Prime Minister, and Dick guaranteed the same
amount of money, or more, to go to the charity which would have
benefited from the ball.

When the news was made public, influential people wrote to
say thank you. A letter came from the Department of Overseas
Trade: 'May I offer you a word of thanks for giving such a fine
lead? It showed up once more that the feelings of the real public
are the same as ever — good as gold. They only require courageous
leadership. Thank you for giving it,' and on a rather different
level, from Oliver Lodge: 'I expect I am rather prejudiced, but
I hate these modern dances . . .'

Earl Cavan wrote from the War Office: 'What were the first
words uttered by the Army when it became officially known that
an Armistice would begin at 11.00 a.m. on November 11th,
1918? "Thank God". Never mind what real motives prompted
those words. They were said by everybody. Therefore November
11th should be, in my humble view, a day of thankfulness.'

Sir Alfred Tripp wrote of

the incalculable service you have done our nation, our empire,
our race, our civilisation, by arousing once more what is best
in us, with the result that we feel ashamed to dance on the
dead.

To my mind [he said] it is far the greatest happening since
the war left us all in darkness. It is a new dawning: once
again we all see some light. Archbishops could not do it—

Dick did it. And Dick will do lots more. And if he is forced to give up his beloved cure at St. Martin's, well, it's one of those inscrutable things that will be revealed in the future. It means that you are wanted for still greater work, because you are one of the great powers in the world today, and the world knows it.

Bishop Gilbert Talbot wrote of 'pluck, decision, and flair, for the working of the country's true and best mind. You threw these in,' he said, 'and the result came out, of a sort not often reached, that will last and leaven and tell.'

'The whole bench of bishops could not do what you have accomplished,' said a City vicar. 'Or at any rate, they did not try. It fills one with exultation to see how powerful the Church is when properly voiced.'

In the short time left, Dick printed a form of service which he led himself with no choir but the four thousand people in the auditorium. It was to be the forerunner of the annual Service of Remembrance still held at the Albert Hall today. After it was over, he kept his own service sheet, and the letters which were sent to him, and years later, he scribbled 'Of course Pacifism must be written into this' on the cover.

The General Council of the League of Nations Union adopted a formal resolution of thanks for his action, and Lord Ponsonby wrote on Peace protest paper. 'Dear Dick,' he said, 'to have succeeded single handed in substituting a service for an Albert Hall Fancy Dress Ball is an achievement which no one in this country could have done but you.

'It is absolutely amazing!

'I feel my campaign is quite unnecessary. A word from you will stop the next war.'

At St. Martin's it was becoming less and less certain that Dick would preach when his name was advertised. Early in November, he called an emergency meeting of the Parochial Church Council and offered his resignation again. The dismay which greeted his proposal is evident from the report pasted into the Minute book:

Early in November, Mr. Sheppard summoned the P.C.C. and explained that the continuance of his asthma made him feel that it was physically impossible for him to do his work as Vicar on the lines he had always tried to follow. With the greatest reluctance, he felt the only course open to him was to resign. He did not himself see how he could with a happy conscience be absent from London for long periods or adopt any different method of doing his work.

At the meeting the Council could do no more than express what they felt about him and all that he meant to them as individuals and to St. Martin's. They made it perfectly clear that they were trying not to adopt a narrow and selfish outlook but were making his health and peace of mind and the wider cause for which he stood their first consideration. They recognised, further, that St. Martin's was now a great deal more than a parish or a congregation, and that it had been allowed to become of national importance as a spiritual centre.

The meeting adjourned for a fortnight, and reassembled with a unanimous, certain, definite proposal that he could perhaps remain Vicar and that the guidance and inspiration under which St. Martin's had grown to what it now is, might remain available. The Council asked him whether for a definite period, he would try to follow a method that might perhaps entail very considerable personal sacrifice in that it would mean altering the system of work which up to date he had carried out.

They wished him to feel free to make such arrangements to be absent from St. Martin's for at least six months in the year as would not only give him the physical rest which his nature never allowed him while he is on the spot, but would also secure for him freedom of mind from responsibility in the details of the Vicar's work.

The proposal was that the Council should approach the requisite authorities to obtain permission for the Vicar to delegate certain of his official functions and that Mr. Ritchie, acting for him, should be entrusted with definite authority to handle details of the work connected with the parish, the church, and its activities.

Mr. Sheppard gratefully agreed—subject to the Bishop's approval—to attempt to follow this course during 1926. He made it quite clear that he wished this plan to be adopted for twelve months only, the whole situation to be reconsidered at the end of that time. The scheme had his warm approval.

We know that everyone will be immensely relieved that so hopeful an alternative to resignation has commended itself not only to Mr. and Mrs. Sheppard, but also to all those at St. Martin's.

'It is extraordinary that our prayers don't give you bodily strength,' wrote Maude Royden. 'We must pray wrong, I suppose. But at least our love isn't wrong and must help your spirit a little. It must come right, mustn't it? And meanwhile, God has given you broadcasting, and you have spoken to more people already than that dreadful Wesley, with the constitution of a horse, did in all his long and mis-pent life!'

But with even broadcasting denied him, Dick was beginning to resent his illness with a dangerously consuming resentment. Every plan he made was soured by the certainty that when the time came, however much pluck or grim resolve he brought to bear, there would be the same stupid capitulation: exhaustion, bed and bulletins, and other people's pity.

Disgust produced a kind of frustrated self-pity, morose and introverted, governed by the fear of becoming a professional invalid, and he wrote desperately to Lady Asquith, pouring out his heart to her and asking her advice.

She replied in a hastily pencilled letter dated midnight.

I can assure you I am much touched by your letter [she said]. I feel the shortness and uncertainty of life should be a hint to all of us to show our feelings.

All you must do now is to get well, and I am sure you will never be an invalid. I advise you against wind and sea. You are better at home. Journeys are no good, nor do I believe in rest. I only believe in the things you teach us all the time: love, work, and welcome. Then hearts, minds, and churches. I find most of these last three are usually if not closed afar.

Disregarding her advice, Dick and Alison left for Egypt. Tutankhamen's tomb had not been long opened to the public, and there was talk of going up the Nile, but in spite of the dry climate the dust got into Dick's lungs and he stayed in bed.

He slept alone so as not to wake Alison with constant coughing and struggling for breath. They had slept apart for some time: doctors had warned him against exertion, and there could be no hope of physical union or of having any more children. Dick seemed shut away inside himself, depressed, remote and moody.

At last they went to Capri, like a bright blue Instow with the sun always shining, but 'beauty does not lie with loneliness, and the vision of nature is ghastly when one is unhappy'. For a time his eyesight was affected by drugs to control the asthma, and he read letters with a magnifying glass and wrote with difficulty. Many of his letters were reckless and indifferent, striving after his old gaiety.

When he returned home, he dreaded the first sermon from the monstrously high old Grinling Gibbons pulpit, to a church full of indulgent sympathisers.

He wrote to friends at St. Martin's, before returning after Easter:

What I would like most is to step back as unnoticed as possible, and to spend our first Sunday at home quietly at prayer with you. I have a horror—remote though the possibility may be—of a church crowded by well-disposed people, many almost strangers to St. Martin's . . . I have decided not to preach on the Sunday of my return, but to have the simple happiness of taking the Communion Service and my share of the other services.

This decision has nothing to do with my health, which I hope ought not now to prevent my doing any work that falls to me, but it is dictated by the desire to dissociate my return from anything in the nature of an occasion for special effort from the pulpit, or the gathering to hear sermons on the part of those who out of sheer kindness are always ready to show sympathy with a man who has been ill—even to the extent of listening to his sermons.

10

The church bells were silenced so that he could sleep, but Dick's apparent confidence in his health was inevitably misplaced, as he must have known it would be. In May, the General Strike began, with men marching to London and gathering in Trafalgar Square. Charing Cross railway station yard opened a food stall, and helpers manned the canteen in the crypt. Speakers harangued the crowd from Nelson's Column, and fights broke out. The parks were crowded, and during the night, men slept in the Square, on the portico steps, and on the stairway to the crypt, when there was no more room inside the crypt itself.

The conduct of the Labour opposition angered Dick because of its apparent insincerity, with champagne one night and beer the next, and quick changes from evening dress to working clothes. In Bedfordbury the men stayed at home because of street fighting.

On the first Sunday of the Strike, Dick was due to preach. Instead, he was in bed fighting for breath, with doctors carrying out tests which were no help at all. 'I am just jogging along,' he wrote to Housman. 'No use to anyone. I'm trundled across to Martin's for a sermon now and then to pretend I'm active and useful, but otherwise I'm on the sofa all and every day being a nuisance to everyone around.'

At one time, he had agonised over becoming popular in case he deflected people from Christ. Now at least there was the proof that he had created a fellowship of people who were reliant on themselves and the promptings of Christ, and not on him. He was reading John Middleton Murry's *Life of Jesus* several times: 'I do not think his Jesus nearly as likeable as mine.' Murry resolutely avoided him—'God forgive me but I had a resistance against him,' he said later. Nevertheless Dick told him that the book helped to keep a spark of faith alive.

Each day brought extremities of emotion. Occasionally there was a return to the old enthusiasm, chasing a scoop for the *Review* or netting a controversial preacher like the Bishop of Pretoria, who nearly broke the pulpit in half.

I am publishing exactly what I really think on matters of the Christian institution [he wrote to Housman]. I am going out and out for pacifism, disestablishment, the removal of every barrier between sect and sect. My whole idea is that no one — not even a backbiter, a profiteer, a truth-seeker, or a murderer — can be excommunicated from the Universal Church unless he or she excommunicates himself or herself, and that the full hospitality of God must be given by the Church to anyone who merely says with reverence, 'Lord I believe, help thou mine unbelief.'

By the summer he was in bed again for seven weeks, and Alison was tense. There was an immense, immediate depth of love between them, but Dick's illness terrified her, and she had no idea how to cope with her own fear, let alone comfort him in his. Whereas at one time she had pleaded headaches as an excuse for not doing what she had no desire to do, her instinct now was to run away altogether, and she escaped more and more to her home or on holiday, suffering agonies of remorse and guilt, writing Dick unhappy letters of justification.

Dick excused her as he always had done, rationalising her behaviour and blaming himself: it was misery for her and stupid of him to be such a failure, 'She needs a rest. She's not well. Of course, she had to go . . .' When she came back, arriving impulsively and unexpectedly, they never talked about his illness, especially to the children, and Dick enlisted friends to take her to concerts and the theatre, or out to dinner at exciting restaurants.

In September, he was in a Broadstairs nursing-home reading Housman: 'All my life I shall remember the story of St. Francis kissing the hands of the priest of evil reputation — I will try to be more like that.' He had been at St. Martin's twelve years, and called them the happiest in his life. During that time, he had been away over eighteen months.

'I am a miserable cripple,' he wrote bitterly, thanking Housman for the St. Francis plays. 'I have had to resign St. Martin's, and my heart is almost broken. Everything I cared for is being pushed out of my life. If I were more of a Christian, I shouldn't be such a damn fool.'

As Anson had said, Dick was incapable of doing things by

halves, whether it was a sermon, a cricket match, or an incurable desire to see men take off their hats to the Church as the old man in Bethnal Green had taken off his hat to the Excelsior Hall.

'We felt our friend was going away,' remembers an old Bedfordbury parishioner. 'When he came, he was young and full of life. Then his health gradually broke and broke . . .'

Punch printed a full-page sketch of Dick with a cigarette between his fingers and a picture of St. Martin's hanging on the wall behind him:

> To stronger hands the stricken shepherd yields
> The flock he folded in St. Martin's Fields;
> Gentle at heart to others' need and pain,
> May Richard shortly be himself again!

12

Why Be Patient?

NEXT YEAR, if I'm alive [Dick wrote to Housman], I shall be like Saint Francis in that I shall be shying stones at authority. I have come to the conclusion that nothing can be done that needs doing without at least verbal violence.

Judge me, and judge me finally on this book of mine. I am saying all that I really believe and I'll never get a job in the Church of England after it appears.

He was preparing *The Impatience of a Parson* for the publishers and experimenting on a new communion with Maude Royden. To his surprise he was made a Companion of Honour in the New Year lists, and from then on he wore the little silver cross at the neck of his cassock. He was less sure now of what he really believed than at any time since his ordination.

I must remain what I am [he said]. That is, a seeker after Truth who has found and grown to love quite terribly Jesus Christ, and is content to believe, without any theological definitions, that Jesus Christ represents God.

That is all that I know and swear by, and if God is not like Jesus Christ, I wish to cock a snook at him.

The strength of this rock-bottom faith was impressive, and the award gave him a sense of reassurance. 'What the Church of England needs to regain its position is a thousand Dick Sheppards,' said the Bishop of Birmingham.

Over the last years, his attitude to suffering had changed. 'I do not like suffering,' he wrote emphatically to Housman soon after leaving St. Martin's. 'I dislike all that talk about how lovely it is to suffer. I think it is a rotten process which has nothing to do with God. At least, if God causes suffering and delights in it, I do not delight in believing in Him.'

Emil Coué, the celebrated French faith-healer, had tried unsuccessfully to cure him of insomnia — Dick thought he was the night nurse — and at the start of 1927, Dick was paraphrasing Coué: 'Every day in every way, I get stronger and stronger and stronger,' he said. 'I must tie a knot in my handkerchief lest I forget it.'

He and Alison moved to a house in Holland Road in Kensington, near to the fresh air and flowers of Holland Park, and Alison indulged her delight in making a new home welcoming and comfortable. When the house was finished, she opened an interior-decorating business on an impulse with an arty friend, and socialites who called her Alice came to her for advice. Dick viewed the enterprise with enthusiasm: even if it was to prove a novelty and a passing phase, it absorbed her for the moment and made her happy.

Oliver Lodge wrote telling him to take life more easily — 'There are plenty of good men upstairs; we want some down here' — and Housman paid a visit to the new home, admiring Alison's green bathroom, but confounding her by saying there were too many pictures in the bedroom.

Dick was worrying about money and idealising marriage much as he was apt to idealise the Church. 'I don't care a hoot for myself,' he said, 'but Alison, though she'd make any sacrifice for me and would never grouse, has never lived in poverty, and the prospect worries me badly.' In spite of the peacocks and the fresh air of the park, and constant repetition of what Dick called the asthmatic's prayer — 'Give us this day our daily breath' — by April, he was in Berne, wishing he knew more about Jesus Christ and having 'a hundred thousand million bugs squirted into me daily' by an instrument he insisted looked like a garden syringe.

The *Morning Post* was advertising a pre-publication series

of extracts from his book, and the *Sunday Express* chased him to Switzerland trying to secure articles to run at the same time. While Alison stayed in England searching for a house in the country, Dick wrote despondent letters likening himself to Robert Louis Stevenson, who, when he was exiled through illness, found the letters of friends like a breath of sweet fresh air.

He wrote to Housman at length on faith, posing problems and sitting at Housman's feet:

I want to reform the Church radically [he said]. I believe that a fresh edition of Christianity, with the teaching of the Sermon on the Mount as its creed, is years overdue.

Frankly, I want to spell references to Him with a capital H, and to bow my head at the name of Jesus, but beyond that I know almost nothing save that my world would be infinitely better if I lived more according to His Spirit. I am getting to hate all definitions of Jesus Christ, because they seem to exclude so many who are approaching God and Him from a different angle from my own. I cannot say such a terrific dogma as 'Jesus was God Himself.' I don't disbelieve it. I don't deny it. But frankly it is enough for me to try and follow, and then see what happens.

I suppose I ought to be interested in turning men into keen Church people, but I'm not. I am only interested in trying to make men think with Jesus Christ in their horizon, and then, provided they are living decently, I will gladly accept their own version of religion, not for myself, but as the right version for them.

He had agreed at last to give four interviews to the *Sunday Express*, professing more reluctance than he probably felt. The paper likened him to Shaw, calling both men humorous evangelists, and heralding the pieces as a daring experiment, which would be read eagerly by millions who never darkened the church's doors. 'He has only one aim,' they said: 'to transform belief into living.'

After the interviews, Dick signed a contract with the paper

for a weekly column which convinced him again, as broadcasting
had done, 'that Jesus Christ has no rival in the hearts of men'.
He called the articles 'only little stuff', adapting his preaching
style easily to journalism, with the result that its simplicity
confounded the intellectuals, who called it facile, and its swift
epigrammatic wit led others to call him a born journalist. More
thoughtful friends chided him for writing instant religion in
what they called a cheap newspaper, and theologians mis-
trusted him as much as he constantly and publicly displayed his
mistrust of them.

Week by week, he wrote on Christ and humanity: marriage,
love, friendship, war, faith and pride and remorse. Much of
what he said indicated the great torrent of accumulated disappointment for which the *Bookseller* was already predicting an
unusually big demand.

The average man [he said] is ready for a surprising amount
of Christianity, if only its leaders would show him the vital
heart of the Gospel. The clergy must come right down from
their pedestals of aloofness and archaic reflections and meet
men and women where they actually are, so that they may
hear in their own tongue the wonderful works of God.

I am well aware that no great cause can for long hold the
allegiance of the virile if, in an amiable desire to make con-
verts, it covers or makes light of its essential notes of sternness.
And yet I resent with all my soul, the fact that the orthodox
have so complicated the perfectly straightforward teaching
of Christ that common people neither hear Him gladly nor
with understanding.

When all's said and done, I believe that the Christian
Church is the best thing left in this chaotic world, and if its
members would come to vigorous life, they could rescue
their world, and themselves, from its bondage of sin and
impotence.

He was writing from The Red House at Godalming in Surrey,
one of the few private houses Lutyens had built, on a steep
incline, with a red-brick veranda looking through red pillars

down the terraced hillside with an asparagus garden and a flat lawn at the bottom where the children played deck tennis. The house had belonged to Clutton Brock—'a hero of mine'—who had painted murals of *art nouveau* maidens on the walls.

'London is a poor place,' Dick wrote to Housman. 'We decided we'd come and live here until death us do part. Poor Alison has had all the trouble (and joy!) of shifting her whole scheme of decoration, including the green bathroom and the (to you) too profuse row of pictures, from London to here.'

He was reading Tyrrell, the revolutionary Jesuit, on mysticism, charity, and the eucharist: 'It's wholly inadequate of me, but I can't make out what I think about the Communion of Saints— I fancy there must be wonderful gold in the ecclesiastical ore around it.' The Shaws came to visit and called the house a magical one, clinging to the hillside, but years earlier Dick had walked through Epping Forest from the East End, hardly concealing his yawns, and his appreciation had not changed.

Rosemary was six years old, left alone to amuse herself, sitting on the hillside for hours on end, watching the rabbits play. Peggie was boarding at St. Paul's school for girls. Soon after the autumn term began, she saw a newspaper placard which said BISHOP ATTACKS DICK SHEPPARD, and thought her father had been involved in a fight.

The Impatience of a Parson was on sale, displayed unexpectedly at Hatchards in Piccadilly and in bookshops all over the country.

'It is just the ill-written, muddle-headed convictions of a man who knows little except that everything in Institutional Religion is wrong,' Dick wrote to Housman. He had compiled it, he said, with Maude Royden in mind. 'You inspired it,' he told her, 'by telling me not to be so damned diffident.' It appeared on the bookstalls in October, price three-and-sixpence, at the same time as a book by Professor Julian Huxley called *Religion Without Revelation*, and a book by Maude Royden in which she disputed the Virgin Birth. The Bishop of Birmingham was making heretical headlines by casting doubt on Adam and Eve.

'What *can* our youth believe?' asked the *Sunday Pictorial* peevishly.

'Dick found it hard to allow for the tardiness of the human spirit,' Temple said later. 'His optimism was an inspiration, but if untempered, it prepared the way for disappointment. So he came to write *The Impatience of a Parson*, which was widely misunderstood. Being impatient, he forgot to mention his most fundamental convictions. He took them for granted, but many of his readers did not.'

In comparison with *The Human Parson*, Dick's series of Cambridge lectures which had appeared as a small book in 1924, *The Impatience* seemed to many to be the obsessive outpourings of a disillusioned invalid, but as always with Dick, when they began to argue, they were up against something so simple that there was no room for manœuvre.

'Why be patient if we believe the Holy Spirit presses on the hearts of men?' Dick asked. 'Pentecost is normal Christianity.'

DICK SHEPPARD HITS OUT, said the *Standard* headline. ROUND COLLAR NOT A SLIPPED HALO said the *Mirror*. STARTLING VIEWS OF WELL-KNOWN CLERGYMAN . . . DICK SHEPPARD'S DARING OUTBURST . . . PARSONS IN REVOLT! . . . THE GOSPEL ACCORDING TO SAINT DICK . . . A WHIP FOR THE BISHOPS.

The nub of the book lay in the idea that the Church of Christ on earth could be no better and no worse than the individual Christians within it. 'It is possible to love one's Church passionately,' Dick wrote in it, echoing the same sentiment he had once expressed about the League of Nations,

and perhaps with equal passion to believe in it, not perhaps exactly as it is, but as it might be, and yet to feel that a great deal of its energy is at the moment being spent on work to which its Founder would attach little, if any, importance.

I am compelled, with the greatest reluctance, to believe that the Churches have corporately so misunderstood the message of their Founder, and so mishandled and mislaid His values, that what survives and does duty nowadays, through the Churches, as Christianity, is a caricature of what Christ intended.

I could more easily see Our Lord sweeping the streets of London than issuing edicts from its cathedral.

An immense revolution is inevitable if the common people are again to hear Christ gladly. Men today are not looking for a religious system, and yet the soul of the world, consciously or unconsciously, is crying for Christ, and I feel that Western civilisation will go up in the smoke of another World War long before Christianity, moving at its present pace, takes possession.

I want a disturbance. I want almost anything rather than an unchallenged continuation of these smothered institutional versions of the fire which Jesus Christ came to cast upon the earth.

In a chapter headed 'In Three Years' Time', he talked of the next Lambeth Conference. 'The last very nearly achieved greatness,' he said. 'The Bishops did their best—and their best was nothing like good enough.' In 1930, he suggested, the Conference should issue an encyclical letter saying 'certain things, some of which may seem in the nature of platitudes to instructed Church people, but which as a matter of fact are not known or recognised by the vast majority, whose ideas about the Church, are, to say the least, confused.'

Following the letter were to be issued a number of explanatory resolutions:

I That the Anglican Communion feels the necessity of asserting that the one fundamental demand which Christianity makes on the individual is that he should accept the values of God which Jesus Christ revealed and endeavour to follow the example of our Lord in incorruptness of living.

II That the Anglican Communion believes it essential that all men should think out their Christianity for themselves and not merely accept it on authority: and that Christianity presupposes that its truths can only be apprehended by those who are living true to their own highest ideals and are facing their doubts in all honesty.

III That the Anglican Communion while believing that the Christian Church is essential for the welfare of the Christian faith, yet recognises that it exists for the service of mankind and is not indispensable for Christian discipleship. At the same time it believes that men and women will be the more strengthened and the cause of Christianity better served if they are sincerely able to give their allegiance to the Christian society.

IV That the Anglican Communion does not believe that a Christian Church has any right to insist upon intellectual tests for would-be disciples.

V That the Anglican Communion believes that, according to the mind of Christ, His Church should be within the world for the salvation of all men. It believes that the attitude of God towards men is that of the father in the story of the Prodigal Son, and that consequently the Christian Church should be ready at any moment, without question or condition, to welcome into its communion all who reverently ask that they may be admitted. It cannot deny the full hospitality of God to any seeker after Him; and it renounces all desire to make moral judgement upon men or to excommunicate or anathematize any single person whatever may have been his short-comings.

VI That the earnest prayer and desire of the Anglican Communion is that it may be allowed, through sacrifice, to assist in outlining to all men a larger edition of Christianity in which all may be literally at one in their common loyalty to Jesus Christ, their fellowship one with another and their common belief that such loyalty and fellowship transcend all differences of interpretation and administration.

VII That the Anglican Communion confesses that men must be won to the cause of Christ by no other methods than by the revelation of God's Love, and that they are not to be importuned into the Christian Society by methods of magic, fear or superstition which Christ Himself refused. It definitely asserts that there is no magic attached to its sacraments or ministry, but that their undoubted benefits are dependent on the attitude of those who reverently seek them.

VIII That the Anglican Communion conceives that its duty is to be a witness in the world to the actual values of Jesus Christ which are plainly to be seen in the Sermon on the Mount. Only by the acceptance of these values on the part of individuals can the remedy be found for the distractions of the world. There is no other panacea. The Anglican Communion will no longer acquiesce in the belief that literal Christianity is impossible and unpractical.

IX That the Anglican Communion denies that the brotherhood of all men — irrespective of their class or nationality or race — can be reconciled with any competitive ideal of human life which necessitates that the weak must go to the wall for the benefit of the strong or that requires men to slay their brother men. It is obliged to outlaw all war and to demand from its members that they should refuse to kill their brethren.

X That the Anglican Communion feels it essential that the presentation of Christianity should be enlarged by radical simplification, and that much that is complicated and now misunderstood should be rephrased or restated.

XI That the Anglican Communion resolves that its teaching and official literature should be purged forthwith of any suggestions that ascribe to God a desire for vengeance or a willingness to punish eternally those who have strayed from the Father's home. Any suggestion that the Christian God is cruel or capricious in His judgements, unjust in His punishments, or less wholly lovable than a perfect father of human conception must be removed both from the teaching of the Church and from its prayer book. In particular the teaching of Jesus Christ about God cannot be reconciled with the current conception of Hell.

XII That the Anglican Communion confesses with shame its share of blame for the fact that the Christian Church has been split into a multitude of isolated sects, and it recognises that men cannot be expected to understand the Gospel of Jesus Christ while it is presented in sectional forms.

XIII   That the Anglican Communion denies that this state of confusion cannot be immediately remedied, but recognises that the remedy is impossible without an infinity of sacrifice on its own part.

XIV   That the Anglican Communion desires every barrier which separates the adherents of one Church from another to be removed without delay: and especially the barriers that prevent fellow Christians from kneeling together at the Holy Communion.

XV   That the Anglican Communion is determined no longer to compete with the kingdoms of this world for prestige. It does not believe in national churches in so far as they exalt the interests of the universal Kingdom of God, or stimulate national prejudices and national jealousies. It believes that titles such as 'Your Grace' and 'My Lord' must be renounced by the leaders of Anglicanism.

XVI   That the Anglican Communion does not desire for itself any privileges which are denied to other Christian Churches, and as one token of its sincerity in this respect it demands its own disestablishment and if necessary is prepared to accept disendowment. Yet believing it to be essential that Christianity should remain the acknowledged religion it asks the State to permit it, together with such other Christian bodies as are willing to assist, to suggest how the establishment of Christianity could be maintained and made effective.

XVII   That the Anglican Communion asks the co-operation of other Churches in order that a way may be discovered by which all who in future so desire may be ordained into One Universal Church with power to minister the Word and Sacraments to any congregation, provided that in exercising such ministry they loyally abide by the rules and practice of that particular branch of the One Universal Church.

XVIII That the Anglican Communion while it believes in the expediency of Episcopal government dissociates itself from the belief that the Apostolic succession is the essential test of the validity of a Christian Church. It expects diversity of views on this subject but it cannot believe the doctrine to be sufficiently proven to permit it any longer to retard the reunion of Christendom.

'What optimism,' said the *Star*. 'Mr. Sheppard might as well expect the House of Lords to reform itself.'

The *Observer* called it a missed opportunity, neither a programme nor a persuasive plea. *Time and Tide* said it was not heroic enough. The *Spectator* blamed him for 'picking and choosing, and leaving on one side the really serious intellectual difficulties' and the *Times Literary Supplement* said it was ill-balanced and deficient in constructive policy, though they were glad it had been written.

The Times reviewed it reprovingly as their book of the week, and said 'we must confess that if this book were the only material before us to judge the worth of Mr. Sheppard's work, we should be puzzled to account for his influence.' 'My only consolation is that it is exactly what *The Times* would have written about Saint Francis,' wrote Maude Royden. 'Indeed, it is just what *The Times* would have said about Our Lord. And anyway, you reach the common people: they can't.'

The *Church Times*, who called Dick as certain a draw in the Sunday newspapers as a popular novelist or an ex-convict, sincerely regretted that they were obliged to regard his teaching as mischievous and dangerous, and the *Universe*, whose reviewer 'had been told' that Dick was loved of thousands, said he reflected 'the very vague opinions and very honourable aspirations of large numbers of English folk at the present day who are seeking a religion half-way between orthodox Protestantism and crude Paganism.' 'The blunt truth,' said Iremonger, in the *Sunday Times*, 'is that Mr. Sheppard expects too much of the Church.'

'He has asked for trouble,' said the *Methodist Recorder*, and 'he will get it.'

Support, predictably, came from the popular press. 'He speaks like a man,' said the *Express*. The *Standard* called the book 'a trenchant attack on all branches of the Christian Church', and the *Mirror*, 'sound commonsense, reasonable arguments and outspoken truths which will probably cause considerable controversy in the Church.' Support also came from a less expected quarter. Hewlett Johnson, who was then Dean of Manchester, wrote to the *Daily Telegraph*, whose critic, C. B. Mortlock, had praised what he called the pent-up doubts of years.

I find myself unable to join in the chorus of clerical regret at the publication of the Rev. H. R. L. Sheppard's book, *The Impatience of a Parson* [he said]. Everybody recognises in Mr. Sheppard the most popular preacher in England today. His broadcast audiences number millions, and are to be found in the most unlikely places. But he is more than a popular preacher. He is a personality of very rare sympathy, with a sensitive perception as to spiritual movements. Perhaps also his judgement in intellectual matters and his reading on theological subjects are greater than he would himself allow.

I believe the book contains a serious criticism of our organised Christianity, and a criticism by no means devoid of constructive ideas.

Lang referred to it, less charitably, as tiresome and unhelpful, which was hardly surprising, since Dick had written that 'it seems almost impossible for any man to retain his reforming zeal after he has obtained to high office. Frankly I doubt if any bishop on the present bench is capable of leading the Church on the road of sacrifice,' he said. 'The Church needs a bigger man than any of them.'

'I don't in the least resent Dick's criticism of our failings,' Randall Davidson remarked to Harold Anson one evening before dinner. 'What I do resent is that he never tells us what we *should* be doing.'

As Anson saw it, Dick was like the Hebrew prophets, who

told the priests that God loathed and despised their bullocks and goats and incense, but when the priests asked what they could do instead, replied, 'All we know is that God hates what you *are* doing.'

Over dinner, they were joined by the Scottish Old Testament scholar, Sir George Adam Smith, and the Archbishop raised the subject again. 'What *did* the prophets tell the priests they were to do?' he asked.

'Some of the prophets said "You must offer fat lambs instead of lean ones",' replied Sir George. 'But the great prophets had no advice to offer except that men should love justice and mercy and walk humbly with their God.'

'I'm bound to admit that is very much what Dick says,' agreed the Archbishop.

The *Bookseller* announced the week's ill-assorted best-sellers— *Now We Are Six*, King Edward's biography and *The Impatience of a Parson*—and the *Newsagent* called it the undoubted bestseller of the moment: 'during my thirty years' experience of bookselling, I cannot remember any book of that type which has had such a tremendous sale.' Before Dick died, it was to sell over one hundred thousand.

A Friends' Meeting House in Southampton, and an East End missioner, made the book the subject of their Sunday talk, and so did the Bishop of London, preaching in Westminster Abbey. 'We are very narrow-minded and often too stodgy,' he said, inadequately, 'we perhaps do not attack the evils of overcrowding and housing as we should, but I say don't scrap the Church of England . . .'

At Maude Royden's independent Guild House, a passage was read out in place of the second lesson.

Local papers reviewed it, from the main Cardiff, Glasgow, Bristol, Manchester and Liverpool press to the *Muswell Hill Record* and the *Birkenhead News*. 'It comes in the nature of a surprise to hear that a parson has at last really become impatient enough to give us the naked truth,' remarked an obscure twenty-one-year-old provincial clerk, indicative of millions. By the end of the year, it was still selling back to back with Housman in Hatchards, and Dick was receiving up to two hundred letters a

day, including anonymous postcards addressed 'Fool', 'Fat-
head', and 'Judas'.

'I don't worry when the Bishop of Gloucester calls me a fool,
for I am a fool,' he wrote to Housman, one 'fighting-for-breath
day'. 'But I do think that I may have made the Bishop sit up a
little, otherwise he wouldn't have got quite so angry with a fool.'

The following year, Randall Davidson died. Cosmo Gordon
Lang became Archbishop of Canterbury, and William Temple
moved from Manchester to York. Lang was sixty-four, and
wrote hopefully to Dick of 'some invincible youth hiding within
me, and a late lark singing. I could not refuse, could I, merely
because I did not answer to the Archbishop of your dreams?'
he said. 'I look to you and others to keep me in touch with youth
and spring.'

Housman sent Dick a cat burglar he had befriended, and Dick
put him to live in Jef's hostel, suggesting facetiously that he
should give an address at St. Martin's with a demonstration up
the steeple afterwards. He was attending uninspired debates
in the Commons on the Revision of the Prayer Book, sitting under
the gallery in Ramsay MacDonald's seat. Those who used to
wait on his doorstep at St. Martin's came instead to Godalming,
and he displayed a genuinely selfless curiosity in other people
and an ability to make shrewd and unexpected judgements, which
had only come with confidence.

He was warm and demonstrative, writing to his friends, male
and female, as if he was in love with them. 'I love Dick Sheppard,'
wrote elegant, ugly, Lady Oxford to Maggie Ponsonby. 'I would
rather be a door-keeper in the house of Dick Sheppard than dwell
in Lambeth Palace,' wrote Maude Royden.

In America, a man died who loved Dick and St. Martin's,
and he left a legacy of twenty thousand pounds to the Sheppards
—Dick's detractors found his wealthy friends an embarrassment—
and one hundred thousand pounds to the church. Dick was
travelling and broadcasting and addressing meetings, giving the
impression to those who met him that he suffered from nothing
more than slightly short breath. Sometimes when he preached
he had to apologise afterwards for the emotion he had roused.
Although his immediate money worries were solved, the asthma

hung on stubbornly, and he went from place to place in England and abroad trying to find somewhere to breathe. If it let up for a moment, there were the side-effects to cope with — depression and tension and nervous exhaustion, as drugs to combat the asthma created their own problems, and necessitated further drugs.

Alison could still make another, magical world, dispelling darkness and minimising the pain, but she was becoming tired and worn-out and scared. The fantasy house on the hillside with its grotesquely tall Elizabethan chimneys had lost its novelty, and it was impossible to play the hostess without the gay host she had married. '*You* will understand how awful it is for a woman who sees her man breaking down under the load of work he has to do, or, still more, under the weight of the consciousness of the work he has to leave undone,' Shaw's wife had written to Dick. 'This world is worst to the best. Yes, of course I know that is a privilege and a tall feather in their caps. Still, it does not make it easier for their wives. Or does it? Yes: if they are the right sort of wives.'

Rosemary was lonely with Peggie away at school. She played with the cook's airedale dog and bought food from the Charterhouse boys' tuck shop, and sat for hours by herself in the garden, lost in an imaginary world. Nannies who came and went told stories that frightened her of bulls who would chase her home if she dawdled and insects that killed you when you sucked grass, and one night, searching for chocolate, she saw the pistol in her father's drawer and Alison found her wide-eyed on the landing, saying she had had a bad dream.

When the holidays came, the children were sent to stay with grandparents and aunts and uncles. Grandfather Carver was preoccupied and melancholy, but Granny gave them sweets to suck in church from a silver pill-box. Aunts and uncles noticed that they arrived looking lost, with insufficient clothes in their suitcases.

Early in 1929, Dick preached on friendship.

I get tired of hearing preachers say that God cannot do his work without us [he said]. I feel sure God wants to work through us, but I hate the very suggestion that he cannot do anything if we fail, because we fail so frequently and so badly.

God has not needed me for his mighty works. He did not need me to create the souls of good men or to bring the spring flowers to life again. God can, as a matter of fact, get on perfectly well without us, though his home circle would never be complete unless we were in it.

He was ill again, protesting against invalid's food and hankering after cold beef and cheese, or even tripe and onions, blancmange and prunes; hating the dependence that required a nurse to empty the slop pail. 'I am now a pacifist,' he wrote to Housman, who had for a long time been backing Ponsonby in peace protests and the No More War campaign. 'I do not think a Christian can take part in any work of killing, or do anything that he cannot believe that Christ would have done.' Housman wanted him to go on a tour to preach pacifism, but 'I am a trifle reluctant to make pacifism my only love . . .'

He had never set out to be a revolutionary. Even at St. Martin's, he had followed where love led only within the prescribed framework. In spite of reassurance which left him, like a naughty child, longing for someone to be really angry with him, he felt certain that the views expressed in *The Impatience* meant the end of his tempestuous love affair with the Church. He had laid his heart bare, and even Lang's 'Whenever you are ready for a post of boot-cleaner at Lambeth, let me know' seemed to take little account of the sacrifice.

It was a surprise, therefore, when he received a letter in May 1929 asking him to pay a visit to No. 10 Downing Street, where he was offered the Deanery of Canterbury.

13

The Best Thing Since Augustine

CANTERBURY WAS TO be a last desperate throw at the dice. Dick was to love it and agonise over it and ache for it after he had gone. And when he had gone, there were those who wondered what might have happened to Canterbury and to the whole of the Church of England, if he had been able to stay.

'We loved our Dick,' they said, surprised into open confession. 'We might have written the words in large letters . . .'

Cosmo Gordon Lang had been enthroned as Archbishop of Canterbury the previous year, and was already famous for boasting that he had never been inside a shop. Cathedral clergy were formal Trollopian characters. Archdeacons, deans and bishops wore aprons, gaiters and wide-brimmed hats with strings securing them. The Dean only appeared when a verger carrying a silver mace rang on the Deanery doorbell and escorted him to the cathedral.

When Dick arrived, he refused to wear gaiters. He visited the cathedral at all hours of the day and night in a black cassock over an ordinary shirt, and he wandered round the streets making friends, sporting an I Zingari tie in deference to a city irrationally devoted to cricket.

These shrines stand at the level of the weakest, doors wide

open [he said]. Ideally the Church of Christ is no frowning fortress from which to hurl the anathemas of Jehovah, no mere casket for precious stones and relics which because the dead could not take with them, the living have commercialised, no majestic political force. It is attempts, poor and misused if you like, ineffectual if you wish, soulless sometimes if you must, but sincere attempts none the less, to assist sorrowing, sinful, blundering men like you and me to keep our heads above the waters.

King's School boys said his arrival was like a bomb dropping in the cloisters.

'It was one of the best things that happened to Canterbury since Augustine and his forty monks,' said Campbell Crum, one of the cathedral canons. 'It was like the coming of a spring day into a world which had its east winds and cold wintry airs. You felt there was a change: a turn of the year.'

Dick called Canterbury a sphinx, smiling at him in the moonlight. 'It's colossal,' he wrote to Harold Anson. 'Services, at least in the Choir, should be severe: plainsong at its most monotonous, with bursts of jazz at intervals. And I should like all services in Latin or Greek or Esperanto.'

After accepting the post, breaking in on Lang during a Lambeth meeting of bishops to ask his advice, he had spent three days of 'drivelling futility' listening to Church Assembly debates.

'They are so shocked that I won't wear gaiters that I feel inclined to chuck the Deanery job in sheer despair at people who *can* be interested in what a padre wears on his legs,' he said. A clerical outfitter who threw up his hands at Dean Inge's dress-sense and Bishop Gore's carelessness, 'hinted that my legs must be a laughing stock,' and Housman indulged in facetious doggerel:

> Dick says that wearing gaiters,
> His legs are in a pen;
> They act as separators
> 'Twixt him and other men.

'Since I won't wear gaiters, I hope I may at least retain my humour,' Dick wrote back. 'I said all I had to say—badly as it

was said—in my *Impatience*, and was told at once by authority
that I had put myself in consequence, outside the pale. I accepted
that with regret, feeling it was inevitable. Now, to my amazement, authority suddenly says "Come and help at the centre".
I think it would be churlish to say "I won't play—boo to you!" '

The previous Dean, George Bell, who had gone to be Bishop
of Chichester, had already done a great deal in his more formal
way towards breaking down barriers between the cathedral
and the city. He had promoted joyous festivals of music, drama,
poetry, and dancing, invited Non-Conformist speakers, and
formed a society of cathedral friends. Announcing Dick's appointment, he called it passing on the torch. 'I commend to you my
personal friend,' he said, 'who has such a special gift of friendship.'

'George has left you, as a legacy, a mass of work in which
you will want all the aid we can give you,' wrote the Senior Canon.
'And the worst of it is, that I am by no means sure you will not
add to it.'

The Installation took place in the middle of a glorious summer.
As the long procession of choristers and lay clerks, rural deans
and clergy of the city, residential canons, honorary canons,
minor canons and six-preachers, made its way through the cold
grey stone of St. Andrew's Chapel and into the body of the
cathedral, leading the Archbishop to Augustine's marble throne
beyond the Sanctuary, Dick was left alone in the bare, monastic
Treasury. The words of the psalms hit the walls:

'I was glad when they said unto me, we will go into the house
of the Lord . . . I will lift up mine eyes unto the hills from whence
cometh my help.'

The thudding pendulum of the old clock on the wall in St.
Andrew's Chapel punctuated the words of the first lesson:
'Everyone that thirsteth, come ye to the waters, and he that hath
no money, come ye, buy and eat . . .' Dick accepted it all with a
wry ambivalence, at once overjoyed and overwhelmed, much
like Erasmus who had delighted in the jewels heaped on Thomas
Becket's tomb, while observing that the saint himself would
probably have preferred leaves and flowers.

'For ye shall go out with joy and be led forth with peace.

The mountains and the hills shall break forth before you into singing, and all the trees of the field shall clap their hands . . .' Canterbury was to be a testing-ground. It was a calculated risk: the city was low-lying and unhealthy, and to be Dean meant to be tied by statutes, and by a Chapter of canons many of whom might expect those statutes to be rigidly observed, invoking them mercilessly to prevent change or unorthodoxy.

'. . . Instead of the thorn shall come up the fir; and instead of the briar, the myrtle.'

As the lesson ended, Dick was collected from his chilly ante-room by two canons and the Precentor, led out of the Treasury, through St. Andrew's Chapel, down the worn stone steps into the body of the cathedral, to walk the long length of the choir and chancel to the sanctuary and the corona beyond, where Cosmo Lang waited on the marble throne.

The formal Mandate was long and unwieldy: 'Cosmo Gordon, by Divine Providence Archbishop of Canterbury, Primate of All England, have admitted Our well beloved in Christ, Hugh Richard Lawrie Sheppard, Clerk, Member of . . .'

'Otherwise known as Dick,' barked Dr. Palmer, the irascible organist, from his organ loft up a winding staircase on the south side of the cathedral. Deaf as a post, at loggerheads with Dr. Bell, he was Dick's first and most spectacular convert, only reverting to his crusty anti-decanal attitude when Dick left and Hewlett Johnson arrived.

'Beloved, let us love, for love is of God. Every one that loveth is born of God and knoweth God . . .' As the public part of the service ended, Lang blessed the new Dean with the familiar, affectionate words: 'The Lord bless thee and keep thee, and make his face to shine upon thee,' and words of comfort echoed through the high fretted stonework as they moved in procession again, down the body of the cathedral, through the well-worn steps of the Martyrdom where pilgrims had kissed the stones, into the cloisters and the Chapter House:

> Father-like he tends and spares us,
> Well our feeble frame he knows,
> In his hands he gently bears us . . .

There were those who had queried Dick's appointment. Apart from an honorary Doctorate from the University of Glasgow, he was not an academic. Many people considered him to be a left-wing revolutionary, a superficial idealist, all heart and no head. There must have been apprehension among the canons as they promised 'due obedience to thee as Dean'; apprehension too, on Dick's side, as he promised 'well and faithfully to rule and govern'.

He was, in fact, quite a-political; hungry for genuine criticism and indifferent to the rest: because of St. Martin's, his broadcasting and his writing, he was used to it. He displayed, in his regard for Canterbury, the dichotomy inherited from his parents, impatient with pomposity and pretence, and yet respecting tradition with genuine humility. He was already well known as a radio personality. He was also remembered as one of the great First World War padres, and Canterbury still counted itself a garrison city. Derek Ingram-Hill was a teenager at King's; today he is a canon at Canterbury. 'In a miraculously short time,' he says, 'Sheppard had everyone in the hollow of his hand.'

The Tudor Deanery, built for the earliest Dean, had red-brick gables. From a parapet outside a long window at the turn of the stairs, it was possible to see the flag-pole on the little tower of St. Martin's church, so old that Augustine probably saw it too. Dick's study, with its lovely Chinese carpet, looked out across the Green Court, where boys from King's cut across to the cloisters.

Reginald Tophill, the Dean's secretary, worked through an archway off the study, in a little room with a vaulted ceiling. His office uniform was a black jacket and pin-stripe trousers, and he calls Dick the best that ever walked in shoe leather.

When we were first introduced, Dean Bell left us to get to know each other [he says], I said 'Yes, Sir' to Dick, and he said 'If we're going to work together, we have to be comrades. There must be no "Sir". Other people call you Toppie and so can I.'

He was a surprise, and he got to me immediately. We knelt

down and said a prayer about working together, and the whole atmosphere of the Deanery changed.

Even today, Toppie has notes from Dick, and memories of him, which bring tears to his eyes: Dick in top-hat and tails going off to London—'Don't I look a gun!'; Dick arriving by the sick bed with a magnum of champagne; Dick in tears after a tough Chapter meeting, trying to push through paid holidays for the cathedral workers, and succeeding only on condition that he made up the discrepancy himself, one week's wages for forty men: 'They don't understand, Toppie. They don't understand.'

Derek Ingram-Hill calls it a magical golden summer.

He appeared at the King's School speech day and convulsed everyone. We'd never seen a clergyman making jokes. He said 'I'm terrified of you boys; I've addressed communist meetings in Bethnal Green, but I wasn't half so frightened of them!'

We didn't take him seriously, it was a phenomen, and we fell for him straight away. Schools under the shadow of a cathedral are extremely hard-boiled where clergy are concerned. Bell was a very, very great man, probably a greater man than Sheppard, but he was rather formal to us boys. As for cathedral clergy, you didn't talk to them. You took off your hat to them. They were hieratic figures in the background. Suddenly to have a clergyman who was likely to turn up anywhere, at any time, disdaining the frills with his own peculiar style of dress and behaviour, was astonishing and wholly charming.

When visitors stopped to stare at their new Dean disrobing in St. Andrew's chapel which was used as a vestry, Dick laughed at their faces pressed up against the wrought iron railings, and suggested they should bring him buns. Within a few weeks, the Dean's service, held traditionally in the nave on Sunday evenings, was attracting more than two thousand people and being relayed into the precincts.

Alison was temporarily happy again, with fresh hopes and

fresh enthusiasms. She measured up for carpets to cover what Housman called 'corridors for Christians to wear and tear in,' and made a boudoir from a dreary box of a room, by papering the walls with scarlet wallpaper and painting the ceiling midnight blue with gold stars on it. She wore striking clothes, slacks and a long cigarette holder, and she loved to make herself comfortable on a sofa with a book to read, the light at the right angle, the wireless where she could reach it, a drink on a table beside her, and a shawl draped along the back of the sofa in case her legs were cold.

Rose was nearly nine, exploring the garden with its ancient mulberry trees and wandering along the old city wall that bordered the grounds. The house was full of magic, with a spiral staircase haunted by monks and the watchful eyes of all the deans whose portraits hung round the dining-room walls. She was a fanciful, frightened little girl, living in a fantasy world of secrets and mystery, creeping into the cloisters at night to see the glowing picture of a grey girl sweeping, and to listen for her cries.

Peggie threw moods of black depression and wrote Russian diaries—'God! life is awful! How unhappy I am!'—and Dick saw in her the beginnings of a self-pity which he guarded against in himself. When Alison was angry with Rose, Peggie shouted and screamed and created a hysteria far worse than the injustice she was protesting about.

Dick sat on Rose's bed at night, telling her stories. He found it hard to talk about religion, and gave her a book about Jesus as awkwardly as if it had been a book about the facts of life. During term time, when speech days came, Alison sent word by Dick that she had a headache. 'Of course she's quite right,' Dick explained, as if he really believed what he was saying. 'She couldn't possibly have made the journey.' When holidays came, Peggie was entranced with the idea of coming home, but Alison found it impossible to simulate an interest in cricket matches and end-of-term concerts, and Peggie, overwhelmed by a sense of anticlimax, spent the first night of the holidays crying.

Both Dick and Alison had their own full-time lives to lead, and it never occurred to them to alter their lifestyle to suit their children. There were no museums or pantomimes or special outings, only, 'Darling, would you like to come shopping with me?' 'What's the point of life?' Peggie wrote dramatically in her diary. 'How bloody unhappy I am!'

A pretty twenty-one-year-old called Nancy Browne came to live at the Deanery, partly to help with secretarial work and partly to keep Alison company. Soon she was used by the family as a pillar box, receiving the confidences they had never shared with each other. She had a quick, caustic wit which appealed to Dick, and when the children returned to school, it was Nancy they wrote to.

Dick caused havoc at mealtimes, making up terrible tales about the food they were eating: vulgar remarks about the cook's toe-nail parings which convulsed the children and revolted Alison. At night, as always, the light was on under his door. On Sunday evenings he stood in the cathedral shaking hands with everyone as they left. Sometimes there were up to two thousand people. Sermons were an effort, preached without the aid of microphones, which had not yet been installed, and only assisted by old-fashioned sounding boards. One evening, as the last person left, he fell flat on his back with exhaustion and had to be helped to the Deanery. Thoroughly irritated by his own weakness, he consistently ignored it, smoking and working and provoking retribution.

Between the Deanery and the cathedral there was a steep flight of twenty-two worn stone steps. 'I remember standing at the top of the Dean's Stairs one day, watching him pull himself up step by step, coughing on every step,' says Derek Ingram-Hill. 'I said, "Your cough's very bad today, sir". And he laughed and said "Yes, it's terrible, isn't it". It was a frightening cough to hear when you're a boy who doesn't know much about that kind of thing.'

Dick went away for treatment in the Auvergne, but was back again in October, as ill as ever and considering resigning: 'Last night I lay blubbing in bed for over two hours. I couldn't breathe and I couldn't die and I just displayed the coward that I am.' Unanimously against resignation, the Chapter sent him to Italy, hoping for a miracle.

Alison, Rose and Nancy went with him, and they stayed in a castle at the top of the cliffs at Portofino, a tiny picturesque promontory near Genoa. According to legends, St. Martin of Tours was said to have lived in Liguria, and Portofino's only church, its crumbling façade half-hidden by a spectacular date palm, was called the church of St. Martin. The fairytale Castello — Dornford Yates had used it as the background to one of his novels — had flower-grown battlements, and a view through olives and cypresses down to the sea and the square quay where cloth merchants and tinkers bargained and fishermen mended their nets outside coloured cottages.

Bernard Montgomery came to stay, married late and idyllically to the young widow of Alison's youngest brother who had been killed at Gallipoli. So did Hugo Johnston and his fiancée Elaine — Dick gave them the money for an engagement ring — and Alan Carver, one of Alison's brothers, with his wife Dorothy. Alan had had a tough time in the war, and Dick was doing all he could to encourage him in an unproductive small-holding.

On the way out, Dick cheated the customs, taking a gramophone, which was illegal, into the train lavatory and coughing and retching and moaning so realistically that the sympathetic customs official left him alone. They arrived in the dark, with porters carrying the luggage up the hillside on their shoulders. In the morning, it was Instow all over again: the smell of blossom and the sparkle of the sea. 'It's all beautiful,' Dick said, 'But when I feel so ill, loveliness doesn't help.'

The castle was full of ghosts and legends, and Rose, put to bed early on her own, sleeping on a camp bed in the dark, woke up to find the furniture moving and strangers talking Italian round her bed, but when they suddenly disappeared, she told no one in case they said she had been dreaming. In the morning, they walked to the village on the next hill before breakfast, and waved to Dick across the valley, where he stood on the castle terrace pouring sherry for them when they returned.

One day Theresa the maid stunned everyone by announcing the arrival of a famous baroness, a wealthy champagne heiress, who was said to live nearby. Everyone stood up and made fatuous conversation until they realised they were talking to Dick wearing stout flowing clothes and a wig with side curls. In the evenings, they played rowdy games of bridge for enormous imaginary fortunes, and when Rose decided that the model man and woman who ran her model farmyard were to be married, Dick lit candles and made the ladies wear hats, and performed a solemn wedding ceremony.

At a fancy-dress party, Betty Montgomery arrived wearing her husband's evening clothes with a moustache painted on her lip. Aristic, witty, and eccentric she was everything her husband was not, pacifist to the point of refusing to allow her children to play with toy soldiers. Montgomery, who never dressed up and found frivolity incomprehensible, came into his own when it rained, organising a game of table-tennis like a battle manoeuvre in the round room at the top of the castle tower.

Max Beerbohm came to visit from his holiday home along the coast at Rapallo. He arrived exhausted, and went away saying he was under the wand of an enchanter. 'The Dean looked worn and pale,' he said, 'but he radiated youthfulness. Hardly had I beheld him than I felt perfectly fresh and in the best of health. He made me feel younger than my years and better than my character, generous, unselfish, altruistic—I might even have felt a little clerical if he had seemed less signally lay.'

Both were witty, affectionate and immediate. 'I am fifty-seven years old,' said Beerbohm, bowling down the hill, round and fastidious, 'I had long ago thought I shouldn't meet again a man of whom I could say to myself, "a new friend".'

Alison and Rose bathed off the rocks, and Dick lay full-length on the patio in the sun. Alison had always found it a fact of life that the next best thing to efficiency was to look helpless, and she let other people darn Dick's socks for her and then said nothing when Dick congratulated her on doing them well. When a guest criticised her idleness, he was up in arms, defending and justifying and demanding an apology.

Alison was trying to track down a suitable nurse to look after him when they were in England. 'Please,' he said, 'get a nurse by all means, but find one without a secret sorrow.'

They travelled back to a winter of gales and rain. Hurricanes from the south damaged the Norman tower and the south-east gable, and one morning there was three hundred-weight of stone and rubble on the ground. The grass in the cloisters was bright and bleak, and Dick tried to resign again, but the canons, backed by Alison and the cathedral workmen, persuaded him to stay. 'I didn't believe I could go into such darkness,' he said, convalescing in Cornwall, and returning too early to Canterbury.

It was 1930, the year of the Lambeth Conference. 'I can only remain where I am by imitating the ostrich, head in sand,' he wrote to Housman. 'Yet I swear that Jesus Christ lives somewhere, and isn't there a lot to be said for following intuition when reason is baffled?

'But I can't join the Roman Church, and I shan't be an officer in the Church of England for long . . .'

In spite of his responsibility to his Chapter, Dick did things his own way. Taking the rigid morning service, the words 'In the name of the Father, and of the Son, and of the Holy *Spirit*' were delivered like a punch on the jaw. He introduced a collection for the South African' diocese of Bloemfontein by remarking that the Bishop was a great rugger player, and stopped hymns in the middle as he used to at St. Martin's to change the tune or tell the congregation they were singing badly.

Once he prayed for children born illegitimately. 'One didn't talk about those sort of things in church then,' says Ingram-Hill. 'I'd never heard any other clergyman pray like it. He'd probably had dealings that week with somebody, and there it was on his mind and coming into his prayers. You felt he was a man who really brought everything from ordinary life into prayer.'

The Senior Vesturer and Sub-Sacrist, a stiff Scotsman, called Dick the first real Christian he had known in forty-five years at the cathedral. 'He used the simplest words, and yet I have never seen anyone approach him in his power of stirring men's souls,' he said. 'He was full of life and fun and gaiety, and he loved to see others happy. When he was announced to preach the cathedral was thronged and I had to have the doors closed. He loved Christ, he taught Christ, and men came to see Christ in him.'

Canon Crum called it one of the sums that baffles human arithmetic. 'I remember a Sunday early in the year,' he said, 'the communicants numbering perhaps four times as many as the corresponding Sunday a year ago, and Dick ministering to them at the altar rail, not hesitating to make his ministry personal as well as sacred by some sign of gladness that "you are there my dear . . ." '

Often he took a torch and went through the cloisters at night, letting himself into the intimate side chapel of St. Edward the Confessor, or the Dean's Chapel with its newly polished silver lamps. At first his kneeling figure startled the nightwatchman, but gradually the cathedral workers became used to seeing their Dean in the cathedral at all hours of the day and night wearing his black cassock with the Companion of Honour cross round his neck. Often he was there when the cleaners arrived at six, and they told him all their family news.

Dick called it clearing a space around the soul.

It was my habit to enter my cathedral in the stillness of early dawn that I might listen [he said once]. One early summer morning, I had entered with my master-key, and thought myself alone. I was sitting before the altar. There it was in its setting of ethereal beauty, almost uncannily holy and aloof. And there was I, an entirely inconsiderable minute thing below, in a black cassock. I was dead from the neck up. It was crushing, and I cried out to those dead stones to speak.

'Can you not unfreeze? Why don't you become human? Why frown on me and my like with such alien majesty? Can you not speak so that I can understand and take heart and hope?'

Then something happened. There was the noise of broom and bucket, and from behind the High Altar emerged a friend of mine, a cleaner, a carpenter by trade, a servant—as I was—of the Cathedral, a brother Old Contemptible in our Canterbury branch. We nodded and went on with our essential and immediate tasks, but a moment later my friend commissioned me from the High Altar. Using the appellation with which one Old Contemptible addresses another, he said, 'Chum Sheppard, I wish you'd go and see Chum So-and-So, he isn't half having a rotten time.'

I asked to what address I must go. Getting a pencil and an old envelope from his pocket, turning to the East to use the altar of Canterbury Cathedral as a desk, and bending over his task as a priest might bend over the holy Mysteries, he slowly traced, with much elbow work, the name and address of the suffering brother.

He did not know how symbolic this was. He came slowly down those great steps, as I was wont to do with the Bread of Life, and handed me his rough bit of paper.

Later, after I had executed my commission and returned from the city, with the cup empty of cold water, it was then that I had learned something of my cathedral and what it had to say to the city that nestles below it.

He was receiving up to a hundred letters a day, many of them containing weird asthma cures. Toppie kept some of the begging letters from him, for fear he would become bankrupt: most of the time, Dick dispensed charity deviously, hating to be thanked. He had the formidable iron railings removed from the stone wall in front of the Deanery and asked Housman for poetic prayers to use in cathedral services—services for which people began queuing an hour-and-a-half early. He had been made a member of the Canterbury Cricket Club, the Gentlemen of Kent—'you won't be expected to go in against fast bowlers!'—and he played some cricket using friends to run for him, and enjoyed Canterbury Cricket Week with Peggie, arranging to finance a friend of hers who could not afford to go to Cambridge University.

'I really am so much better, and able to pull my weight here now,' he wrote optimistically to Housman. Starting a new commonplace book, he noted down Beverley Nichols's choice of four great Christians—Gandhi, George Bernard Shaw as music critic, Delius and Walford Davies—and jotted down stories that amused him: the university wit who said, 'Well, Lord, we're both Trinity men' and the woman who dressed up smartly and went out holding a lavatory brush instead of an umbrella.

'Hebrew mythology was quite right,' he noted, 'a snake always gets into the garden.'

The Lambeth Conference was taking place with great panoply

and intent, but not one of the resolutions contained in *The Impatience* was debated or even mentioned. Lang wrote to say thank you for a massive cathedral service organised for all the bishops and their wives, with a garden party afterwards. Dick had read the only lesson in the service, and it was impudently apt:

'I therefore, the prisoner of the Lord, beseech you that you walk worthily of the vocation wherewith ye are called, with all lowliness and meekness, with long-suffering, forbearing one another in love . . .'

From then onwards, many of his writings contain words of deep disillusion. He asked B.B.C. audiences, in an exasperated sermon from what he called the wilderness:

Why are the great people, as the world calls them, in Church and State, so dull, pompous, and disappointing? Isn't it because they are nearly always so completely safe?

We know exactly what they are going to say even before they open their mouths. We know they are about to bid us do nothing in a hurry; to explore the situation; to remember that we are only trustees of our great heritage; and we know that they are going, if possible, to charm us back into the old, old grooves with fair words than mean almost nothing.

I am clear now beyond any shadow of doubt that we must either turn back, or go on with granite-like courage and dare to do what He bids us do, at those great moments when on our knees we seek to find His guidance. We do know it then much better than we like to confess. The danger point for us is that moment when, rising from our knees with the call of God upon our soul, we enter the council chamber where wise men are gathered together to tame us. Good men, many of them vastly better than we are, but still men who desire to remove the sting from the Gospel.

They bid us compromise, saying, 'My friend, I quite agree that that is all splendid, only it is terribly unpractical. It would never work. Don't ask too much at the moment. Take the little you can get and be thankful. Let us progressively advance, until ultimately what you, and indeed we, desire, will arrive. One step enough.'

What is the use of one step? Did anyone accomplish anything by going up one step? Even an asthmatic can do that
without boasting of achievement. We need to know when to
be patient [he said, echoing a younger, more daring Temple]
but also we need more to know when to be impatient.

He tried unsuccessfully to persuade the Chapter to adopt the
new 1928 Prayer Book for use in the cathedral, began openly
advocating pacifism — 'there must at times be conflict between
Christ and State, and our place is every time with Christ' — and
announced his intention of celebrating Holy Communion in a
Presbyterian Church, an action which earned Temple's immediate disapproval.

He wrote to another rebel, Guy Rogers:

I'm going off the deep end (I promised to when I was Dean
of Canterbury), and am assisting Herbert Gray at his Presbyterian Communion service. Rightly or wrongly, I just can't
hold back any longer and feel the only hope now is in making a
blazing row.

If only the Church will consent to fight. Cosmo and William
Ebor are in despair at what I propose to do. I wish to God
they would attack me publicly and get the issue raised, but I
fear they'll only say 'Poor Dick! we must not take him
seriously.'

I'm worried about the Church of England. My whole soul
tells me that half-a-dozen of us ought to go out into the wilderness and hold a mission to England, which would necessitate
saying things that would be disloyal to our denominations.

I just cannot take any interest in admirable statements.

Paul Robeson, in England to play Othello, came to stay at
the Deanery, sitting Rose on his knee and singing to her, and
delighting Dick with 'Were You There When They Crucified
My Lord?' and Dick wrote to Shaw, asking him to come and
address an informal meeting in the precincts. Shaw wrote back
from the Malvern Festival where he had 'almost as much sordid
business to transact as a bishop', rehearsing five of his plays.

Some time ago, at St. Martin's, Dick had asked him to write on Prayer Book reform.

What could I do except get you into trouble, which you are only too well able to do for yourself [Shaw asked]. From the point of view of pietistic Canterbury I am a heathen. From its political point of view I am a Bolshevik. How much of the Apostles' Creed do you suppose I believe? Do you realise that I am much more pro-Russian than Trotsky? And the worst (or best) of it is that these questions cannot be amiably side-tracked any longer. And even if this were not so, I am too old to temporize or to behave considerately: I am passing through my second youth on my way to second childhood, and find myself, to my alarm, talking very much as I did when I was 25.

You asked me to write in the *St. Martin's Review* about the revision of the prayer book, which I used to hear you over the wireless revising yourself very freely every Sunday. Well, I did this, and the result was that you did not get the article. It would have blown St. Martin's into Trafalgar Square. I found that the whole book was saturated with Transubstantiation to such an extent than an attempt to eliminate it would be like an attempt to restore the spires of Chartres: the first stone taken out for numbering would have brought down the whole edifice.

I had already found, when my mother was cremated, and I had the Church of England service read because it seemed so mean to do the Chaplain out of his half-guinea, that the skulls and crossbones of the fifteenth century were grinning and rattling all through it in so heathenish a manner that when my sister followed my mother, I had to improvise a service and officiate myself.

At a wedding in St. George's Hanover Square, my wife and I agreed that we could not have stood it, and that but for the alternative of the registrar, we should have lived in sin rather than endure it . . . the vows to remain until death in a state of feeling and judgement which might and indeed must vary not only from decade to decade but even to some

extent from hour to hour, were so unreal that I was not surprised to find that the parson made no more pretence of taking
them seriously than any of the smart people and theatrical
celebrities assembled there.

The baptism service is the best, but I find people asking
me to act as godfather to their infants, and being amazed
when I reply that I cannot pledge myself to see that their
children are taught doctrines some of which (the atonement, for
instance) I not only disbelieve but abhor as ungentlemanly and
destructive of the human conscience by putting it on the dole.

Last Easter I attended a service dedicating a window to
the memory of my sister-in-law. Her husband read the lessons.
One of them was that perfectly infernal chapter from Exodus
which describes the spoiling of the Egyptians (by borrowing
their jewels and running away with them at the express suggestion of God) and the slaughter of the first-born. It made
a horrible impression on me, but the congregation took it
without turning a hair because it had ceased to have any
reality for them.

How can I tell your people that I am a Friend of the Cathedral
because I attach an enormous value to its atmosphere when
there is no service going on, and Christian and Jew, Deist
and Atheist, can make their souls there without disturbance
by any priest or any reminders of a rascally old tribal god with
the morals of Fagin in Oliver Twist?

You see how it is. If I spoke to your people I should seem
to be trying to tear off your gaiters, and I should perhaps dis-
courage you, although my desire is to keep you in the Church
so that the people may still get some genuine religion in the
place where they habitually look for it.

Our love to Mrs. Sheppard, and such blessings as our very
limited credit can command on yourself . . .'

It was an autumn of disasters. Unrest in India, with Gandhi
in gaol again and Housman attending Home Rule meetings
where Communists rushed the platform and fought with Labour
ministers. Hunger marchers in Trafalgar Square. Seagrave
exploded at one hundred miles an hour on Lake Windermere,

and the R101 airship crashed in France. Pioneers talked of jet propulsion, television, and atomic physics. Dick was thoughtful and withdrawn, longing to stay at the Deanery and knowing he would be unable to. A friend who stayed the night heard him in his bedroom next door praying and pleading and struggling for breath, but by the morning he was laughing and well again.

His broadcast services became shorter, simpler, and more infrequent: 'Asthma not only causes a man to make noises like nothing on earth except an asthmatic, but it also makes it hard for him, while it is on, to use his head.' At one of them, he pleaded for a 'divine and radiant carelessness'. 'Oh, my dears,' he said, 'it would be so lovely for those who live with us if now and then we could make ourselves a little more carefree.'

More and more he was talking of those who felt unable to pray, as if he was experiencing some kind of spiritual destitution himself, and as winter drew nearer, exacerbating the asthma, Alison went off to stay with friends, leaving Nancy to take care of Dick. A Canterbury photographer, providing pictures of him for those who wanted them as souvenirs, commented on his smile. 'It lit up his face,' she said. 'Christianity bubbled out of him. But he didn't look as if he was happy deep down.'

Alison longed to entertain, but Dick was so unpredictable, out at all hours, giving himself utterly to other people, then coming home spent and ill. When he entertained, Alison was either out, or she would yawn and stretch around nine o'clock and say how extraordinarily tired she was, so that guests scuttled away. Dick took Peggie to an exhibition of Flemish art at Antwerp, staying at the Bath Club on the way and chain-smoking Craven 'A'. He was unsure of himself, too ingratiating to the servants, confusing and sometimes offending them by treating them self-consciously as friends, and he referred nostalgically to 'my babies', although Peggie was nearly fifteen, already angry at Alison's lack of commitment and ferociously defensive of Dick, who was a hero in all but his excruciating use of Edwardian slang.

As often as possible, he gave the nave sermons on Sunday evenings, typed out like poetry, few lines to a page and persuasively rhythmic:

> Why, you cannot even love
> Without sorrow,

for

> the moment you gain that prize
> of all prizes,
> soon comes suffering in its train.

Wherever life and love are, there is pain [he said]. In Jesus Christ the mystery reaches its acutest form. There you have the spectacle of an ideally good man brought to an ideally bad end, as a consequence of his devotion to God and Man. It is a test case—*the* test case.

Presiding at a big Armistice meeting at the Canterbury Drill Hall, he stayed until the last person had been spoken too, and then collapsed. He had been suffering from heart pains, and London specialists ordered him to give up his job and rest. Christmas came and went. 'Come on, Pegs, don't be so glum!' he chivvied, making an effort to sing 'Good Christian Men Rejoice', in the bathroom on Christmas morning. 'I am incurably insistent on insisting that Xmas is real and true,' he wrote to Housman, quoting Mary Coleridge: 'The safety of the world was there, and the world's danger.'

Christianity [he said] is the only religion that has faced the problem of suffering and dared to believe that out of darkness there will one day come light. Christians are told to go on through the world holding their heads high and believing that ultimately love and goodness will triumph. Every day that the attempt is made, the adventure seems justified.

But it helps sometimes, even in my own small troubles, if someone holds my hand and says 'Yes, it is dreadful, isn't it' rather than for ever trying to brace me up. There are times when we cannot think of God in terms of love, and we want merely the sympathy of a silent friend.

But Alison was exhausted too, and bitterly disappointed. She loved the Deanery, the prestige, and the excitement, and was neither capable enough, nor willing, to spend the rest of her life nursing Dick and straining to give him the help and peace and security that he needed. She resented the fading of a beautiful dream of popularity and success and easy pleasure, and despised herself for being resentful. She had wanted to be so good and strong—a beautiful, adored heroine—but even backed by Dick's love and adoration, she had neither the strength nor the inclination to battle on much more.

His resignation was to take place formally from February 28th, 1931, but he left for a London nursing-home before then. Resignations, it seemed, were always to take place in the winter. 'He passed like a meteor of light and love,' said Lang sorrowfully. When the news was made public, seventeen-year-old Derek Ingram-Hill went to the Deanery with a desperate last-minute desire to see him before he went, but the man-servant answered the door and said, 'I'm sorry, Dr. Sheppard left an hour ago and he won't be back.' Before Dick went, he had emptied his study and said a prayer in it, 'that the fellow who has it next may make a better show of things than I have.'

Ramsay MacDonald wrote his condolences—'to make Church appointments I find more difficult than to rule Indian Conferences,' he said, 'perhaps you will be dropping in at No. 10: I wish I saw you oftener'—and Campbell Crum wrote in the poetic way which Dick loved.

> How can anyone say anything? [he asked]. Do you know the stones in a ring at Stonehenge? And do you know the angels in the Botticelli Nativity at the National Gallery? Well, you were just beginning to fiddle to us Stonehenge stones and make us feel in our stony toes that presently we might join hands and dance like Botticelli's angels.
>
> We shan't forget the air you were playing—I think it was caught from the music you hear when you look at the picture. And that music will go on long after we are done with the sort of gloom it puts me in to sit and write this letter.
>
> The wind is howling. The idiot it is: it has no self-control.

It ought to think of that dance which is going to make all
Stonehenge dance some day.

Toppie said Dick was a rebellious man, broken-hearted because
he had failed, and some time later, Dick wrote to him: 'How I'd
love to come and smash Canterbury and then rebuild it,' he said.
'It should be the power house for universal Christianity,' he told
friends sadly, 'but what is it? Just a beautiful monument.

'I ache for Canterbury,' he said. Later, he left instructions
asking to be buried there, as if he felt that failure and resignation
yet again meant the end of his useful life in the Church.

14

A Real and Lovable Problem

AFTER DICK HAD gone, Lang talked of 'poor Canterbury . . .' and at the end of the Second World War, windows were blessed in the cloisters showing Dick with St. Martin and Thomas Becket.

'It is pure pleasure to think of our Lord and his Lord saying as he said in Martin's dream, "See what a beautiful coat my servant Richard has given me," ' said Canon Crum. 'But St. Thomas and the sword. That asks for more difficult believing. Love and cruel violence. Love and war. It cost St. Thomas his life to prove that the world's swords will ever break.'

When Dick left Canterbury, he planned to write his autobiography: inevitably it was never finished. He had neither the time nor the inclination to do more than the first few chapters, on which he heaped an accumulation of frustration and failure which only obliquely belonged there: 'Nothing would induce me to go over my childhood days again . . .'

Bismark's quotation was on his mind: he had used it in recent sermons, and he was to use it again. 'When you want to take any fence in life, throw your heart over it first, and then you and your horse will follow.'

Oxford House, St. Martin's, Canterbury, each one ending in ill health and resignation; a marriage with so much love in it, degenerating into an awkward, bitter charade, polite but relent-

less. There were times when the successes—warmth in the East
End, excitement at St. Martin's, the moments of intense, perceptive joy which he and Alison could still create—were all
non-existent.

Outside Dick's window, the Surrey countryside stretched
through orchards to open hills. Above his desk there was the
little sham splinter from the Cross. There had to be a fence in
life: he needed to give everything to someone or to something.

Since the 1930 Lambeth Conference, his enthusiasm had
turned from Church Reform, and he was reading Huxley, thriv-
ing on it, but bewildered: 'I don't know what I *do* believe.'
Housman was fidgeting about immortality, reassured by hearing
the call of the cuckoo. 'I hope you are going to be well enough
to speak for Disarmament in the Christ and Peace Movement,'
he wrote. 'It is touch and go: now or never.'

Dick's militarist brother, Edgar, heard with a certain resignation
that Dick had decided to join 'these damned pacifists'.

'He did not reach his final convictions as a pacifist without
struggle and difficulty,' said Housman later. 'But before he saw
his way clear, he had already said to me, speaking of his work
as an Army chaplain, "My position was indefensible, for I was
urging men to do what I would not do myself . . ." '

The house, Shoelands, was at Seale near Guildford, and Alison
decorated it with flair, surprising Dick anew with imaginative
touches which made a room vivacious and welcoming. The
move absorbed her attention, but when she had finished, the
old tensions returned, and the childlike inability to hide her
feelings which had once attracted Dick challenged him instead.

Dick tormented himself in his room, trying to fathom the
future while the famous and the infamous came knocking at the
door. Alison, headstrong, loving and resentful, craving attention—
if not Dick's, then anyone's—drove off to spend money, glancing in
her driving mirror to see if men turned their heads as she passed.

Peggie was fifteen, emotional, dramatic and intense, falling
in love and weeping extravagantly at the cinema. 'Won't it be
lovely for you when you can leave home and live on your own,'
Dick said, to her astonishment.

Rose was ten, lonely and imaginative, listening in astonished

admiration as Peggie declaimed her diary aloud in the bath:
'Oh the hell of another morning! Why doesn't he ring! Where
is he! I wept through English, history, maths and latin!'

'It was worse for Peggie than for me,' says Rose, who climbed
through holes in the hedges and went bird-watching, listening
for the liquid call of curlews. 'I retreated into a world of imagination, and I was blissfully happy roaming round the countryside
with invisible friends of my own.

'I did everything the wrong way, buying hopelessly difficult
books on nature study just because they looked big and impressive,
and deciding to collect bird's feathers, which was disheartening,
because they never dropped them.

'Peggie read Rupert Brooke and Yeats, sobbing quietly under
the trees while I was busy climbing them.'

Peggie went with Dick to Lords and to the Canterbury Cricket
Week, and when Alison was too tired to go with him to supper
with the Shaws, Peggie went instead, thrilled because Shaw
showed off by addressing all his conversation to her. Rose cleaned
out the fish tank and dropped the biggest, fattest goldfish behind
the radiator. When Dick came in she was sitting sobbing on a
chair listening to the fish sizzling.

Dick hooked the fish out, put on his robes, and led a solemn
procession round the house to the lavatory, chanting and dropping
the fish into the lavatory bowl, pulling the chain three times
and saying with great reverence: 'Flesh to water! Flesh to water!
Flesh to water!'

Throughout the summer, he was ill again and unable to walk
more than a hundred yards. 'I do wonder what our Lord would
have us do now,' he wrote to Harold Anson. 'It seems to me
that the alternatives are simply going on as we are, trying to
make life a little less ugly and cruel, or else really trying to be
Christian, which would seem to mean pacifism, poverty, and a
hundred other things that I funk.'

The phrase *diabolo non obstante* was an increasingly frequent
proviso, with the unspoken parenthesis, 'but if he does . . .' Church
meetings were chaired by bishops who congratulated the Government and applauded caution.

'What I hate is just sitting still and watching this civilisation

of ours going bust for want of—what? I don't know. For myself,
I should like either to get very well and do ten years' hard work
inside the Church but outside high office, or else just to die. And
what a lot there is to be said for that.'

Gandhi was in England, collecting curious, devoted crowds
and angry onlookers, preaching voluntary poverty and non-
resistance to police who had come to keep order. Baldwin resigned,
in spite of the bishops' enthusiasm, and there was an autumn
General Election.

Dick was taking broadcast services again from St. Martin's,
using prayers for peace composed by Housman: 'I suppose it
might shock those to whom "The blood of the Lamb"—a phrase
that makes me almost sick—is highly significant and sacred,' he
said, 'but I fear they must be shocked, poor dears.' Preaching
just before the election, he was accused of broadcasting a seditious
sermon.

'Almost at the outset the preacher spoke of the political antics
which would be prominent during the next few weeks,' complained *Daily Telegraph* readers. 'Surely at such a critical period
as the present, our true politicians are not interested in antics.'
Others talked of 'music hall discourse'. 'I fear many B.B.C.
listeners were shocked by the use of slang words which amounted
to blasphemy in the St. Martin-in-the-Fields sermon last night,'
wrote one. 'The offending expressions were "Getting it in the
neck" and "guts".'

'People who object to your saying "guts" are quite willing
to chant, in sweet Anglicans or Gregorians, David's descriptions
of physical symptoms which are not usually referred to in polite
conversation,' said Housman. 'It's queer what tradition and
custom will do for us, making quite diabolical things like war,
slavery, and torture, almost sacred institutions.'

Taking part in his first big peace meeting, Dick was advertised
as principal speaker on a platform with George Lansbury, Maude
Royden and Laurence Housman, who called the event his 'Albert
haul'. Before he could finish his speech, Dick collapsed and
cornered the headlines. Alison was abroad, she and Dick pursuing
their own paths with reckless tenacity, longing to be necessary
to one another, Dick forgiving when he should have been furious,

Alison bored to tears with her own restlessness. Seale was snow-bound, the moors looking bleak and beautiful. Ramsay Mac-Donald was at the head of a compromise National Government, and Japan and China were at war. Sir Gerald Kelly was painting Dick's portrait for St. Martin's. Later, Lang was to comment: 'That portrait is looking down at me and saying "You hypocrite!" '

Maude Royden was as impatient as Dick, small and fiery, with an intense determination strengthened by her lameness. In February, she took over a fourteenth-century cottage two miles outside Sevenoaks and invited Dick and Herbert Gray to join her in retreat. They made a strange threesome, fiery, infirm and idealistic, convinced that Dick was right when he dismissed the creed of Collective Security as meaning that if war came, every-one would be in it. A small raised garden overlooked thirty miles of Weald, and from it, the wide horizons of a new Peace Army were born.

As a result of the meeting, the three of them signed a letter to the Press inviting volunteers to form an army to stand between enemy firing lines, and calling on the League of Nations to make use of such an army.

'Most of those who read it will laugh at it and us,' Dick wrote to Housman, 'but the urgency of the times compelled us to go right ahead.'

I don't laugh when people are sincere in protest against anything shameful and scandalous [replied Housman]. As a symbol it is all right, and will I hope attract sympathy; as a practical proposal I think it is addressed to the wrong organisation, and under circumstances when it could not be made to work.

Even if the League of Nations accepted the offer, what at best would happen? You and your fellow volunteers would be sent out and set down somewhere between the opposing forces. And just where you were set down, or wherever you moved, they would carefully fire over your heads to avoid hitting you, until you were tired of nothing happening and of being of no use except to provide the papers with picturesque headlines which would cut no ice and put out no fire.

The only practical way that I can see for actively intervening pacifists is for them to come up out of the ranks and trenches of the opposing armies (with arms out for a sign) and probably get shot as deserters by their own side, till the thing sickened those who shot them; or to be numerous and powerful enough to dump themselves willy nilly between the lines at a moment of impending assault. And that has great practical difficulties.

With the dazzling illogicality of idealism, Dick set out for Tilbury docks accompanied by Maude Royden, Herbert Gray, Brigadier-General Frank Crozier, who had resigned his commission rather than take part in the Irish Black and Tan atrocities, and Donald Soper, who was then a prominent young Islington Methodist minister still in his twenties.

Heading for a place called Chopei, where the fighting was fiercest, they were never allowed out of the country.

Soper calls Dick debonair in the best sense of the word, in spite of his shameless air of aristocracy: 'It is one thing to find someone engaging at a cocktail party; another to find someone engaging in a vestry.' Proud to have been among the first recruits to the Peace Army, he calls himself an office boy: a naive junior partner.

It could have been a revolution [he says now]. It could have been a situation in which radical changes were demanded instead of more moderate ones. Dick was always saying 'Give me a million: what we need are numbers'.

He bubbled with infectious enthusiasm, but he never looked ahead, and the practical difficulties were colossal. It was like little boats today, going out into the South Pacific to protest against nuclear tests.

French, German and Swiss soldiers called it *une idée sublime* but quite impractical, and a French First World War captain who had ordered his troops to lay down their arms instead of firing on fifteen thousand rioting Germans, suggested forming a shock force from within the International Red Cross.

> We think of holding a meeting some time down at the docks, here in London, to protest against the sending of munitions of war to the Far East [wrote Maude Royden]. It isn't easy to know just when ships are starting for Japan with guns, and the difficulty of finding out suggests that those concerned are aware of some public criticism.
>
> It is just possible that some of us might get arrested, and we want to be sure you wouldn't object . . .

Against a background of military tattoos and air-displays, Ellen Wilkinson led the Jarrow marchers to London, and Trafalgar Square again housed the homeless and the unemployed. Naval recruiting films sent to schools were captioned 'Arm! Arm! Arm!'

The great Einstein, soon to flee from Berlin where he was Director of the Kaiser Wilhelm Physical Institute, collaborated with Freud on a book called *Why War?*, and held a peace demonstration at The Hague. On his way to attend it, ambivalent as ever, Dick questioned within himself, bound hand and foot to the instinctive certainty that Christ could not have killed, and yet despising some of the cowards collecting around him.

He came back with Einstein's words hammering in his head: 'I appeal to all men and women to declare that they will refuse to give any further assistance to war or the preparations for war. I ask them to tell their Governments this in writing . . .'

'I want to smash the churches and reform them,' he said savagely, preaching in Canterbury and putting down his ill-temper to reading Conrad's letters and a bad attack of asthma. 'I am in despair, utter despair, at the world.'

'If you really despaired, would you ever trouble to broadcast from St. Martin's again?' asked Housman, setting off on a circuit of peace meetings. 'If I despaired, I shouldn't bother to give one address. Being of a religious temperament, you focus on a personal love of Christ, and on the elements or instances of evil in the world which are opposed to him, and big mountains as they are, you make bigger mountains still.'

Dick tried unsuccessfully to enlist Lloyd George at the head of the pacifists. All through the summer and autumn he was frustrated and incapacitated by asthma, heart attacks and pleurisy, and in desperation he booked a villa at St. Raphael in the South of France, where he and Alison, Nancy and the children, could spend the winter. He was reading, but not enjoying, Lilley's *Religion and Revelation*, and determined to call at Venice to try and think charitable thoughts over D. H. Lawrence's grave.

'I feel terribly lonely in the Church of England,' he said.

While they were in France, visiting the little casino and sitting up early, watching the sea, he listened to the Albert Hall Armistice celebrations, and was disturbed to hear the shrieks and whistles of revellers, which he called ugly and inane. 'The walls of Jericho look like standing for many a long day,' he wrote in a New Year article. 'We must compel goodness and decency, laughter and hope, to come in and live with us.'

Sir John Simon, middle-of-the-road Foreign Secretary, was doing well on the fence against an ominous background. 'What we want is not Sir John Simon, but Saint John Baptist, with the passion of a million hearts behind him.'

'Simon, Simon,' wrote Housman blasphemously, 'behold Satan hath desired to have you that he may sift you like wheat . . .' He and Dick were saying 'Lead Kindly Light' once a week as a bond of the spirit with Gandhi and his followers.

'There may be something in your sub-conscious mind, against which, unbeknown to yourself, you are fighting,' Housman added, more seriously. 'You may be trying to shut yourself off from some growing conviction which, if you declared it, would give great pain to your friends and admirers . . .'

On the way home, Dick read the agenda for the summer meeting of the Church Assembly, a body which he called bereft of imagination, proportion and humour. At the head was a wordy summary of the Banns of Matrimony Measure, and the *Church Times* printed a report under the title SUMMER TASK OF THE CHURCH ASSEMBLY.

'Isn't impatience justified?' asked Dick bitterly, recalling the first fiery days of Life and Liberty and likening the whole affair to peddlars in Baghdad crying 'In the name of Allah! Figs!'

'He was certainly not happy about the Assembly,' said Temple mildly.

13

Lord Ponsonby was preaching the futility of war and Baldwin was talking of its horrors. Ramsay MacDonald was begging the churches to prod the Government into pacifism. Vera Brittain published an idealistically outspoken autobiography called *Testament of Youth*, and Storm Jameson was called a hysterical woman novelist for supporting it. Housman talked grandiloquently of dying on the pacifist barricades, while Crozier announced dryly that if war broke out, he wanted merely to die without discussing the matter in the interval.

'The Church is a frightened Church,' said Dick, writing to ask Housman for good arguments to use at the Oxford Peace Congress: 'You give me the intelligent rounding off my simplicity requires.'

At Shoelands, Alison contrived to pass the time. She spent extravagantly and rested in the afternoon. Cocktail hour was the high-spot of the day. She did a little gardening, and had probably never made a cup of tea in her life. Dick smoked fifty or sixty cigarettes a day and shrugged his shoulders when friends said it was bad for him. It was irritating enough to feel like an invalid: he refused to behave like one.

They never quarrelled, but 'relationships seep into you', says Peggie, who was beginning to realise why Dick was encouraging her to leave home. 'I had always imagined they were happy, but then there was the gradual dawning that there was something wrong: something menacing.'

'I saw how miserable they made each other, and it became my preoccupation. Dick wasn't the gay extrovert he seemed to be. He was sadder, more ill and tortured and uncertain. He was only really happy when Alison was happy. They never had rows: they were just unhappy in their separate rooms.'

Shoelands was half-way between the villages of Seale and Puttenham, off the Hog's Back, but callers still found their way there, many of them scroungers, to whom Dick was polite but shrewd. Basil Jellicoe came asking for a post at St. Martin's. Harold Davidson, notorious Rector of Stiffkey, begged Dick's support. Many, like a young artist called Arthur Wragg who had 'found out that starving is not so bad as it sounds,' came despairing of 'finding the essence of sincerity in anyone'. Dick came in from the garden apologising for looking like a third-rate gigolo, and proceded to change Wragg's life for him by fixing him up with an agent, promoting his bitter black and white illustrations which the timid called blasphemous, and preaching sermons which Wragg said made him feel as if he could draw the whole world and everyone in it.

By the summer, the Peace Army was several thousand strong, with nothing much to do. 'It was amusing,' Dick wrote wickedly to Kingsley Martin, 'to see Osbert Sitwell and Beverley Nichols walking away wearing our new Peace badges.'

Young, cynical and brilliant, Kingsley Martin called Dick 'an unusual parson whose reputation did not at first recommend him to me'. Editor of the *Statesman*, he thought Dick's *Sunday Express* journalism indifferent, and he had heard him referred to as an aristocrat, a popular preacher and a practical joker.

When I met him [he said later], I found all the things I had heard against him were trivial. He seemed totally uninterested in himself. Shaw spoke of him as a superb actor, and no doubt he could have been successful as a comedian in the West End, but he endeared himself to me by his honesty and his desire to get at the truth. I think it really was a fact that he felt love for almost every human being he met, but this selfless and affectionate quality did not make him a wise politician.

It was enough for him that an increasing number of people joined his Peace Army. Perhaps it might become so big that it could prevent the next war? He would write little postcards to me recording its growth.

As Mussolini began preparing for war with Abyssinia, Dick rang Kingsley to ask whether to send his Peace Army to Geneva.

I explained that in Geneva the League would be discussing sanctions against Mussolini as a way of stopping him from attacking Abyssinia [said the younger man patiently]. There was, of course, some risk that war would result from sanctions, but if the pacifists protested at Geneva, they would be lining up against the one policy that might prevent war.

If they wanted to make a relevant protest, they had better

go to Rome as tourists and demonstrate there. Some of them
would no doubt be arrested, but they would really be opposing
the war, not impeding those who were already trying to stop it.

Dick had never thought of it like that. But 'the Peace Army
did not go to Rome,' said Kingsley Martin later. 'I never heard of
it doing anything.'

'Dear Lord, what *can* be done?' asked Dick, in France again
for the winter, writing prosaically about brown boats in the
harbour, and spending three hours early every morning, from
four o'clock until seven o'clock, sitting at his bedroom window.
'Must you raise up another civilisation to do your will? If we can
help, may I? And what do you want done?'

He was feeling much better, playing golf every day and taking
fewer drugs because of a new German inhaling machine which
he took with him everywhere. 'I cannot spend another hour
trying to reform the Church of England,' he decided arrogantly,
embarking on a six-month stint as proxy Vicar at St. Martin's
while Pat McCormick took a break, and heralding his arrival by
writing a provocatively subjective piece in the *Sunday Express*
on what London would do to Christ.

I think we should soon be saying that our Lord is disappointing and curiously ineffective [he wrote]. As a social
reformer, he lacks a programme. As an orator, he is uncon-
vincing. A good man, no doubt, but unpractical and unwise.

Obviously he loves deeply, almost desperately, but his
speech is careless and too spontaneous, and lends itself to
misunderstanding. He talks nothing but the dialect of the
human heart, very persuasively, but it is rather embarrassing
and too painfully direct. Altogether an interesting and considerable personage, but—forgive us hazarding the suggestion
—is he not a little extravagant and emotional? And one cannot
run this modern world on extravagance and emotion.

'Why, once he blazed out at a number of quite excellent
people who were merely tightening up their creed in the interest
of religion itself, and twice he was seen to cry in public, once in
Park Lane, and again in Poplar.

Clearly, too, he is no match for the learned. He will not
counter their arguments with arguments of his own. He says
that it is useless to argue with those who will not unlearn,
and he merely tells them to forget their dull theories and to
think instead of men, women and children.

And he makes the mistake of allowing passion to creep into
his message. He says that only through passion can man
attain to wisdom and that God is as passionate as the Father
in the story of the Prodigal Son. He says that the cold wisdom
of this world is lunacy, and that sanity comes as surely from
warmth as insanity from coldness. He bids men be passionate,
and, of course, that is a great mistake and a little dangerous.

A man whose message is coloured by his emotions is not a
safe guide. Anyhow, with much courtesy we should ask our
Lord to leave our coasts, for a time at any rate. And meanwhile, to placate his strange followers, we might appoint a
committee of erudite ecclesiastics, with a Privy Councillor
or two, and, of course, one woman and one representative
of Labour to assist, to investigate with a view to obtaining
from his teaching some practical scheme which would be
generally acceptable for national improvement and international security.

'The vision of Christ that thou does see,' said Blake, 'has a
great hook nose like thine; mine has a snub nose like to mine . . .'
Dick was similarly subjective.

London, when Dick returned to it, was a 'damnable and gut-
rotting affair'. 'I am very unpopular with the higher ecclesiastics,
but they won't strike me, which they ought to do. They only
say "We love dear Dick, of course, only no one can take him
seriously—he's a dear funny, that's all." It's a good policy, but
annoying for the victim.'

He was up at five in the morning and working through until
seven at night, but without purpose: 'I am not anxious to do any
real work except lie around at home and try to do my terribly
indifferent journalism and a wild book or two.' St. Martin's
was a renewal: intense activity, enthusiasm, and no time to
think ahead, dressing up as W. G. Grace for cricket matches in

the courtyard, fretting about kissing lepers, and entertaining Temple who puffed up the stairs, bluff and broad, thankful not to be called upon to believe in the resurrection of the flesh.

He worked eighteen hours a day, looking in on clubs and meetings and writing notes of encouragement to the curates who ran them. 'A church without enthusiasm should have its roof ripped off', he said. 'It will never make an impact unless it is not only militant, but working flat out.' Unable to believe that not all church people would be prepared to work flat out, he paced up and down thumping one hand on the other. 'Why not, in God's name?' he asked. 'Why not? Time's too short for anything less.'

Setting a compulsive example, one Sunday's appointments overflowed his diary:

6.00 a.m.	Letter writing
7.30	Celebration Charing Cross Hospital
8.15	Assist at St. Martin's
9.00–10.00	Three ward services at the hospital
10.15	Assist at St. Martin's
11.30	Conduct service at St. Martin's
1.00–2.15 p.m.	Sandwich lunch with friend
2.30	Two personal interviews
3.30	Christening
4.00–6.00	Four ward services at the hospital
6.15	Preach at St. Martin's
7.30	Dinner at the Bath Club
9.00–10.00	Visiting the Crypt
10.15	B.B.C. Epilogue
11.00–4.00 a.m.	Letter writing.

One Sunday he preached about Ruskin, who suddenly saw on how many hills which he had thought desolate, the hosts of Heaven still moved in chariots of fire. He was also preaching, inevitably, and to many people's annoyance, on war and peace:

> We're still spending millions on arms and deplore
> That we're all just a little less safe than before . . .

He who says 'I believe in God' without going on to say, 'I believe in man', has a long way to go [he said].

I believe in man—sinful, struggling, failing, faltering man; but inherently, potentially noble—little lower than the angels and made in the likeness of God. Of course his failures are many. Of course they are disastrous, recurring, inexplicable. Of course he may be and often is a beast and a hero on one and the same day. But to Christ he is infinitely precious and there is always a place reserved for him and for no one else to occupy, not very far removed from the right hand of God.

I believe that one of the greatest gifts that Christianity can contribute today towards the healing of the nations lies in its belief in the inherent goodness of man. It was the way of Christ to make men better by finding so much that was already good within them. He loved them into the Kingdom. George Tyrrell used to say that he was sure God intended us to find him in our fellows or else he would have given us eyes with which to pierce Heaven.

'Would you mind telling me if Mr. Sheppard is preaching today?' asked an old lady who had clambered laboriously up the steps. When a clergyman told her he wasn't, she said, 'In that case would you help me down again, please.'

Dick was disconcerting, laughing one minute and in tears the next, sick and then well again, joking and serious, dropping with exhaustion and prepared to do anything but sit quietly drinking a cup of tea until he got his breath back, producing a snap of the children and asking anxiously, 'Do you think they have sex appeal? It matters a lot, you know.'

Sometimes, trying to sleep the night through, lying half-conscious watching for the dawn, he was persuaded that one day it would not come: '*Diabolo non obstante*—if he does, I may be dead in bed.' He manoeuvred his pillows so that he faced the crack in the curtains, purposely left two or three inches apart, and when the first light came he felt flooded with relief, saying, 'Thank you, Jesus. All's well.'

One day he bought up a job lot of iron lasts, thinking of the unemployed queuing in the crypt for food and accommodation, many without soles on their uppers. Charles Wardell was in his late teens, studying hard, hungry, cold and short of cash. Missing his train from Charing Cross one evening, he wandered up the steps of St. Martin's to wait in the warm.

'This funny little figure darted out of the shadows and across the portico,' he says. 'He'd never seen me before, but he seized my arm and said "D'you know anything about mending boots?" I didn't, except for what I'd seen my father do, but before I knew where I was, I was down in the crypt trying to help him.'

Later, shaking hands with Dick—'You will come again, won't you Charles?'—there was the inevitable reaction:

His eyes were tired, but smiling just the same, and I said 'Of course, Mr. Sheppard.' And the look in his eyes and the pleading in his voice kept coming back to me all the way home in the train. One half of me was saying 'You utter clot. With all you have on your plate at the moment, how can you?' and the other half was saying 'You can't let him down. You know you can't.'

There was a magnetism about him that you couldn't resist, and it drew you right into his world. I remember once thinking I would turn into St. Martin's during a lunch-time. I thought it would be quiet and I could think. Quiet? Was it heck! I had forgotten Dick's lunchtime services, and as I opened the door, gales of laughter swept around me. The place was packed and he was preaching.

I enjoyed the service, and hardly had he pronounced the last word of the Benediction than he was bounding down the steps, down the aisle like a whirlwind, with his draperies flying out behind him, his hand outstretched—to me, at the very back of the church. And, 'How are you Charles? How good to see you, how very good to see you!' Then a whole torrent of questions, 'Are you well? Can you spend long with us? Have you had any lunch? Will you have a cup of tea with us? Tell me all about what has been happening.'

He gave you his all without you having even a chance to ask for it, and I came away eventually feeling ten feet tall.

Charles was a Baptist from south-east London, where the Baptist minister stood on his church steps declaiming against Roman Catholics passing in their Corpus Christi procession. Once Dick said, 'What would you think if I refused you communion, Charles?'

'I would never enter your church again,' Charles replied, and Dick said, 'Yes, I know.'

When he came back, Pat McCormick astonished Dick by offering to resign as Vicar of St. Martin's and to work under Dick as his curate. Maude Royden offered him her Guild House — 'as a centre of Peace Work on definitely Christian lines, accepting the position that war is un-Christian' — and other pacifist friends tried to persuade him to travel full-time preaching peace.

In the autumn, the new Dean of St. Paul's, Walter Matthews, was the instigator in the royal offer of a canonry.

Dick's old friend Oliver Quick had left St. Paul's in despair. W. H. Elliott the broadcaster, who had been there before Oliver, called it one of the most miserable and wretched times of his life. Time and again he had watched old Dean Inge put up imaginative ideas which had floundered helplessly because he had been outvoted by his canons.

Lang said Dick was a real and lovable problem.

It is not easy to place you [he said]. But I am bound to say that a Canonry at St. Paul's would in my opinion give you a better opportunity of serving our Lord at this present time than any other, and I know that is what you would wish.

The main thing is that the pulpit and its message should be vitalised. You would do that, for it has been shown that you have things to say which people are eager to hear and which help their lives.

It is a vital voice that St. Paul's needs.

Everyone else was against it. Alison already resented seeing the spark and fire which had attracted her to Dick expended unstintingly on others, when she wanted some of it for herself. Sometimes she longed for him to be angry with her instead of gently trying to justify her most provocative actions. As it was, he had lived at Brown's Hotel most of the time he was at St. Martin's, and when he came home, he was exhausted. St. Paul's would be more tiring still. Peggie and Nancy watched anxiously, and hoped he would turn the offer down.

Dick himself was worrying about what he called the lunacy of the manner in which the nations were pursuing peace. 'It seems essential to discover whether or not it be true, as we are told, that the majority of thoughtful men in this country are now convinced that war of every kind or for any cause, is not only a denial of Christianity, but a crime against humanity which is no longer to be permitted by civilised people,' he said, in a letter which was printed not very prominently by the national and provincial Press.

'The idea behind this letter is not to form any fresh organisation, nor to call pacifists together to abuse those who conscientiously are not able to agree with them. It is an attempt to discover how strong the will to peace has grown.'

In order to do so, he asked for postcards from all those willing to sign a peace pledge which could one day land them in gaol:

'We renounce war and never again, directly or indirectly, will we support or sanction another.'

Replies were to be sent to Brigadier Crozier's home at Walton-on-Thames. For the first few days, there was nothing. Then the village postmaster rang to inquire where he should take several sacks full of postcards. In a few weeks Dick had received thirty thousand replies: an unexpected windfall which Soper calls a natural reaction against the euphoria that followed the First War. 'People thought that was the war to end all wars,' he says. 'Then we began to see that we were moving towards another war, and not the Kingdom of Heaven or even an earthly paradise. Dick's voice was raised at the critical psychological moment.'

Soon over one hundred thousand postcards had arrived. 'I have gone too far,' Dick wrote in the *Sunday Express*. 'I am in hot water and not enjoying it a bit, for I seem to be up against so many of the people I like best and whose opinions, as a rule, I share and respect. The trouble is, I am now what is called a peace crank.'

At St. Paul's, Matthews was regarded with suspicion as an innovator. The news that Dick had accepted the vacant canonry removed all doubt. A letter from William Temple to Dick would have done nothing to quieten the fears ricochetting around the red-brick courtyard.

'The possibilities are vast,' he wrote, 'though most of the ground has to be conquered afresh. Do go, and bring a heart of humanity into that gorgeous place, and make St. Paul's the parish church of the City.'

15

God's Railway Station

'RATS? NOT SINCE we extinguished them. Darkness? Yes. Impossibilities? A matter of opinion.

'I think it very good of you to go to St. Paul's. Few people will know what the cost to you must be.'

In this way, Oliver Quick handed over No. 1, Amen Court.

The house, as he said, was dark. The kitchen in the basement was lighter than the study, which looked out on to a brick wall. Dark books and panelled bookcases made the whole room look brown, except for the gleam of silver decanters on a side table and a silver cigarette box open on the desk full of Craven 'A'. Dick had his blue notepaper out on the desk—he had noticed a long time ago that blue envelopes looked more interesting than white ones—ashtrays everywhere, and an outsize waste-paper basket on the floor.

Elliott and Oliver Quick had found the room too small to use as a study, but Henry Scott Holland had worked there day by day, and there were those who said Dick was like him. Elliott swore that Scott Holland's secret prayers were in the walls of the little three-windowed room.

Except for cats howling, Amen Court was silent day and night, and Dick enjoyed pushing up the window and disturbing the gravity of his fellow canons by calling down to them. When the telephone rang, he mimicked the butler until he knew who was on the other end.

A week before his installation, he wrote an article which the

Daily Mail refused to print. In it, he challenged the two Archbishops to come out unequivocally on the side of peace.

'Retired colonels will write to the papers demanding that they
be unfrocked,' he said, equating worldly failure with Calvary.
'Bellicose Primrose Leaguers might storm the gates of Lambeth
Palace. But they will save the soul of the Church.' Arthur Wragg
drew a bitter cartoon for the *Sunday Express*, who rejected it as
too depressing for Sunday breakfast reading.

In the middle of November, Dick was installed at St. Paul's
in a ceremony which was 'grim and in a fog inside me and everywhere else'. Before the end of the month, he was complaining
that the only instruction he had received was never to allow any
outside ecclesiastic, however exalted, to give the blessing in the
cathedral, but to do it himself to preserve the dignity of the
Dean and Chapter. Before Christmas, he had been appointed
'an entirely incompetent Precentor', and had meekly performed
hack tasks like writing up Chapter Minutes in his distinctive and
undecipherable hand-writing.

On Christmas Day, he fulfilled the worst fears of his fellow
canons by kneeling down while everyone else stood to sing the
complex Athanasian Creed, as a protest against its use at a
popular service. 'To open with a highly technical and intellectual
statement that makes no reference to the Kingdom of God—
our Lord's main preoccupation and passion—and no mention
of ethics, is bad Christianity and bad propaganda,' he said.

He was taking the Minutes himself during the row that followed
in Chapter. 'The Precentor was censored for his attitude to the
Athanasian Creed on Christmas Day in the cathedral,' he wrote
carefully and more clearly than usual. But the reaction was the
same as usual: 'Don't be silly, Dick! Just don't do it again,' and
the words are scored through.

Later he was disconcertingly asking for the recital of the
whole of the Ten Commandments: 'There is a travesty of religion
very common today, which suggests that provided we are all
very jolly together and very kind to granny and the cat, it doesn't
much matter what we do besides . . .'

Taking the words of St. John of the Cross as his New Year
motto—'When the evening of your life comes, you will be judged

on love' — he wandered round the City, talking to those who lived and worked in the area. 'It has been pointed out to me until I am weary of hearing it, that at the one time when passers-by and those who work in the neighbourhood might enter St. Paul's to rest or to make their souls, the cathedral is shut,' he reported, presenting the Chapter with the unwelcome views of a young man who worked within a hundred yards of the cathedral but never worshipped inside it.

'We feel we are quite outside the work and interest of St. Paul's,' he had written out for Dick. 'We do not care for your services. We don't want to be preached at or exhorted any more. What we want is to feel an atmosphere of welcome when we come into the cathedral, and we don't feel that now. We don't believe you care about us a bit.'

Not surprisingly, fellow canons felt he and Matthews were conspiring to turn St. Paul's into St. Martin-in-the-Fields, a view which was strengthened alarmingly when Dick put forward tentative proposals: to illuminate the cross on the dome, to put a lamp by the doors and keep them open until seven o'clock in the evening, to provide clergy for counselling and hearing confessions, and to introduce a series of midday addresses.

'I wonder how we must appear to those who hear us making brave assertions about the fatherhood of God and the brotherhood of man,' Dick said. 'I wonder if we do not seem to them like Alpine climbers, who, having greased their faces and covered them with masks, and having put on their nailed boots and taken ice-axes in their hands, then proceed to walk gravely up the mild heights of Ludgate Hill?'

William Morris had picturesquely called St. Paul's God's railway station, but so far as Dick was concerned, Housman was nearer the mark when he talked of a great marble hall. Dick called his first months there abysmal days of disillusion. Elliott, with hindsight, referred to them as a Gethsemane.

'I shall either be hopeful at St. Paul's in six months, or have left in disgust,' Dick wrote to Housman.

Canon Alexander lived next door, embittered and disappointed. In the past he had deputised for deaf old Dean Inge who had treated him with consistent sarcasm and contempt. When Inge retired, Alexander, dignified and statuesque, steeped in cathedral tradition, had expected to become Dean. 'In these drawers are all my plans for St. Paul's,' he had said, tapping his desk, when Matthews was appointed. 'Now nobody will ever see them.'

Dean Matthews expected hostility, and therefore received it, treating Alexander with suspicion instead of charity. In Alexander's eyes, Dick was a Matthews man, and although he was forced into fondness for Dick, when Dick blew his head off at meetings and made a grand exit tripping over the carpet and laughing at himself, he nevertheless retained complete antipathy for everything that Dick tried to do with the cathedral.

Kenneth Mozley, Dick's other neighbour, preached on the doctrine of the Atonement at a service for working men and was rewarded with blank incomprehension and disinterest. Matthews called him curiously liberal in theory and conservative in practice. Dick thought him a medieval man living six hundred years too late.

Dark and hawk-eyed, Mozley had read *The Impatience of a Parson*. 'I did not greet his appointment with enthusiasm,' he said flatly. 'I had the impression that he was a man whose belief in experiment meant a readiness to engage in stunts for their own sake.' Dick displayed an unexpected diffidence, entreating the other clergy not to listen to his sermons, and reacting with surprised pleasure when they did listen and congratulated him afterwards.

I discovered that the estimate of him as a sugary preacher who might reach the heart but not the head would not do at all [Mozley said]. The giving of his own friendship, and the desire he had for the same gift to come to himself, did away with the narrowness and the wrong assumptions from which I had suffered.

Only a lunatic could have thought Dick an exhibitionist after any length of time spent in his company.

In Germany, gipsies prophesied Hitler's death, and Goering advertised guns before butter. 'Guns,' he said, 'make history,' and Germans, waiting in butter queues talked of spreading history

on their bread. In England, rumours circulated of prominent
Nazis recanting and the impossibility of war. Dick called St.
Paul's a place without a soul, and used its pulpit to declaim
against the thirty-seventh Article of the Church of England
which states that 'It is lawful for Christian men, at the command
of the Magistrate, to wear weapons and serve in the wars.'

One day he came home mimicking the Bishop of London,
who had met him on Ludgate Hill and called out vacuously,
'Hallo, old chap! Still keen on peace?' Temple maintained that
the choice was between using force rightly or using it wrongly.

'The Church has not yet begun to take its Lord seriously,'
Dick said. 'And I shall continue to say that whenever I get the
opportunity. And I shall go on denying the right of either the
Archbishop of York or the Bishop of London to say that a
Christian may kill his brother.'

> I'm a bit puzzled [wrote Housman, reading of his appoint-
> ment as Chaplain to the King]. Here have you been rampaging
> unpatriotically against war and breaking most of the 39 articles
> of our modern social belief, and the King goes and makes you
> one of his Chaplains. Is he a stealthy pacifist, or is it only his
> Charlie Chaplain he intends you to be?
> I used to be inclined to think that people like you ought to
> come out of the Establishment,' he went on, 'but I'm more
> inclined to think now that they do better to stay explosively
> within it, and only come out if they are turned out. My vote
> is that you stay on at St. Paul's and try to blow off its dome
> of silence with doses of internal combustion, for anyway the
> dear Lord did not leave the world in disgust, but let it do its
> damnedest to down him, both then and since.

Dick took over the pastoral care of the cathedral workmen—
no one else knew their names—and pushed through improvements
and a new mess-room. Not surprisingly the choirboys loved
him, and they went for tea and buns after Evensong at the A.B.C.
on Ludgate Hill where Walter de la Mare had once talked poetry
with Edward Thomas. When the Dean wanted to get to know
the cathedral staff better and found his efforts hampered by

tradition, Dick suggested Matthews should pay the weekly wages himself.

When he was not in residence, he was travelling round the country speaking at peace meetings, writing notes and reading on railway trains, coming home late at night to avoid staying away. In Bristol for a meeting, he visited friends, buttoning up his jacket as soon as their twelve-year-old daughter came in from school and playing hide-and-seek with her, collecting cobwebs at the top of the house.

'I like that man,' she said when he had gone. 'He didn't ask me if I liked school. He just said "I want a game!"'

Dick and Alison moved from Shoelands to Amen Court, hanging pictures of Napoleon round the walls and Dick did everything he could to make Alison comfortable. When he was unhappy, he cut himself off, determined not to worry her. Alison over-spent, consulting spiritualists in the East End of London and leaving Rose waiting nervously in the car for hours on end with nothing to do, embarrassing Dick when newspapers reported her attendance at seances.

When she missed the country, complaining that she must have a life of her own, they bought a cottage in Surrey at Ewhurst, and then moved on to another at Rudgwick.

'I knew a man that had health and riches and several houses, all beautiful and ready furnished, and would often trouble himself and family to be removing from one house to another,' said Dick in a sermon, quoting Izaak Walton. 'And being asked by a friend: Why he removed so often from one house to another, replied: It was to find content in some one of them.'

Archie Macdonell and his wife Mona lived at Hascombe Place in the next village, and in the summer, Dick led a cricket team against Archie's eleven, wearing his I Zingari cap and sweater. The teams included Professor da Costa Andrade, Eric Gillett, Howard Marshall and Alec Waugh. Kingsley Martin was among the spectators, and Archie was good-looking, amusing, and easy to talk to.

It rained, but even so, it was reminiscent of the village-green atmosphere Archie had created in a light-weight spoof of Evelyn Waugh called *England Their England*. Alec Waugh was caught off a long hop, and Dick provoked so much laughter that someone quoted Dr. Johnson on the unseemly merry-making of parsons.

Peggie was down from Cambridge, where she was preoccupied with the problems of poverty and of falling in and out of love. She had, as Dick wanted, made her own life, considering belief in God naive, while enjoying the emotive, sensual side of religion. Illogically she never considered Dick to be naive, omitting to tell him of her loss of faith, because she knew it would hurt him.

In the evening, they went to the Macdonells' for dinner, and Peggie noticed a politeness between Dick and Alison, as if they were avoiding each other and yet trying to be natural.

Rose was developing an intense, primitive, childlike faith much like Alison's; a kind of intuitive certainty. She was shrewd at chess, beating her aunts and uncles easily. At home, she was less shrewd, going for long happy walks with Archie and Alison and watching them talking under the trees.

Peggie found Archie charming, but commented tersely that she disliked his behaviour.

When Max Beerbohm and his wife went to Rapallo for the summer, Dick went out to join them. 'I read *The Times* eagerly each morning,' Max said sadly, 'and then I try to shut Europe out of my mind. What can you hope for when even the people of Rapallo think the people of Santa Margherita all devils?'

Max's wife was a Jewess, and he displayed a ferocious and uncharacteristic hatred of Fascism. 'Will you join my Kickshaw Club?' he asked Dick facetiously, professing not to know whether he loved or hated Shaw. Underneath the brittle wit there lurked a new dis-ease and disillusion.

Dick noted down his impressions: 'Max met me,' he said, 'a little older—cheeks redder but same blue eyes that gaze into vacancy and see everything—same inside chuckling that comes out suddenly . . .'

In the evening, Max burlesqued the Kaiser's visit to the Castello, and imitated a cleric giving a banal public statement. Afterwards he laughed for a long time at his own humour, tears coming into his eyes. 'He obviously enjoys his lazy, quiet, undisturbed life,' Dick noted with envious incomprehension.

In a few months, Mussolini had invaded Abyssinia. 'It simply beats me,' Dick said to Housman. 'I don't know what we pacifists ought to be at.'

Following in the footsteps of A. A. Milne, Bertrand Russell and Beverley Nichols, he published a book called *We Say 'No'*.

In September 1914, I knelt by a dying soldier [it began]. I had just arrived in France. He was the first soldier I saw die, and he died thanking God that if his child was a boy, he would never have to go through the hell of war.

That man believed what he had been told—that he was fighting in the war to end war. Innumerable others also believed it and died, as he did, at least happy in the thought that their sons would be spared their Calvary.

These sons are of military age today.

Then he sent out invitations to every one of the thousands who had pledged themselves against war, calling them to a mass meeting at the Albert Hall. When the day came, a hot Sunday evening in July, he waited anxiously in a room behind the platform. 'We didn't know what the dickens would happen,' he confessed later. 'We didn't know whether anybody would turn up or not. And then to our amazement and astonishment, young and old men, mostly young, some of them ex-service people, packed into the Hall.'

Arthur Wragg had drawn the picture for the cover of the programme—a sponge of vinegar on the end of a spear offered to a First World War soldier, with the caption 'Weep not for me but for yourselves'—and Sassoon read war poems.

'It was the finest pacifist meeting I was ever at,' Dick said.

Later he went to the Devil's Dyke up on the South Downs outside Brighton to talk to an open-air meeting of young people. It was a beautiful summer evening, and members of the Brighton branch of the International Friendship League came up on the old Dyke Railway with a party of Germans among their friends from abroad. The green slopes of the Dyke were gay with colourful clothes, and Dick talked of love and peace in words that are still remembered forty years later.

At the end, they all said the Lord's Prayer together in different languages, and there was a sense of emotion and elation and a certainty of the unconquerable power of good.

New members of Dick's Peace Movement were averaging four hundred a day: the gale of God blowing too strong to last. Alison was spending more and more time in the country, and he went back alone at night to the eerie stillness of Amen Court, where rats still skirmished with cats in the corners, sniffing the rubbish bins. He had been elected President of the undenominational Brotherhood Movement, and the honour thrilled him. Presiding over their annual summer meeting, he celebrated communion and was promptly accused of sacrilege and cold-shouldered by Anglo-Catholics, who cancelled an invitation to speak at their Congress.

'I am tired and dispirited,' he said. 'I feel I am swimming against the tide all the time.'

In Chapter, he was learning to get his own way by guile rather than pungent sarcasm or obstinacy, persuading the King to offer Christmas trees for the cathedral steps before asking the canons if they would be willing to put them there. Many of his suggested reforms had been carried out: there were clergy available for counselling, shortened services, no Athanasian Creed scheduled for the Christmas Day service, and the cathedral doors were open until seven.

On New Year's Eve, in spite of tough opposition, he insisted on holding an open-air service with the Salvation Army, while the Dean conducted a Watchnight service inside. Both were innovations. Standing up on a small prefabricated wooden platform supported by scaffolding, unable to make himself heard above the din, Dick was greeted with howls of derision and pelted with empty whisky bottles. The next morning there was debris and filth inside and outside the cathedral and Dick was utterly and magnificently apologetic, sending Alexander a barrel of oysters. Alexander loved oysters but he did not propose to withdraw his opposition to Dick's attempts to destroy the dignity of the cathedral.

Dick talked despairingly of the cold, cold stones of St. Paul's. 'They crush all that is human in the place,' he said. 'How can I bear to stay here any longer? Wren did a wonderful job, but he left one thing out. He didn't give it a soul, and nobody knows how to remedy the omission.'

When Housman's brother died, waspish and independent, Lawrence sent Dick a page of A. E.'s beloved *Propertius* in his own flawless handwriting, and Dick framed it and hung it in his study. 'I suppose we all covet gifts we don't possess,' he said. 'The thing I covet most is the kind of power your brother had, and even the strange and interesting attitudes to life that he adopted.

'My Peggie tells me she would love to possess your present when I am gone. She is strangely like me in some ways, poor kid.'

16

'These Damned Pacifists'

AS MUSSOLINI'S TANKS rumbled through the mountains and into the city fort of Addis Ababa, the Dean and Chapter of St. Paul's were considering the breeding of ravens in order that they might destroy the cathedral pigeons. So much importance was attached to the issue that Professor Julian Huxley was invited to address the Chapter on the habits of ravens, and to give an assurance 'that they would not prey on the pigeons in public'.

'It is the decisive hour for Christianity,' Dick exploded, appealing on the radio for money to help Ethiopian evacuees. 'All other solutions are bankrupt; all other prescriptions discredited. I cannot understand why professing Christians lack an overwhelming sense of mission—unless they do not really believe in their religion.'

He had scandalised the canons—and Alison—by walking up and down in sandwich boards advertising an open-air peace meeting in Hyde Park, and said he had never felt so conspicuous in his life as he had done outside the Cavendish Club. At the meeting he had stood for a long time in sleet and snow, addressing the crowds through a megaphone.

'The churches have lost the accents of the Holy Ghost,' he wrote to Housman. 'I am continually wondering if one oughtn't

to leave the Anglican communion and butt at it from the outside . . .'

Disenchanted with himself, overcome with a sense of his own
futility, he changed the name of his Movement from the Dick
Sheppard Peace Pledge to the Peace Pledge Union, saying his
own name stank in his nostrils. Writing to the papers, he called
for a million members and a vigorous and constructive peace
organisation. Headquarters were opened in London, and famous
men and women were announced as sponsors: Aldous Huxley,
Gerald Heard, Siegfried Sassoon, Bertrand Russell, Arthur
Ponsonby, Donald Soper, Charles Raven, Rose Macaulay and
Storm Jameson.

Huxley wrote to Dick from his goldfish bowl study in Albany,
where he sat and typed, to the discomfort of the other inhabitants.
Called the man who hates God by the newspapers, he believed
the only hope for the future lay in pacifists being better dis-
ciplined than militarists, and prepared to put up with as much
danger. Meeting Dick with suspicion, as all intellectuals did, he
found himself blinded by 'absolutes so simple that only an angel
could follow them', and wrote to ask if he had left his eyeglass
behind.

Ever since lunching with you the other day, I have been
feeling very much ashamed of the glibness with which I
talked of the project of organising the Peace Movement [he
wrote]. When one has been endowed with that curious thing,
the gift of the gab, one is sadly tempted to make use of it for
elegantly expressing ideas which one knows as ideas and not by
experience.

That *I* should have talked so much to *you*—the theoretician
to the man who knows the business of dealing with people
by the process of self-dedication—is frankly comic, and it is
only by laughing at myself that I can take the edge off my
shame.

Thinking, reading, talking and writing have been my opium
and alcohol, and I am trying to get off them on to listening and
doing. Meanwhile, excuse me.

Pale and willowy, with thick spectacles, Huxley sailed up Ave
Maria Lane to Amen Court, his long coat billowing round him.
Bertrand Russell came, laughing like a horse and suggesting that
P.P.U. members refuse to pay income tax. There was C. E. M.
Joad, the Brains Trust man, and Rose Macaulay, tall and gaunt
with a fascinating face, calling Haile Selassie her black Emperor:
'I *do* wish someone would shoot the Duce. Do you think I ought
to go out and have a try as I feel so strongly about it?'

Visiting Dick for the first time sandwiched between a meeting
with Haile Selassie—'we didn't talk to him, but saw him'—
and seeing *The Littlest Rebel*—'a very nice American-Civil War
film, with Shirley Temple'—she wrote the next day to her
sister:

> I think I never met a clergyman so genuinely and pleasantly
> interested in people and their affairs. I had to try not to waste
> time answering his questions about when and how I worked,
> my sisters, where I went for my holidays, did I go to church,
> etc., etc. I was there an hour, and alone, but must go again
> sometime, he says, and finish discussing Peace.
>
> He thinks it is bad for clergy to become bishops and arch-
> bishops, and that both Canterbury and York have become
> conventional and timid. However he still has hope for the
> Church.
>
> I told him I had too, despite its curious and disappointing
> history.

Intellectuals, political activists and literary personalities, met
in the upstairs drawing-room at No. 1, Amen Court for cider
and iced coffee. One night in the summer, Kingsley Martin was
there. 'It was hot, and I remember my growing dismay as the
speaker developed in ponderous detail his theory about the
technique of group meetings for the practice of non-violence,'
he wrote later. 'Dick, who was lying on the floor in his shirt-
sleeves, whispered to me: "Can't you get up and tell them we
haven't time for all this intensive cultivation and that our job is
to stop the next bloody war?"'

'That meeting settled none of my doubts about Canon

Sheppard's Peace Movement, but it reassured me about Dick,' he said.

Max Plowman was there too, the first General Secretary of the P.P.U., who called himself Dick's tenacious lackey. A poet and devotee of Blake, committed to 'what we love, for God must be fully incarnate in the face of some dear son of his,' he had craggy features and deep eyes — what Middleton Murry called 'a bloody lovely face'.

Max called Dick an inaugurator of new things in an old world; the Peace Pledge Union, akin to signing a death warrant. 'I know Sheppard has got the goods,' he said. 'I want people to discover it.' Temple, he said, was tobogganing to hell.

'Sheppard spoke his bit near the end,' he wrote to a friend afterwards. 'His simplicity and sincerity really carry the guns that are going to count when the firing begins. The man who knows something out of his own experience, knows something which makes the finest and wisest opinion look shadowy, and with all his obvious faults, Dick Sheppard is a truly devoted soul who is ready to go down before the truth every time he sees it.'

When the P.P.U. Headquarters opened, there was nothing to do. Margery Rayne, the Secretary, said Dick's concern saved her from perpetual loneliness and boredom. 'My only 'phone calls were from him,' she said, 'and the daily letter of cheer came in the familiar blue envelope.' When letters started pouring in, 'Dick was always there, ready to answer questions about filing; how to send a package to some un-heard-of place in Wales; who was the cheapest stationer in London; how to draft a letter to the press. I have a picture in my mind of him sitting surrounded by letters on the floor of the little room that was our only office, boasting that he could stick on stamps quicker than any professional.'

There was no furniture and Charles Wardell came to help, sitting on the floor with Dick, addressing envelopes, so did David Spreckley, a young cavalry officer who resigned his commission and came to be a group organiser.

I was 21 [he said] and Dick inspired me. He was absolutely straight and undevious. Some of us young radicals weren't happy about his life-style. We thought he was living it up a bit, being in a house attached to a cathedral, dressing for dinner and holding elaborate dinner parties with silver candlesticks. We kicked against that, but it was counter-balanced by the actual physical work that he did, with his heart and his asthma.

He went on and on and on, working on all-night trains, visiting and speaking. He must have known he was a very sick man, and yet I never saw him depressed or cross. He generated happiness.

Of course, it wasn't true. Dick was depressed, isolating the depression like a virus deep inside him. And he did get cross, moved to tears of anger at Canon Alexander's obstinacy, and kicking the office door behind a sycophantic pacifist worker.

'There are cranks who run in and out of every forward movement, and they get dreadfully in the way,' he commented realistically. 'People who hate being with the minority and are only there for conscience sake, are generally right, but those who delight to take what is called the freakish position and glory in being in opposition, are usually wrong.'

Enthusiasts dashed in and came away with short shrift: 'Dick! I've a marvellous idea!'

'Go away and do it then.'

One day Margery gave a cocktail party and invited an ex-L.S.E. friend called Priscilla. Priscilla was a left-wing ex-Communist agnostic, nurtured on Harold Laski, whose wife had fed her ham sandwiches when she was hard up. Dick was introduced as Dr. Sheppard and was wearing a soft collar, and Priscilla thought he was a doctor.

We talked about Mussolini's attempt to infuse aggressive national feeling into Italy [she says]. The little Bloomsbury flat was warm with cigarettes and wine, and the atmosphere relaxed. I was almost asleep when I heard Dick's voice say 'I don't pretend to know much about Christianity, but I always think Jesus Christ would have said . . .'

In that place and at that time it was like a sudden electric shock. Such a shock that I lost track of what Dick was actually saying. I only knew that to this Dr. Sheppard, Jesus Christ was a real, living, present person.

When the party broke up, she went home to her bed-sitter—'I came to the L.S.E. with one skirt, one pair of shoes and a jumper'—and walked round and round Mecklenburgh Square where she lived. 'If this Dr. Sheppard is right—though he can't be,' she thought, 'what are the implications for the world? What are the implications for me?'

Later, she learned that Dr. Sheppard was Dick Sheppard of St. Martin's, and she embarked on a tentative road to faith, helping at the P.P.U. and sharing her doubts and certainties with Dick, who said, 'Yes, I know, it is almost impossible to believe. I'm certain of nothing. But I'd rather base my whole life on a mistake than give up Christ.'

When she told him her sins and mistakes, he said, 'I am certain that God can bring a blessing even out of our sins', and when she took him to dinner one evening in a favourite haunt off the Charing Cross Road, 'he turned my rather squalid little Indian meal into a banquet, praising the food, joking with the waiters, interested in everything.'

Once they talked about loneliness. 'Do you know,' Dick said, 'one of the loneliest things in the world is to be popular. People have this image of me as a popular parson, and it's so hard to be myself with them. They never share the ordinary parts of their lives with me. They feel they must be experiencing a spiritual crisis.

'For God's sake, Priscilla,' he said, pulling out a piece of paper and writing down his telephone number. 'the next time you burn a saucepan, ring me up and tell me.'

Low drew a cartoon of Dick and George Lansbury astride a horse, stopping at a sign-post pointing to '100 per cent pacifism' one way and 'Organisation of law and order' the other. The caption said, 'Sorry boys, I can't go both ways at once.' Dick was criticised for being anti-British, a cloistered intellectual, a coward and a misguided Imperialist labouring under the illusion that if Britain laid down her arms, the whole world would follow

suit. The Bishop of London said pacifism was convincing
Ribbentrop that Britain would never fight.

> I was sorry you missed Dick Sheppard on the wireless
> [Rose Macaulay wrote to her sister]. It was quite the best
> sermon I have ever heard, very stirring and keen. I wish more
> sermons were like that. He really did make goodness sound
> like an urgent and desperately important job to be tackled.
> His idea was that we should all tackle it for 24 hours on
> Monday, just to try it. I wonder how many people did, and
> what were the results! Perhaps huge gifts of money to useful
> things, businesses ruined through a day of honesty, quarrels
> made up or crimes confessed.

Dick wrote a letter to Hitler, asking to go and preach peace
in Germany, but there was no reply. Instead, Low drew another
cartoon of Hitler and Mussolini bursting into sentimental tears.
Later, when Dick wanted to fly to Spain and intercede with
Franco for the people of Madrid, the Foreign Office prevented
him. In the late summer, he travelled with George Lansbury,
Donald Soper and Vera Brittain to address an open-air Peace
meeting near Dorchester in a natural amphitheatre which seated
fifteen thousand people. It was to be chaired by Housman,
who had just obtained permission for his long-banned series
of plays, *Victoria Regina*, to be shown on the London stage,
incorporating many of Dick's stories of Windsor days.

When Vera Brittain followed her fiery *Testament of Youth*
with *Testament of Experience*, she included an account of the
meeting:

> As I travelled to Dorchester through a sudden shimmering
> heat-wave, I felt intimidated by the status of the other speakers,
> and especially by the overwhelming reputation of Canon
> Sheppard. This man of genius—preacher, broadcaster, peace
> crusader—was one of the most popular human beings ever
> to tread London's crowded pavements . . .
> When the demonstrations began, a huge audience from all
> over Wessex crowded the great Ring in beating sunlight.

On the raised platform, scintillating with heat, the speakers addressed their listeners from beneath a striped sun umbrella.

George Lansbury followed the chairman; shrewd and benign, sturdily erect in his black alpaca coat, he appeared in spite of his 76 years to be the only person unaffected by the temperature. At the end of the row sat Dick Sheppard in his customary informal attire. As he listened to George Lansbury he inhaled oxygen from a rubber apparatus which he carried to relieve his chronic asthma.

With half London I had seen and heard Dick Sheppard preach at St. Martin's. Now, as he rose to speak in his light friendly voice with its underlying note of infectious laughter, I realised that he could play on the emotions of a crowd with a master's skill.

By the time my own turn came I was panic-stricken. This Christian pacifist platform was like no other on which I had stood; here my customary little speech in support of collective security would strike a discordant note. Its basis was political, but the message of my fellow-speakers sprang from the love of God.

Yet I had prepared nothing else. Struggling to my feet I quoted Bunyan, improvised a feeble little story about the pilgrimage of the *Anciens Combattants* at Verdun, and sat down—the biggest disappointment to thousands on that spectacular afternoon.

The hilarious gaiety of the journey back to London all but obliterated this humiliation.

A cavalcade of organisers and audience accompanied us to the station, and insisted upon photographing us before we boarded the train. Being the only woman speaker, I had been presented with a bouquet of luxuriant roses. As Donald Soper was then a young man and I still appeared deceptively immature, the finished picture suggested a bride and bridegroom being sent off for the honeymoon by their respective fathers.

In the train the four of us shared a restaurant table, and talked all the way home. In the railway carriage, though our conversation was glorious, the heat became excessive, and one after another we took off all the outer garments that we could decently remove. Dick Sheppard's popularity sprang from his deep humanity and magnetic charm; he was not a handsome man, and even in his canonicals did not look impressive. Now, with his coat thrown on the table and shirt-sleeves rolled up, he resembled a tipsy cricketer going home at the end of a too enjoyable afternoon.

The railway officials had immediately recognised both him and George Lansbury, but not all the passengers were equally enlightened. One sour-faced elderly woman at the next table appeared particularly scandalised by Dick's informality.

'Pick up your coat!' she reprimanded him severely. 'Fancy putting it down where people have to eat!'

With a sidelong wink at me, Dick meekly obeyed her. When we reached Waterloo the porters ushered us off the train as though we were Royalty, and we shook hands and parted.

Shortly after the Dorchester demonstration, Dick invited me to become a sponsor of his Peace Pledge Union . . . Passionately and repeatedly I wished that I had never gone to Dorchester to be thus diverted from the accepted policies, endorsed by millions who desired peace but did not want to pay for it, which stopped short at the final sacrifice. As I had perceived all too clearly on that pacifist platform, to follow Dick meant treading the Way of the Cross in modern guise. He pointed to a path which might end, not in crucifixion or a den of lions, but at internment, the concentration camp, and the shooting squad.

It was not surprising that the rulers and most of the people in Britain—for three centuries an aggressive country which had lived by conquest and domination—could not receive Dick Sheppard's message. They could no more accept it than they or any other powerful nation had ever accepted the teaching of his Master and Friend—for 'To take him seriously,' as H. G. Wells wrote of 'this Galilean' in *The Outline of History*, 'was to enter upon a strange and alarming life, to abandon habits, to control instincts and impulses, to essay an incredible happiness . . .'

Soon after Christmas, I wrote to Dick and told him that I would become a sponsor of his movement.

All through the autumn, Dick worked with Aldous Huxley

producing peace propaganda and wishing Christ had been more explicit on the Christian attitude to violence. 'Do you agree with Aldous that one cannot build rightly with the wrong materials?' he asked Kingsley Martin once, popping his head unexpectedly round Kingsley's office door. 'It so often seems that one can . . .'

Huxley was preparing an *Encyclopaedia on Pacifism*, speaking with Dick on pacifist platforms throughout the country, reading haltingly and holding his notes an inch from his eyes. His French wife, Maria, organised practical work, aiding destitute families, released prisoners and Jewish refugees, running along to post letters in Piccadilly in her dressing-gown and slippers.

'We have spent the whole winter, September to December, in London, where we worked like slaves,' she wrote. 'Aldous for the Peace Pledge Movement with Dick Sheppard, and I as secretary and slavy to those two men. But we were happy.

'Weather grey and grey and grey.'

Dick took on arduous weeks of one-night stands, travelling many miles for meetings an hour or two hours long. Often he caught the early morning newspaper trains back to London to avoid talking all night in someone else's house, and sat in the guard's van talking instead, arriving back too exhausted to go home without calling in at the hospital first. Entering into fiery conversations with friends, he insisted with passionate certainty that if war broke out, the Peace Pledge Union would have failed.

When Oswald Mosley's Fascist meetings had started in London, his mother had asked Dick to attend one of them. Horrified at the thug tactics used to quieten opposition, he had gone straight to the night editor of *The Times*, who refused to print his story, and then, in a temper, to the *Daily Telegraph*, who ran it the next day. Now youngsters from the Peace Pledge Union banded together in a formidable army and sat down across Commercial Road in the path of the Black Shirts, chewing gum and singing:

> Loving Sheppard of thy sheep,
> Keep us all in Peace Pledge keep.
> Where thou leadest, we will go,
> On the tramlines row by row!

At St. Paul's it was said that Matthews was saving Dick from dying of a broken heart, and that Dick was saving Matthews from despair. Canon Mozley commented that if Dick was doing his job properly, he would be attending more cathedral services, and Dick wrote a stormy letter of resignation to the Dean.

'Please don't go off the deep end,' begged Matthews, who was ill with worry. 'Your departure from St. Paul's would be a disaster to me, and to the place.

'I *think* you are a prophet,' he added cautiously.

Little things gave disproportionate pleasure: one night when he had just been stung for a fortune, a taxi-driver refused to take any fare, and then came to tea afterwards when Dick wrote about him in the papers; and there were rare evenings when everyone was at home, singing ludicrous five-part anthems with stupid words and acting grotesque melodramas, compelling his audience to laugh and resentful if they tried to dissuade him, breathlessly resuming his place by the fire afterwards to continue quietly with his asthma.

But however cheerfully he behaved, criticism hurt deeply, and friends, angry with him for disregarding his health, said he had already died a hundred deaths. 'I do hope somebody is near,' he said to Charles Wardell, terrified of dying alone. Sometimes, after the effort of preaching, he walked out of the cathedral in a dream, saying, 'Have I finished?'

> The Church let Dick down, and so did we [says Charles]. He thought and hoped and lived and prayed in a dimension quite beyond the capabilities of the minds and personalities of people like myself; beyond people like the Dean of St. Paul's and the Archbishops of Canterbury and York.
>
> We did not live and think big enough or daringly enough or constructively enough. We all agreed with him and went with him up to a point. We admired him for his thinking and wished we could go all the way with him. And we left him trudging on alone in the dark.

Alison was having an affair with Archie Macdonell. Dick had invited Dorothy Carver up to the Athenaeum to ask her about it, but Dorothy had been loyal and non-committal. Now Alison wanted to leave, haunted by the certainty that she had lost Dick's affection and calling him a different man after years of illness and recourse to drugs.

She used Nancy as a confidante, and then blamed her for coming between them. Nancy loved Dick, but she told Alison how much Dick needed her—and he did. Alison's remoteness attracted him more than Nancy's consuming concern, albeit laced with a wit as quick and caustic as his own.

Alison had provoked scandal and strained other people's marriages before, but Dick's friends had formed a loyal conspiracy of silence and apparent ignorance. Restless infatuations had blown themselves out, and she had returned to safety again. Dick thought of her as a lost child, and dreaded seeing her embark on a course which would only lead deeper into trouble and unhappiness.

Lang called Dick a man of two worlds, never wholly integrated, and the dichotomy gave rise both to his disarming sincerity, and to a continual inner struggle. Those who called themselves his friends commandeered that in him which spoke to them, and tried, with some embarrassment, to dismiss the rest. After bright, packed halls full of thrill and hope and adulation, Amen Court was lonely and dark to go home to late at night.

'It would be so easy,' he said, 'to bring everything to an end.'

Instead, he preached a sermon on renewal. 'Ask to be brought back to life again, even if the process hurts,' he said, praying from Donne:

> Batter my heart, three person'd God, for you
> As yet but knocke, breathe, shine, and seeke to mend;
> That I may rise, and stand, o'erthrow mee, and bend
> Your force, to breake, blowe, burn and make me new.

On Armistice Day, he wore a white poppy, like everyone else in the P.P.U., but the cathedral Chapter passed permission for a bombing range on their land. 'Do you think I ought to come out of the Church?' he asked Plowman, ringing him up out of the blue.

Plowman laughed and said, 'Yes, of course,' before realising that Dick was serious. 'I know of only two men who might be said to have "Kept the Divine Vision in the day of trouble,"' he said. 'They are Dick Sheppard and George Lansbury, and both of them are in the Church of England. So the question might as lief be asked should we come *in!*'

Dick and Alison went to Cannes for Christmas to try and talk about the future. Rose went with them, and caught 'flu on the train. When they arrived at the hotel, it was desolate, with hardly any visitors.

As Rose was getting better, Alison caught 'flu, and Rose tried to look after her. Dick was weighed down with depression, playing table-tennis with Rose until he was panting and had to stop, trying his best to amuse her and make her laugh. He promised to take her to the casino, but soon after they began the walk there, he was exhausted and they had to go back.

Alison spent Christmas in bed. Dick put Rose on a train home, and then collapsed and had to be taken to hospital. It was the most miserable Christmas any of them could remember.

When Rose arrived home, she was met by Peggie and Nancy, who plied her with questions, but she had no idea what they were talking about. 'It was part of my defence system to put a happy face on things,' she says. 'I was determined to make my mother into a proper mother. I was determined to force everything into a happy picture. I refused to accept that life wasn't perfect.'

Dick came back to a full diary and an arduous series of one-night stands: Sheffield, Bradford, Leeds, Nottingham, Leicester, Hull and Newcastle. Nothing had been decided.

To Dick, pacifism was an ardent adventure [said Rose Macaulay]. It was a crusade. It might not work yet, he would admit, but it was worth a throw, worth taking a chance on, and he made the throw and took the chance with a white-hot enthusiasm that swept the more cautious and timid and sceptical along with him.

The amount of personality that he threw into a friendship, a committee meeting, a conversation, would have left most people exhausted and inert, but he seemed to generate and radiate energy, even when most physically frail, and to electrify and warm the temperature about him so that every one's blood heat rose by several degrees.

He always seemed to have more friends, more irons in the fire, more appointments and engagements to the minute, more letters to deal with, more jobs on hand, than any one man could maintain.

He had to live life hard, throttle full out. It was not to be expected that it could last. The pace was too hot. It had to run down or break.

17

An Infinite Sorrow

AT THE START of 1937, Dick spoke on pacifism at the Church Assembly and was greeted with hostile silence. William Temple spoke against him. 'It looks as though these people are going to get the war they want,' said Huxley. 'It's as though they were possessed by devils.'

Dick wrote to Temple asking his advice, and Temple wrote back lengthily and diplomatically. 'I do not think the fact that you are in a minority in an official assembly is any reason why you should resign,' he said. 'If I were in your position, I should continue to officiate as a minister of the Church of England, trying to leaven it from within.'

Dick carried the letter round in his pocket until it was falling apart. 'Don't be an ass!' said Matthews. 'Why on earth should the fact that the Archbishop of York and others disagreed with your views of the application of Christianity to war make you give up being a Christian minister?'

'We haven't yet, I hope, assented to the dogma of the infallibility of the Archbishop of York.'

Matthews also disagreed with Dick. Housman called him full of hope in a hopeless minority. 'Lord Ponsonby once likened his political usefulness to that of a pike put into a tank of fish,' he said. 'So are you, among those betrayers of Christ with a kiss.'

In the spring, John Middleton Murry joined the Peace Pledge Union, and Dick said it was the best thing that had ever happened.

'When those two know and trust one another,' said Plowman, 'the mountains will begin to move.'

Murry was indifferent to look at, with arresting eyes and tweeds that hung off him when he walked. 'I hope I won't be tongue-tied,' he wrote before they met. 'I seem to find it more and more difficult to say what I mean. The more the issue clarifies, the more simple and unutterable it becomes. It can then, I suppose, only be lived.'

Committed to the Adelphi Centre—which he called a training centre for real socialists—he was battling with a destructive marriage in an effort to rediscover the truth that God is love. Saying psalms before meals and toying with the idea of becoming a priest, he had only just capitulated to pacifism.

Dick asked Murry if he should come out of the Church, and Murry gazed into the distance. 'One,' he said concisely, 'that is for you to decide. Two, the fact that you ask me means that the moment for decision is not come. Three, that means you must wait.'

Plowman called Murry the poet of all their lives. 'Saw Dick Sheppard on Friday and took to him very much,' Murry wrote in his diary, betraying a certain surprise. 'He said he felt isolated and asked me if I would mind his coming to "yarn" to me when he felt the need. I found him easy and natural to talk to and felt that good would come of our meeting.'

Later he admitted there was more to it than that. 'The seed of a deep and swiftly growing affection was quickened in my heart; and at the same time a kind of fear,' he said. 'I have learned to grow afraid for people that I love.'

The Executive of the Peace Pledge Union was meeting once a week. Bertrand Russell held strategic dinners at the House of Lords and pacifists put up as candidates at local elections. Basque evacuees were being supported, and it was decided to subsidise the *Peace News* and open a bookshop.

It is my profound conviction that the teaching of Christ two thousand years ago is not only the word of God for yesterday but the last word in concrete contemporary reality and commonsense for today [Dick said in a City church sermon].

Even if the so-called wisdom of this world were ranged

against the pacifist it should not make any difference what-
soever to the attitude which the Christian must adopt. If he
is asked to prepare for war there is only one answer that he
can give—an uncompromising and resolute refusal.

The art of killing is the essence of war, and no Christian
can uphold war unlesss he is prepared to kill his brother. If a
man believes in the Fatherhood of God and the Brotherhood
of man, war is murder and all war is civil war. The core of
Christian pacifism is the belief that it is never right to take
human life. It has nothing to do with quietism in the sense
of immoral apathy or cowardice. Its basis is not utilitarian.
It does not condemn all use of force. It is a constructive
philosophy of life. It does not make an unconditional surrender to evil. It attacks it with something much more effective
than violence, namely the constructive power of non-violent
resistance.

The man who says that Christian pacifism is a superhuman
and an unnatural ideal is expressing the truth with theological
exactitude, for it is a supernatural ideal, and if it is to be
more than the fleeting hope of a disillusioned generation it
must be sought with supernatural aid. It can be pursued only
in the strength of God.

I am persuaded that the supreme test today of adherence to
Christ as Lord and Master is provided by the conflict between
those who say that war is inevitable and under certain unhappy
circumstances justifiable, and those who when asked to prepare
for it and take part in it are able to answer: Not on my life—
God being my helper.

Young enthusiasts planned to gate-crash the Hendon Air
Pageant with a plane flying a trailer with the words 'Dick Sheppard
says "Remember Guernica"' on it, and newspapers blockaded
attempts to print peace propaganda.

'What we want is a bloody massacre!' said Dick one day,
storming into the bookshop, where Peggie helped in the holidays
and leading pacifists gave lunch-time lectures.

'Are you a Christian?' shouted a man from the back of the
crowd one day when he was speaking in the park.

'He's a parson!' shouted someone else.

'Yes, but are you a Christian?' persisted the man.

'Why do you ask me that?' said Dick.

'Because you Christians have let us down,' was the reply, and it added to the increasing sadness Dick's friends noticed in his eyes when he was off-guard.

'I never knew him when he was not suffering,' said Matthews, who felt he was wasting his time. 'I imagine that he can hardly have ever known what it was to live without pain, and his greatest pain arose from the fact that he suffered always in the suffering of others.

'To the general public he seemed to be just a wonderful stage manager, a master of the art of publicity. But to those who knew him, he seemed to spend all his time either in prayer for others or in working for them, quite regardless of his own reputation.'

In May, he set sail on the *Europa* for what he called ten eccentric days in New York.

Lord Ponsonby knew of a wealthy, idiosyncratic American woman willing to give money to the P.P.U. Dick had written asking for fifty thousand pounds and been promised one thousand two hundred pounds. At New York, there was no one to meet him, and reporters 'told me I was a fool to think I'd get a dollar from her'.

Rung at seven every morning with alterations to a list of engagements that never took place, Dick organised his own preaching and speaking arrangements in Yale, New Haven, Philadelphia and New York.

'No money in them,' he noted, 'only enthusiasm. 37 talks in nine days. Heat awful.'

Sensing there was no money forthcoming, he consulted lawyers and commented casually that he was sending daily postcards to Princess Margaret and Princess Elizabeth in London.

'The day I was due to sail at eleven on the *Queen Mary*, I stormed her room, although the hotel porter had orders not to admit me,' he said. 'I stood over her as she reclined on a sofa and told her that directly I landed I should have to tell the King she had let me down. After a little thought, she gave in: £1,000. Our contest didn't end until 10.30 and I only caught my boat

as the gangways were being taken up.' He fainted as he stepped
on board, and was in bed for three days. The cheque was dis-
honoured.

While he was away, Alison finally made up her mind to leave
him for Archie Macdonell. Archie had been persuasive for over
a year, and 'I must have a life of my own,' Alison said emotionally,
exhausted by Dick's ups and downs.

'My Alison has left me for someone she loves differently,' Dick
wrote to Housman. 'The bottom has gone out of my world. We
had real happiness for 22 years.'

Alison tried to justify herself. She said Dick was impossible
to live with, as he probably was. She cried with guilt, but was
determined this time to free herself from a life she disliked and
for which she was ill-equipped.

She had promised Dick never to see Archie again, but she had
been unable to keep the promise. She said she was in love with
Archie as she had never been in love with anyone before, and
because she believed what she was saying, she was very persuasive.

'I have never been upset by the moral lapses of my friends,'
said Alec Waugh. 'Who am I to throw a stone? But I *was* shocked
at A.G.M.'s elopement with Dick's wife.'

Dick blamed himself. For an apparent extrovert he was
illogically independent, private, desperate, and difficult to help.

'How can I go and preach from the pulpit when I know that
it must be because of me that she's left?' he asked Hugo and
Elaine Johnston, sitting in their drawing-room at Cranleigh
with tears running down his face. 'It must be my fault.' He went
to a Harrogate nursing-home, and those who understood left
him alone; those who did not understand tried to follow and to
help, and he pretended to be grateful.

He was ill, exhausted and disillusioned, vulnerable and in
need of love. 'What can I preach except love?' he asked time and
again, full of self-reproach. 'How can I ever preach love again?'

When he came back to Amen Court, the spirit had gone out
of the place. Nancy stayed with Dick, and the servants gossiped.
Everyone, including her own family, condemned Alison. 'Don't
let your instinct to sacrifice yourself overpower your judgement
of what is best in the long run,' warned Matthews. 'The one

thing you can do for me,' Dick wrote to his friends, 'is to look after Alison. And if anything happens to me, don't take it out on her.'

'He never blamed her,' says Peggie. 'In a way it made me angry that he didn't. He never talked bitterly. He just kept on saying that he had failed. He loved her: they loved each other. He did everything in the world that he could for her. Perhaps he did too much.'

When Peggie met her mother, Alison sobbed and said no one knew how difficult life had been. Peggie was fiercely and furiously puritanical, shouting and swearing. When Rose came home, Dick said Alison had gone on holiday. He disliked taking the hard way—sometimes in the past his prevarication had caused trouble. 'She's a little bit tired,' he said lamely. 'She won't be here for a while.'

When Rose went up to the top of the house where she and Peggie had attic rooms, Peggie was lying on her bed sobbing: 'She's a bitch and she's living with Archie!' Memories of walks in the country and strange incomprehensible telephone calls came into Rose's mind, but she pushed them resolutely away, deep inside her. She was determined to make her mother a proper mother.

'I think I can truly say that all that is in my heart now, over and above a great dull ache, is an infinite tenderness towards her, and an infinite sorrow that I failed her,' Dick wrote to Housman.

'One day she may wish to come back or to have her divorce. Of course, I shall stand by her whatever happens, though I pray it may be the former.' It seemed to his friends that he was too meek, too complaisant, too loving.

Aldous Huxley and Gerald Heard proposed to corner the German nickel market, and were condemned by Chamberlain as impractical. P.P.U. Minutes carry reckless suggestions from Canon Sheppard: processions to Lambeth Palace, pickets outside the Houses of Parliament, refusals to support the Government re-armament plan by withholding income tax.

Dick had never been so low in his life. Characteristically he reacted by organising a P.P.U. holiday camp in Hampshire for five hundred people. For many, it was to be their last memory of him.

Max Plowman was there, talking of lone sheep pasturing alone and lecturing in the sun. Kingsley Martin was brilliantly gloomy. Murry spoke on God or the Nation, and watched Dick closely. 'The thing I had despaired of ever seeing was there before my eyes, laughing at me and I at him,' he said. 'A great democratic and Christian leader.'

Dick displayed baffling extremes, darting into the office tent — 'I say, we're looking up, three girls with red toenails!' — and refusing to preach because he had no faith, only hope and love. 'Confident people inspire me,' he said. 'But they make me feel inferior.'

'I'm a good mixer,' he admitted cheerfully, dressing up in a black beard and helmet and brandishing a sword. 'When a man has had as much experience as I've had, he gets to know what he can do and what he can't. I know that I can't preach, and I know that I can't write. But I'm a good mixer.'

Fastidious to a fault, he opened someone else's suitcase and leaped away from it in horror. 'Quick! I must wash! I've touched his pyjamas!'

One night he collapsed with a bad attack of asthma, and an anxious helper rushed for his inhaler. When she brought a brown medicine bottle that was standing beside it, Dick laughed a lot and made his asthma worse.

'Oh, that's so funny!' he gasped when he had enough breath. 'You've brought my shampoo.'

On the last night, sitting and singing together round the camp fire, five hundred people of all ages, old people and children among them, Dick asked almost hesitantly for a moment's silence. Afterwards he said, 'That was unity'. As a result of that brief unity, he went back to London feeling less alone. 'That camp was the most worthwhile experience of my life,' he said.

'Dick was extraordinary,' said Max Plowman, 'though I'm rather worried about his health.'

At St. Paul's, Chapter meetings were intransigent, obtuse and trivial. After a particularly acrimonious exchange, Dick told the P.P.U. he would be a free agent by Christmas, and agreed to stand at the Glasgow Rectorial elections in October. He wrote indignantly to Matthews of what he called the scandal of St. Paul's:

I came to St. Paul's originally at the request of the Arch-bishop of Canterbury to assist the Dean in making the needful reforms which everyone not living in Amen Court knows to be essential [he said]. I found the conditions much worse than I believed possible—and I am not without experience of Cathedrals.

It is impossible to describe the inhumanity of the place itself, and I should appear to exaggerate if I attempted to give the criticisms which I have heard at the doors of the cathedral, and from the lips of young and old—and by no means un-intelligent—who have attempted from time to time to make their souls and find spiritual strength at its worship.

As to the cathedral's attitude towards social problems and the values that really matter in this war-saturated world, I dare not express myself. Until I came to St. Paul's I would not have believed that such aloofness from reality on the part of almost everyone concerned could exist in a corporate body. And I, therefore, with gratitude to my colleagues for their personal kindness to me, am compelled to give my resignation to the Prime Minister.

If I were younger and saw any hope of reforming what now is, I should not resign my canonry, but at my age, and holding the views I do, I am not proposing to spend my remaining years in tolerating what I consider to be the spoiling of a great cathedral.

I see St. Paul's as it might be—a place of reverent worship, understood and loved by the people, but I know that dream is impossible of attainment without drastic and radical altera-tions which my colleagues in Amen Court neither desire nor would approve.

Every night, Peggie and Nancy stayed awake to help Dick up the stairs to bed when he came in, pushing and pulling him until he reached the top. It was frustrating and humiliating to be such a nuisance. 'You don't know what it's like to struggle day after day, unable to breathe,' he said to them cruelly. 'You're so used to it that you don't even bother to sympathise.' When Peggie left to go back to Cambridge, 'for some reason I couldn't bear to go, and I rang the doorbell to kiss him goodbye again.'

At a small country conference of the P.P.U. Executive, getting together to draw up a national manifesto, Dick gave Middleton Murry a copy of Bernanos's *Diary of a Country Priest*. 'I've no brains, Middleton,' he said, 'but this seems to me the real thing. I wish you'd tell me.' Then he suggested they should take a caravan and tour the country together, addressing everyone they met and talking to them about peace.

They talked about faith. 'Faith? I don't believe I know anything about faith, Middleton,' Dick said. 'But Jesus is my God. I don't believe I have any faith except that: but I have a love for men. Somewhere in me I have love. I hang on to that.'

Soon afterwards, Murry decided to become a priest. It was a short-lived decision; its main purpose was to support Dick. 'Something in his tired face, maybe, something in his quiet voice, made it echo in my mind for days,' he said. 'The "hanging on": desperate, but without despair. Faith? The very essence of it.'

'For God's sake don't kill yourself, as I fear you are doing,' he wrote to Dick.

On the birthday of his dead first wife, Katherine Mansfield, with whom Dick felt a strange, sad affinity, Murry was restless and uneasy. In the end, he composed a prayer and sent it to Dick: '. . . take possession of our hearts, we beseech Thee, that we may become humble, joyful, and entire servants of Thy mighty purposes . . . that men may know that in the faithfulness of love alone is the issue from the world's despair.'

'It was made for Dick,' said Murry later. 'It is the only thing I can say that may not be unworthy of him.'

'Dick is killing himself.' In the offices of the Peace Pledge Union, it was a daily observation. Within three weeks, he spoke at Ely, Wigan, Aberdeen, Sutton Coldfield, Hornsey, Carmarthen, Acton, Coventry, Newcastle, Epsom, Guildford, Saffron Walden and Eastbourne, standing for long periods and gasping for breath between sentences. Dean Matthews, who was not a pacifist, disapproved, but priorities were everything:

> I was in a very distressed state [writes a woman who met Dick then]. My husband had left me with three young sons. One was eleven and at Prep. school. I had never had a job, and I didn't know what to do.
>
> One day I went into St. Paul's to think and try to resolve the problem. Dick Sheppard walked past. He saw me sitting there, and he came back and asked if he could help.
>
> I started to tell him my worries, and I couldn't stop crying. He took me over to Amen Court and gave me coffee and a sandwich. He told his Secretary to let me in to see him whenever I called. He arranged through various organisations for a school for my eldest son, and promised to get the second into St. Paul's Choir School when he was nine, if I could get him some musical tuition.
>
> Through his encouragement I pulled myself together and managed to get a job, and now my sons are splendid men. I give all the credit to Dick Sheppard for helping me with time, contacts and encouragement through a critical period in my life.

Dick was taking barbiturates to off-set the stimulants he took for his asthma. They helped him to sleep, but meant that he dropped off at the theatre, which worried his friends. It was a time of depression, Plowman calling himself a low-grade pacifist, spiritually in chains.

> I don't suffer fools gladly [he wrote to novelist J. D. Beresford]. And there's no shortage of them on the fringes of the P.P.U.! When I behold people using so intrinsically disinterested a movement as the P.P.U. for the low purposes of personal ambition, when I see them hanging on to Dick's skirts as a means of canalising his efforts into their own pet shows, the very devil of vindictiveness enters into me!
>
> But one compensation I have which is real. And that is an admiration for Dick which I rather think is unique.
>
> I know more than a little, from inside observation (and

from my own experience) of what this whole show has cost
him: and it amounts in plain fact to pretty precisely what
Christ said his discipleship would cost.

He has been, and is, let down left and right. He is left high
and dry time and again. Well-meaning people love him as
they love a sponge. He carries in the practical sense at least
ten men's burdens. And he knows all that—knows the job
has almost taken the skin off his back and meant all manner
of humiliation inconceivable. But there he is: God's own
sublime clown, merry and boyish when any other man I've
ever known would be blue with rage, the soul of good cheer
at moments when any other man with half his troubles would be
Jeremiah.

Oh yes! Make no mistake about it—our Dick is a saint of
the very first water and a hero of the very finest mould. I
wouldn't forego my learning of that for something.

In Portsmouth, Betty Montgomery died suddenly and tragically
of septicaemia, leaving her husband devastated: Dick took the
funeral, with Montgomery crying like a child. In Glasgow,
student newspapers carried banner headlines: A VOTE FOR
SHEPPARD IS A VOTE FOR PEACE. George MacLeod, then the Dick
Sheppard of Glasgow, addressed student meetings. So did
C. E. M. Joad, Aldous Huxley and Middleton Murry. Rose
Macaulay, looking like a spinster in Victorian hat and Victorian
hair-do, had to be rescued from kidnapping and paper bombs.
Bertrand Russell and Laurence Housman sent messages.

Dick's opponents were Macneile Dixon, a Scottish Nationalist,
Professor J. B. S. Haldane and Winston Churchill, described in
turn as a gentle nonentity, a crusader for another Holy War, and
an egotist and a blunderer.

'Glasgow reports that the betting is 6–5 on me,' Dick wrote
to Peggie, forbidden, as a candidate, to go near the place himself. 'I simply don't believe it. But Glasgow is doing well—a
free fight in which my pacifist crowd seem to be splendidly
militant.'

Supporters in sandwich boards paraded through Glasgow
displaying Arthur Wragg's posters, 'Who next, brother?'

'And Jesus said, suffer the little children . . .'

'Lord, that our eyes may be opened.'

'Those who would like Britain to give a lead must vote for Dick Sheppard,' said Rose Macaulay. 'Those who think it safer and wiser to remain barbarians with tomahawks had better vote otherwise.'

On Saturday, October 23rd, 220 students voted for Haldane, 281 for Churchill, 364 for Macneile Dixon, and 538 for Dick Sheppard.

The *Scotsman* called it a remarkable example of what a keen and united minority could accomplish when the majority were apathetic and divided. Equally aghast, the *Glasgow Herald* thought Canon Sheppard 'not quite in the tradition of University Rectors'. The votes cast for him were idealistic and romantic, they said, 'Symptomatic of the spirit of the new world and of young people's dissatisfaction with the old.'

Rose was at home, and she made paper castles of telegrams which collapsed around Dick as he opened the door. Bertrand Russell sent one to say he was overjoyed. 'Read Psalm 29 and apply to Rome for immediate canonisation,' said George MacLeod. 'Glorious news,' said Lansbury. 'This is a great sign of youth's revolt against barbarism and resolve to follow advice of Christ to fight evil with good. God bless and strengthen you.'

'I'm delighted my erstwhile constituents have been able to give a lead,' wrote Compton Mackenzie from the Outer Hebrides. 'I hope you will have as happy a three years office as I had.'

It was the verdict of youth, and it came like an unexpected benediction. Dick went to bed, content for the first time in his life, to lie awake. 'Now it doesn't matter if I die this week,' he said.

18

Nunc dimittis

'Is *l'audace, l'audace, et toujours l'audace* henceforth to be our policy?' asked Housman. Dick was finishing an article on death for the *Sunday Circle*.

Instead of shirking the issue and shrinking from the ordeal, should we not look forward to it in the light of a great adventure [he asked]. The greatest adventure of all.

It would not do for us to know too much. Our mortal eyes could not stand the splendour of the light of that other world. We have our task to accomplish before we set out on the journey. But instead of with dread, may we not look forward to it as one may look forward to that other rather terrifying experience of flight?

The 'plane is on the ground; we take our seats fearfully. The 'plane taxis across the airfield. So far there is nothing unusual—like a motor car on the road. But gently, imperceptibly, we have left the earth; we are rising. Up into the clouds.

There was nothing to dread at all.

In the last week of October, Dick's flight was called.
Alison was pleading for a reconciliation. After a few months, it was all over and Archie was leaving, and Alison was lost and lonely. Dick refused. She was still unsure, and he was emotionally exhausted, only just beginning to sense a new freedom from

tension. He was preparing a sermon on pacifism for St. Paul's on Sunday, and they made a date to talk afterwards.

Rose was at home after a complicated appendicitis operation, pale and thin and disturbed by letters from Alison saying how cruel Dick was. She had been writing stories, and when she showed them to Dick, he read them through with thrilled enthusiasm. It was as if he had loved his children a lot, but never really known them, and sudden glimpses into their lives warmed and surprised him. Later he left money for them in his will, like a compensation.

In the end he agreed to let Rose go to stay with Alison, providing Archie had gone. Like Peggie, suddenly intuitive, Rose kept returning to say goodbye to him, reluctant to leave. 'This is ridiculous,' he laughed. 'We might be saying goodbye to each other for ever.'

Alison and Archie had been living at Rudgwick, scandalising the villagers by using Dick's cottage. Rose stayed indoors instead of going into the garden because she was ashamed of meeting anyone. Alison was lonely and unhappy, and she read Dick's old love letters aloud, but Rose was only sixteen and immature: when Alison tried to explain the life she and Dick had led together, Rose had no idea what she was talking about.

Afterwards, she went upstairs to her bedroom and wondered whether she dare jump out of the window.

At Amen Court, Dick had a vision of a great light shining on St. Martin's, and hundreds of people queueing to climb the steps and pass through its bright inside. There was no one to tell it to but Nancy. 'I don't know what it means,' he said. His asthma was bad, and there were times when he was unsure what he was doing or saying, gasping for breath and moaning for Alison.

On Thursday, there was a meeting of the P.P.U. Executive, and Lord Ponsonby retired to an adjoining room to draft a letter to *The Times*, setting out constructive peace proposals. 'Loud gusts of laughter reached my ears,' he said. 'Dick in the Chair always transformed what might otherwise be a perfunctory, drab, business performance into a gathering of exuberant enthusiasts.'

They had attended a meeting of the Advisory Council of the

War Resisters' International in the morning. Dick had gone on
without lunch to the three-hour meeting in the afternoon. In the
evening they were due to speak at Leyton.

> After a hurried meal, I met him at the station [said Lord
> Ponsonby]. He had had no meal. The journey was short, but
> there was time for an animated discussion on the fallacy of a
> war of defence, with a complete stranger in the carriage. Dick's
> friendliness was disarming and the stranger was impressed.
> The meeting was in a hall with abominable acoustics. It
> was a strain on the speakers, but more especially on one gripped
> with asthma. As usual Dick had to be dragged away because
> he insisted on joking with the stewards, the literature sellers
> and the doorkeepers.
> Arriving at Liverpool Street at 11.00 I said: 'Now you must
> go home, have some food, and go to bed.'
> 'Not yet,' he replied. 'I must go to the hospital to see a
> dying man. He expects me.'

On Friday Dick sent Priscilla a hundred cigarettes and the
news that he had found just the right job for her. Unable to
sleep, he stayed up writing the unnecessary little notes which
arrived unexpectedly, 'like candles on a Christmas tree' said
Rose Macaulay. One was to Kenneth, the son of his old friend
Woollcombe, from Oxford House days. 'Let me know the result
of the Haileybury Scholarship,' he said. 'The betting on the
Stock Exchange is heavily in favour of you winning.'
On Saturday there was a Chapter meeting at St. Paul's. The
Dean talked about a woman they both knew: Dick slightly,
Matthews very well. 'Tell her I pray for her and her husband
every single day,' Dick said. During the meeting, with the
unexpected backing of Canon Mozley, it was agreed that members
of the P.P.U. should be allowed to celebrate Holy Communion
once a week in the crypt. To Dick, it was an unaccustomed
burst of sunshine, and he said in his profligate way that it made
him feel he could spend the rest of his life happily at St. Paul's.
In the afternoon he rang Mozley to thank him, and Mozley was
surprised at the fervour of his gratitude.

The next day was Cosmo Gordon Lang's birthday, and he arranged to have some flowers delivered by hand.

For Dick, the old Jewish saying was true. He really did have two texts in his pockets, one telling him he was dust and ashes and the other that for him the whole of the world was made. Beneath every success there had to be the bitter taste of failure: of failure to please Alison. He wanted her to be happy, and it seemed impossible, and he couldn't get it out of his mind.

He locked the study door as he often did when he wanted to pray or to work undisturbed. His sister was making trouble, spreading gossip, and he began drafting a letter begging her to stop.

Amen Court was black and silent and his asthma was bad again. 'It would be so easy . . .' But there was always an abounding enthusiasm and an incorrigible desire to live, that somehow brought him back to life again.

He put his head in his hands.

'Even while we might not live to see all that we long to see,' he had written once, 'yet in the evening of life we might turn towards the East, in the company of all those who love the Lord Christ, and sing the *Nunc dimittis*.

'Lord, now lettest thou thy servant depart in peace.'

*   *   *

In the morning, Hugo Johnston was preaching at a Surrey hospital. After the service, he was asked to stay to lunch, but he excused himself and went home to Cranleigh. While he and Elaine were having lunch, a call came through from Amen Court from Dick's manservant, saying that the study door was still locked. By the time Hugo arrived, the door had been broken down and Dick was found dead at his desk.

At St. Martin's, the news was announced during the People's Service, and the band of the Welsh Guards played the *Hallelujah Chorus*. At St. Paul's, Canon Mozley gave the announcement during the afternoon Evensong, and worshippers left early to walk down Ludgate Hill to the Fleet Street offices of the *Sunday Express* to buy Dick's last article. Many were bewildered to find themselves moved to tears.

Dorothy Carver read the news on stop-press London newspaper placards and found it impossible to believe. Dick had nearly died so many times, and yet now he was dead, it seemed incomprehensible.

Lang wrote in 'haste and bewilderment' to Peggie:

> The strange and sudden news has brought me a great shock. I cannot realise it.
>
> In the course of this morning I received from him, sent by hand, some beautiful flowers and a characteristically loving note. He had remembered that this was my birthday. In the afternoon I received the news that he had vanished from our sight. I think this remembrance of me must have been one of his very last acts. How can I fail to be deeply moved?
>
> I can't write about him now, my heart is too full, recalling the years he spent as my companion, my son, at Amen Court so many years ago, all his loving kindness since, overflowing any differences of opinion and binding me as it bound all his friends, to him.
>
> I can only let my heart find relief in prayer, and tomorrow, All Saints Day, I shall remember him at the altar here . . .

Rose kept crying, and relatives told her not to be selfish and to think of her mother. When she and Alison arrived back at Amen Court, she went on to meet Peggie, who had been told the news in the middle of a fencing display. They laughed a lot, tense and brittle. At Amen Court there were reporters collecting silly anecdotes and rumours of suicide. In the evening, instead of sitting miserably, they all went to the cinema where newsreels showed pictures of Dick.

'How lovely to see Daddy looking well again,' Rose said.

An autopsy showed the condition of his heart to be so bad that he should have died months ago.

Among his papers was a galley proof of an article on immortality, which he called

> some kind of active and conscious existence when we have gladly embraced the opportunity of making good our failures here.

I do not think it is the mere desire to make myself happy
in a world that is unfriendly that makes me believe with all
my soul in the ultimate triumph of Love [he had written].

It is not often as the conclusion of an argument that men
attain to belief in a future life. It comes more easily in those
deep silences when reason is temporarily baffled, and the
valour within the soul dares to go out beyond to where it
would be, and sun itself in the light of God.

For two days and nights the coffin rested at St. Martin's
surrounded by tall candlesticks. 'He is in his home again,' said
Pat McCormick. Members of St. Martin's staff and congregation and of the P.P.U. kept watch, and one hundred thousand
people came during the day and night, waiters and waitresses,
charwomen, taxi-cab drivers, street-cleaners tramps and prosti-
tutes. Sometimes it took an hour-and-a-quarter to file through.

'He's all right now,' said a cockney coster woman. 'He's happy.
But what's going to happen to the rest of us?'

Up in the gallery, Peggie watched and found it all incomprehensible. It was Dick's vision: St. Martin's, lighted day and
night, with queues of people moving through.

Dick and Alison had talked of his death, and he had left
instructions dictated more than a year earlier. 'I don't want
Alison to feel she need ever see me after I die, or that she ought
to attend any of the services that are held,' he had written. 'I
entirely agree with her point of view in all this.' When the time
came, the Dean of St. Paul's refused to allow her to attend the
funeral, and she was distraught. Lang wrote a letter full of
sympathy, but a friend of Dick's said, 'I think you should know
that I consider you Dick's murderer.'

It was as hard for her as Dick had feared it would be, and
she was haunted with guilt and regret for what might have been.
A friend visiting her the following Christmas saw her mantel-
shelves full of Christmas cards which were two years old.

Crowds four deep lined the streets, men with their hats off
and women in tears. Police held up traffic as a hundred clergy
and people followed the hearse in a procession along the Embankment and up Ludgate Hill to St. Paul's. Police on point duty

saluted, and men came up on board the Thames tugs and barges, taking off their hats. The cathedral was crowded to the doors, with people standing in the courtyard.

Dean Matthews called Dick a primitive Christian and a fool for Christ's sake. 'He did not find the way of love easy,' he said. 'Those who saw only the cheery, delightful, genial, good companion, did not see the real man.'

'The devil seems out reaping this year, especially among our friends,' wrote Vera Brittain's husband, George Catlin, who was there. She was on an American tour, and his letter caught up with her in New York.

'All those clerics, non-committal, using generalisations like blankets,' he said. 'Nothing is more extraordinary than the way in which this man had power. Those who utterly disagreed with him were swayed by him. Those who most thought him wrong, dangerous, almost treasonable, conspired to honour him.'

'One is left thinking about it—very seriously.'

Dick was buried, as he had asked, beside Randall Davidson in the cathedral cloisters at Canterbury—'I much hope no Church dignitary will make an oration over me'—but long afterwards, Beerbohm likened him to the Portofino lighthouse: a silvery recurrence of light on the walls; a friendly intrusion.

'He worked himself to death, of course,' commented Rose Macaulay. 'He was unique, I think. It is nice to have known him.'

Index